THE OFFICIAL
SCOUT-
MASTER
HANDBOOK

Seventh Edition • Sixth Printing • 1985
BOY SCOUTS OF AMERICA • Irving, Texas

Your Name

PEOPLE WHO CAN HELP YOU

Assistant Scoutmaster   (Phone)

Assistant Scoutmaster   (Phone)

Committee Chairman   (Phone)

Scouting Coordinator   (Phone)

Commissioner   (Phone)

District Executive   (Phone)

1

A MESSAGE FROM THE CHIEF

As Chief Scout Executive, I have a personal interest in your success as a Scoutmaster or assistant Scoutmaster; for your success is the future of Scouting.

For more than 75 years boys have wanted to be Boy Scouts and follow the Scouting trail. Men like you have helped them. What Boy Scouts strive for is their own excellence through a program of activities that is in step with the times. What they stand for are the timeless virtures of manhood expressed in the Boy Scout Oath and Law and the positive attitude of "Doing a Good Turn daily" and "Being Prepared." Deep within the soul of every boy there is a yearning to be somebody. Scouting can help them realize that dream.

Boy Scouts can run their own troop with your help and Scouting's secret system of operation: the PATROL METHOD. In this handbook, part 1 will show you how to deal with many Boy Scouts. When you have the troop in hand, using the patrol method, you are ready for part 2. In it you can begin the study of individual boys. As you continue in the role of Scoutmaster, part 3 will provide the tools to meet your needs.

Your Scouting service center and professional and commissioner staff will give you every assistance within their power.

Your troop's chartered organization and the nation need and appreciate your efforts.

Sincerely,

Ben H. Love
Chief Scout Executive

Contents

An Introduction to the World of Boy Scouting

When a boy, Baden-Powell—the founder of Scouting—often eluded his teacher, snared rabbits, and cooked his own dinner.

Sketch by Baden-Powell.

BOY SCOUTING has an exciting and colorful history. It began as a training program for young soldiers under the command of British Army officer Robert S. S. Baden-Powell, who was always dissatisfied with the ability of soldiers to carry out reconnaissance and to care for themselves under primitive conditions.

In India in 1897 with his first regimental command, Baden-Powell had full freedom to use his training ideas. He had men train in small groups; made their training hard but enjoyable, and gave them increasing responsibilities. Soldiers who became efficient were called scouts. To record his methods, Baden-Powell wrote a small volume, *Aids to Scouting*, for military use.

In 1899, the talented but obscure officer found himself in charge of a regiment in Mafeking, South Africa, under siege by a force of 9,000 Boers, descendants of the Dutch settlers who had first colonized South Africa. British forces were badly outnumbered, but Baden-Powell kept the Boers from overrunning the city by a combination of bluff and boldness. As news of relief of the 217-day siege reached England, Baden-Powell became a hero.

Boy Scouting evolved in Baden-Powell's mind as a result of two unrelated developments.

The first was his review, in 1903 and 1904, of the Boys' Brigade, a uniformed, quasimilitary organization for English boys. As the hero of Mafeking, Baden-Powell was accorded a worshipful reception by the boys. He was impressed by their enthusiasm and interest, but he was sorely troubled by the militarism shown in their drilling, uniforms, and toy rifles.

The second development was his review of his manual, *Aids to Scouting*. It had enjoyed an astounding sale to English boys. Baden-Powell realized that it would never do as a book for boys. It was written to prepare men for war. What he wanted was a book to prepare boys for peace.

So began Baden-Powell's quest for all the literature of the world about training boys for manhood. He searched everywhere.

By 1907, Baden-Powell's thinking had crystallized enough to get reactions from men whose opinions he respected. Replies were encouraging, and in the summer of that year he sought the answer to the ultimate question: How would boys take to this idea?

To find out, he organized the world's first Boy Scout camp. Twenty-two boys, from farm and city, went to Brownsea Island off England's southern coast, to camp as Scouts.

The heart of Baden-Powell's idea was the patrol method, and almost the first thing done at the camp was to divide the boys into four patrols.

This first Boy Scout camp was not greatly different from Boy Scout camps today. There was plenty of Scoutcraft practice, games, competition, campfires, and patrol overnight camps away from the troop.

The camp was a rousing success in the eyes of both Baden-Powell and the boys. The secret was the patrol method in which he said: "Each patrol leader was given full responsibility for the behaviour of his patrol at all times, in camp and in the field. . . . Responsibility, discipline, and competitive rivalry were thus at once established and a good standard of development was ensured throughout the troop."

Baden-Powell followed a three-stage procedure. Each night at the campfire B-P told a story about one of his adventures where some Scoutcraft skill helped him. The next morning, B-P showed the Scouts how to acquire the skill. In the afternoon, B-P created a situation in which patrols had to use that skill.

It boiled down to this: (1) get them interested, (2) show them how, and (3) let them compete. If B-P had camped on Brownsea Island in our time he might have used a space adventure like this one:

Scoop the Arcturian rock into a neckerchief that is tied at the corners with sheet bends and stretched tight. Carry the rock 25 meters to the dump site.

THE ARCTURIANS

Get Them Interested. Agents of the third planet from the star Arcturus are among us. The newspapers, radio, and TV have been asked not to report their presence to avoid panic. It is not known what these agents are up to, but they communicate with International Morse code. You can identify the agents because they wear this mark ...-- on their left arms. That is the figure 3 in code and represents their planet which, like ours, is the third from the sun.

Show Them How. Written messages in Morse code can be easily decoded by us. On page 356 of *The Official Boy Scout Handbook* you'll find the code.

```
.--- ..- ... - / .--. ..- - / - .... . / .-.. . - - . .-. /
J     U   S   T   P     U   T     T  H   E     L  E  T  T  E  R

.- -... --- ...- . / - .... . / -.. --- - ... /
A  B    O    V   E    T  H   E    D   O   T  S

.- -. -.. / .--. .- ... .... . ... ///
A  N  D     P    A  S   H    E  S
```

Let Them Compete. An Arcturian agent—a committee member, parent, or older Scout—gives the same written message to each patrol that will answer the first of three questions: Are the Arcturians friendly?

Clue No. 1

WE MEAN/YOU NO/HARM

As soon as a patrol decodes the message it sends one of its members to give the answer to the senior patrol leader. When all have reported, another Arcturian gives the second message to the patrol leaders. This message will answer the second question: Why are the Arcturians interested in us?

Clue No. 2

WE NEED/YOUR/HELP

When the message is decoded by all patrols, the Arcturian agents hand out the third message, which will answer the third question: What are we to do?

Clue No. 3

THE/ROCKS/MARKED/3/
ARE/RADIOACTIVE
THEY/MUST/BE/MOVED/
25/METERS/BUT/DO/
NOT/TOUCH/THEM

First patrol to perform this Good Turn for the Arcturians is the winner.

Scouting is and should be exciting fun for boys and men. If boys find you fun to be with, you'll really enjoy Scouting. If boys find you a good example to follow in their lives, you'll be making a great contribution to our nation.

THE IDEALS OF BOY SCOUTING

TRUTH   KNOWLEDGE

Scout Oath or Promise

On my honor I will do my best
To do my duty to God and my country
   and to obey the Scout Law;
To help other people at all times;
To keep myself physically strong,
   mentally awake, and morally straight.

Scout Motto

"Be Prepared"

BE PREPARED

Scout Slogan

The knot at the bottom of the Second Class badge reminds a Scout to "Do a Good Turn Daily."

Scout Sign

The three upstretched fingers stand for the three parts of the Scout Oath. The other two fingers represent the bond that ties all Scouts together.

Scout Law

Trustworthy. A Scout tells the truth. He keeps his promises. Honesty is part of his code of conduct. People can depend on him.

Loyal. A Scout is true to his family, Scout leaders, friends, school, and nation.

Helpful. A Scout is concerned about other people. He does things willingly for others without pay or reward.

Friendly. A Scout is a friend to all. He is a brother to other Scouts. He seeks to understand others. He respects those with ideas and customs other than his own.

Courteous. A Scout is polite to everyone regardless of age or position. He knows good manners make it easier for people to get along together.

Kind. A Scout understands there is strength in being gentle. He treats others as he wants to be treated. He does not hurt or kill harmless things without reason.

Obedient. A Scout follows the rules of his family, school, and troop. He obeys the laws of his community and country. If he thinks these rules and laws are unfair, he tries to have them changed in an orderly manner rather than disobey them.

Cheerful. A Scout looks for the bright side of things. He cheerfully does tasks that come his way. He tries to make others happy.

Thrifty. A Scout works to pay his way and to help others. He saves for unforeseen needs. He protects and conserves natural resources. He carefully uses time and property.

Brave. A Scout can face danger even if he is afraid. He has the courage to stand for what he thinks is right even if others laugh at or threaten him.

Clean. A Scout keeps his body and mind fit and clean. He goes around with those who believe in living by these same ideals. He helps keep his home and community clean.

Reverent. A Scout is reverent toward God. He is faithful in his religious duties. He respects the beliefs of others.

Part 1

LEADING
THE TROOP

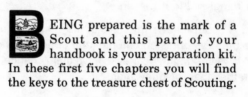 EING prepared is the mark of a Scout and this part of your handbook is your preparation kit. In these first five chapters you will find the keys to the treasure chest of Scouting.

Chapter 1

The Scoutmaster's Role

You are the driving force in making the troop go!

CONGRATULATIONS on your selection as Scoutmaster. A committee or someone convinced you that you were the man for this job, and you "volunteered." We salute you for accepting this important responsibility and trust that you recognize your job as one of the most vital in the Boy Scouts of America.

A troop's success depends heavily upon the effectiveness of its Scoutmaster. You will derive great personal satisfaction as you watch the growth of your Scouts in stature and knowledge and see the plans of your troop unfold into reality. There are others in a troop with important responsibilties. You must be sure to use their talents by seeking them out and delegating tasks to get things done, but you are the key man in making the troop go.

This handbook is written to provide most of what you will need to be a successful Scoutmaster. There are other tools that will be helpful to you, but you will want to keep this book close at hand.

Your Qualifications

You probably have more qualifications for being a Scoutmaster than you suppose.

If you were a Boy Scout, or have served Scouting in some adult capacity, this experience will help—no matter how little actual experience you have had.

Whatever you do for a living will help in some way. Scoutmasters are teachers and plumbers, machinists and doctors, farmers and merchants. Some of what they know how to do helps them—often in surprising ways.

Your lifetime of experience will help. You have been a boy, and if you remember what it was like, you will understand boys better. If you are a parent, your experience in that role will be useful.

You will draw on everything you are and have been to be a good Scoutmaster. In turn, some of what you learn as Scoutmaster you can "plow back" into the other parts of your life.

What qualities should you possess to be a good Scoutmaster? One could make a long list, but that wouldn't help. Basically, you need to be an open person—one who speaks honestly and listens intently. You need a sense of humor—not the ability to tell funny stories, but the ability to smile at yourself and at life. You need to understand the place of the outdoor program in Scouting and your part in it. And then—and this is quite important—you ought to like boys.

Given these basic qualifications, plus your lifetime of experience, you have what it takes. Naturally, though, you will need the knowledge and skill to use the Boy Scout program. This you can get from this book and other Scouting literature, from training experiences, and from fellow Scouters who know their business.

But alone, your qualifications will not get you there, nor do they need to. There are, in addition to you, lots of Scouters who are both eager and able to help. Part of being a Scoutmaster is knowing when and how to look to the able people who surround you.

Although we are always looking for more help, there is no other organization that can boast of the human resources available to the Boy Scouts of America. Ask for help. Contact your council office and find out who can help your troop and what resources are available to make your troop program the best that it can be.

Now let's take a good look at what you'll be doing.

A Quick Look at the Boy Scout Program

You may have read in the introduction how Robert Baden-Powell, the founder of Scouting, perhaps a century ahead of his time insisted that education could be fun. And should be. The PATROL SYSTEM he founded is based on this principle. Scouters have known for decades that Scouting is nothing less than a revolution in education.

While boys will not think of it in this way, your troop is a unique educational unit. Look at some of the things it offers to prospective members. (You probably will mention these to boys when they join.)

The boy can join if he wants to, but he doesn't have to. If he's not satisfied, he can quit anytime. Or he can transfer to another troop if he thinks he can do better.

He will have many chances to learn and improve himself. He can accept them or not; it will not be held against him if he turns them down. He decides what he will learn, and how fast.

As he improves himself, he will be recognized. Those who do the most get the most recognition. Each boy sets his own goals for personal growth.

The troop is governed by boys. They make the rules and plan the program with your guidance.

They will have chances to lead, and to learn how to lead.

The adult leaders give their services to boys without charge. What they do is of such value that if the boys were charged accordingly, few could afford to belong.

So Scouting *is* education. And it looks like fun because it *is* fun. Thus, you have two quick ways to judge your troop and everything it does.

1. Is it fun for the boys? If it's not, it's not Scouting.

2. Is it educational? Does it lead boys to one or more of Scouting's aims? It may be fun, but if it lacks this sense of purpose, it is not Scouting.

Every Scouting activity and way of organizing and doing things has a purpose behind it. Each has something to do with moving boys from where they are toward some basic goals. We call these goals the aims of Scouting. Here they are in general.

Scouting works toward three aims. One is *character*. We may define character as what the boy is himself: his personal qualities, his values, his outlook.

Education through Scouting can be fun and should be.

A second aim is *citizenship*. Used broadly, citizenship means the boy's relationship to others. He comes to learn of his obligations to other people, to the society he lives in, to the government that presides over that society.

A third aim of Scouting is *fitness*. Fitness shows itself in four distinct aspects: of the body (well-tuned and healthy), the mind (able to think and solve problems), the "moral fiber" (as shown by courage, respect for others, etc.), and the emotions (self-control and self-respect).

It is obvious that a variety of methods and activities must be used to attain these aims. You will not make sweeping changes with a single hike, game, or meeting. Yet everything should be done with purpose.

Thus it is important that you know and use the methods of Scouting. They have been designed especially to accomplish the objectives. There are other methods but they may bring different results—results quite different from those we are seeking.

Boy Scouting is for boys ages 11 through 17. The other parts of Scouting are Tiger Cubs, BSA, for 7-year-old boys, Cub Scouting for boys 8 through 9 (at age 10 Cub Scouts become Webelos Scouts), Varsity Scouting for boys 14 through 18, and Exploring for young men and young women ages 14 through 20.

What a Scoutmaster Does

The Scoutmaster is the key to good Scouting. The troop is molded in his image. If he leaves, he must be promptly replaced or the troop goes downhill fast. Whatever abilities the troop committee and assistant Scoutmasters may have, they are not substitutes for a good Scoutmaster.

Yet for all of that, the Scoutmaster is not an obvious or even a very visible part of the best troops. Visit a top troop and you may not even recognize the Scoutmaster by what he does.

A Scoutmaster controls, but does not command. He calls the signals but is rarely "up front." Thus, if you are looking for a comparison, a Scoutmaster is more like a coach than a field commander. He is on the sidelines. His work is done before the action takes place.

A good Scoutmaster works from this base: *never do anything for a boy that the boy can do for himself.*

The crucial part of this is your estimate of what a boy can do.

Would you, as a publisher, let boys buy your material on credit and trust them to deliver it to patrons, collect for it, keep books,

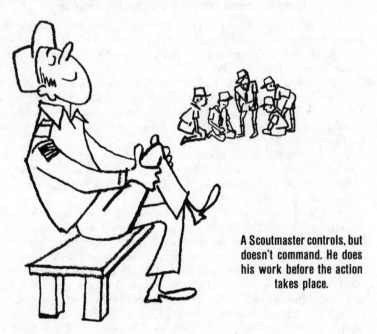

A Scoutmaster controls, but doesn't command. He does his work before the action takes place.

and pay you on time? Daily newspapers have done it for a century, with great results.

Can a boy teach another to swim? Can a boy demonstrate tent pitching? Can a 12-year-old patrol leader keep order in his patrol? Can a 14-year-old run 40 troop meetings a year—or even one?

Boys can do all of these things. In their better moments they also report fires and crimes, drive farm tractors, work for pay, bring up little brothers and sisters, save people from drowning, and play games with a zest few professional athletes can match.

But if you put a bunch of boys in a room together they can generate instant chaos. They punch each other, roll on the floor, break the chairs, and ultimately get thrown out.

Thus boys are great contradictions. They are supremely capable, but they are raw material. They need the guidance of an adult to make the leap. As Scoutmaster, you help them become what they want to become.

Visit a Troop

Suppose we visit a meeting of a good troop. This troop has been going a while. The Scoutmaster is trained and has been on the job for some time.

A Scout directs us to the Scoutmaster. He's in a side room, talking to a Scout. He seems to have time to talk. By the sounds from the meeting room, we judge that the meeting is going on without him. We try a few questions.

"Don't you run the troop meeting?"

"The senior patrol leader does that."

"Don't you keep the records?"

"The scribe does that."

"Who planned this meeting?"

"The patrol leaders' council."

"But who keeps the boys under control in there?"

"Their patrol leaders."

"Do you like to lead boys?"

"Sure. But that's not my job. I teach them to lead themselves. They're supposed to learn to lead. They can't do that if I do the leading."

"Was the troop like this when you started?"

"Shucks no. I had to do everything. But I made up my mind that I was going to teach them to do as much as I could."

"Have you finished?"

"No. This isn't a job you ever finish. But we're getting there."

The history of one Scoutmaster in one troop is likely to be the history of a gradual shift of power. When you take over a troop, you have to be on guard against instant chaos. So you start by taking charge. You quietly, but firmly, establish yourself as the leader.

But as soon as you have established yourself as their leader, you start moving the power back to the Scouts. As fast as they learn to lead and accept responsibility, you give it to them. And they learn fast.

This doesn't mean that you work yourself out of a job. But you do work yourself into a different kind of job. You work yourself into the background and boy leaders into the foreground. You spend more time training them and less time doing their work.

Boys and Adults

You must recognize that there are two things going on at once in the troop, and you are intimately involved in both.

One is the troop's organization and activities. The troop is an ongoing body with plans and program. There are all of the details to be worked out and followed up: who's going, how many cars do we need, who's buying the food, where are the tent stakes, when did Bill get his Second Class badge? If you are going to address yourself to all these details, you will have to quit your job, leave your family, and give up sleeping. So resolve right now that you are not going to play superman and try to know everything and run everthing.

The other part of this program is the individual boys who are involved in it. They are the reason for all the planning and activity and organization, and you do not delegate your concern and interest in each Scout to anyone. You are friend, counselor, and inspirational leader to every boy in the troop.

Scouts will have less trouble seeing you in this role than you will yourself. It is only natural for boys to look to boy leaders for advancement help, details on activities, equipment, etc. It is equally natural for them to look to you for adult guidance and counsel, judgment, and common sense.

The better you know each individual boy in the troop, the more valuable his Scouting experience will be.

So as a Scoutmaster you are a strange combination. At the same time that you are close to every boy, you work hard at placing others in positions of leadership.

Working with adults, your position is much the same. You share problems and needs with the committee and other leaders. You encourage others to carry out their jobs aggressively—yet without your influence, they may go off the track. Here, too, you lead without commanding.

There is a wealth of talent available among committee members, parents, and assistant Scoutmasters. You need these folks. Together they can do dozens of things you can't. They are your best resources.

Some Scoutmasters have trouble getting anything out of these resources. Here are some common reasons for their troubles.

- One Scoutmaster can't delegate. He asks for "cooperation" and "help," but then he ignores it and goes on doing everything himself. Under these circumstances, people just quietly fade away.

Take charge of the troop, then find suitable jobs for others.

- The troop program is poor. It is difficult to get people to cooperate with something that doesn't seem to be getting anywhere. This is why good troops often have more help than they need, while weak ones don't seem to get support from anybody. You won't get much cooperation unless you have something good going.

- Consider the opposite problem, too. It is less obvious but quite common. The troop succeeds and attracts a large group of adults who want to help. Most of them are parents of boys in the troop. In the midst of this surplus, the boy leaders and even the Scoutmaster may find themselves displaced by an army of eager fathers.

The Scoutmaster plays a crucial role in getting a proper balance between too little and too much adult support. He must recognize where support leaves off and interference begins.

Boy leaders help make the troop program go.

Troop Activities and How They Happen

The troop program is what holds the troop together. It is the sticky stuff on the flypaper. It is the mortar in the brick wall. If you take the program out of the troop, all you have left is a bunch of boys standing around with their hands in their pockets. And they don't stand that way long.

Troop program cannot be whipped up on the spot. You can't bring everyone together and then decide what to do. It has to be decided first.

Exactly what the Scoutmaster's part in the program is, depends on where he is in shifting the power. If he has a brand new troop, he will do many things himself. If he and the troop are both experienced, he will do more coaching and less direct program work.

This is equally true with the outdoor program. It is unreasonable to expect a Scoutmaster to be highly skilled in all the outdoor activities of Scouting. But it *is* reasonable to expect him to train boy leaders to do the jobs. Then he can be free to:

- Observe and talk to Scouts.

- Make sure the various events happen.

- Coach boy leaders (praise for good work and help for weaknesses).

- Make sure things are being done safely.

It may sound like a pipe dream that a Scoutmaster is supposed to train boy leaders in things that he is not even good at himself. But nobody says that *he* has to do all the training. Other leaders in the troop, committee members, fathers, merit badge counselors, and your council can all help in the process.

Helping the Boy

As Scoutmaster, you oversee all the activity of the troop. You make sure that it happens, that it's purposeful, that it's safe. That it accomplishes something. But you deliberately work yourself out of direct involvement so you will have time to help boys individually.

You will need to get to know each boy as soon as he joins. You can do this by setting aside some time for him.

This is hard to do during troop meetings. There are too many other demands on your time. Set aside time before or after a meeting when you can meet with the boy alone. Or, set aside a separate evening when you plan to meet all the new boys and their families, one at a time.

However you do it, be sure that you do it for every boy when he joins. Get to know about his family, his interests, what is he good at, how he does in school, what he hopes for in Scouting. This is the first of many conferences you'll have with him. In Scouting, these planned sessions are called Scoutmaster conferences. Their purpose is to help build a relationship between the man and the boy and give the Scout a chance to set some goals for himself.

You'll get to know him that way. And he will get to know you, and he'll know from the start that you take Scouting seriously and you take him seriously.

From your earliest acquaintance with new Scouts, you will recognize some strengths and weaknesses.

Here is a bright one.

This Scout is an athlete.

There is a natural leader.

That one talks well to adults but seems to have no friends his own age.

Such a private catalog will tell you at least two things:

1. What assets these boys have that you can count on as resources in the troop.

2. What problems these boys have that you may be able to help with.

By finding ways to use a boy's good points, you can give him confidence and you may help to get rid of some of his problems.

Having learned what a boy is like at the outset, you can then watch him to see how things go. If he grows as you hope, that's fine. If things don't go so well, you can move in and try to help. In any case, if you can get him to set some goals for himself, then he'll be trying to please himself, not just you.

You should develop a good coach-counselor relationship with each Scout. Every boy in the troop should be able to talk freely with you. This is being able to express one's real feelings, not just talking about the weather and ball games.

You should see yourself as a coach and counselor, as well as an expert in axmanship and tent pitching.

Work Your Strengths—
Delegate Your Weaknesses

Every program skill you have is an advantage. If you know how to teach first aid, build a fire, or tie flies, you have valuable skills that you can share with other leaders and with Scouts. These are all to your credit, and you can use them. On the other hand, it is a rare man who knows all of these things.

The point is, you can have a good troop without being a champion at everything in *The Official Boy Scout Handbook*. You should learn those skills that interest you, but you needn't feel that you have to be an expert in all of them. Let somebody else be the expert. And a lot of these experts can be boys.

It is the other elements in Scout leadership that are essential. You have to be able to work with the troop committee. You have to be able to train boy leaders to lead. You have to coach and sometimes counsel.

As a Scoutmaster, you set up others so that they can run the activities and make the troop go. In turn, you are free to do other important work with individual boys.

The Scoutmaster's Satisfaction

Considering the pay scale of Scoutmasters, there must be something else in it for those who do it. And indeed there is. That something is satisfaction.

It is only reasonable that a Scoutmaster should get some joy from his work. If he is unhappy doing it, he will fail. He must be happy to succeed.

Taking over as Scoutmaster is usually the beginning of a building process. You build the troop, and you try to keep one step ahead. As in building anything, at times you work hard but have little to show for it. There are slips along the way.

For most Scoutmasters, the first year is not overrun with satisfactions. That doesn't mean that it's no fun. But you don't get the feeling, in the early months, that you have conquered the world.

Beginning after a year, more or less, the satisfactions roll in more frequently. They are often not dramatic, but they have intense meaning for the man who worked his head off for them.

The senior patrol leader runs a whole troop meeting like an old pro for the first time, never asking once for help. The troop sets up camp without a word from you. It makes you proud!

Chapter 2

Starting Out as a Scoutmaster

You have an appointment with destiny.

THIS chapter has two sections. The first is for the Scout-master of a new troop while the second is for a new Scout-master in an existing troop. There are differences in the way you operate. But in either case, knowing your commissioner will really help you. Call your Scout service center for your commissioner's name and telephone number. Look in the white pages under Boy Scouts of America.

LEADING A NEW TROOP

In many ways this is an ideal situation. True, the troop so far is just a list of boys' names. But no mistakes have been made either. You can start off right. You won't have to undo anything. You can grow into the Scoutmaster's shoes as the boys grow into a troop.

It is better to wait a couple of weeks to get started than to rush into a first meeting unprepared. But don't wait too long. The boys will be eager to get started. You don't have to be an old pro to get started, but you should be ahead of the Scouts. They'll catch up fast, so you need a little head start.

Find out what it's all about by reading the basic literature. You'll find this *Scoutmaster Handbook, The Official Patrol Leader Handbook,* and *The Official Boy Scout Handbook* great reference tools. Don't try to read them from cover to cover. Use the index to find the things you need.

Getting the Troop Program Started

Start out with weekly troop meetings. The regularity of the weekly meeting is important at the start. Write out your meeting program. At first you'll have to do the planning yourself. Later your boy leaders—the patrol leaders' council—will help and eventually do most of the planning.

Write everything out in detail. List your preopening activity, opening ceremony, announcements, games, demonstrations, and closing activities. List any equipment needed and arrange for it before the meeting.

Make arrangements for the meeting place to be open or get a key. You should arrive early—before any of the boys. Make it a rule that no Scouts go inside until the adult leader arrives.

Follow your written program, but don't be its slave. If an activity doesn't come off, go on to the next one. If interest wears down before the scheduled time to stop, don't keep it going just because the clock hasn't caught up with the schedule.

Keep the program lively. Every minute should be fun. Keep talk down and action up. Alternate sitting and activity. Boys just can't sit still very long, so don't expect them to.

An hour and a half is the maximum length of time for a meeting. Less is OK. It's better to have lots of action for an hour than a dull meeting that lasts for an hour and a half.

Start and close on time. Your preopening activity will take care of early arrivals. When the word gets out that meetings start on time, Scouts will be there on time.

Plan at least two meetings ahead. Then you can make announcements about coming attractions.

Control the group. Don't let them get out of hand for a moment. They must know that while activities will be lots of fun, there's no place for horseplay. Don't lecture on discipline, but let them know right at the start what you will and will not tolerate.

You'll really get the troop off to a good start if you plan and announce a troop hike for the end of the first month's program. Plan for your first overnight camp within 2 months.

SAMPLE MEETING SUGGESTIONS

The following meeting suggestions can be used with a brand new troop, a reorganized troop, or a troop that has not been very active. They are intended to get you started. You and your Scouts will be able to think of all kinds of other activities once you get started. These meetings are based on the Hiking skill award.

Read the meeting notes to become thoroughly familiar with the program. A few days before the meeting talk with the older boys. Show them what you are going to do and give them parts in the program.

Meeting No. 1

MATERIALS NEEDED. Practice compass made from a paper tablet, push pin, tape, and a penny; volleyball or basketball; map of your community, commercial or sketch map you made yourself; *Official Boy Scout Handbooks*.

PREOPENING. As Scouts arrive have them join one of two groups. One group works with a large drawing of a compass, learning each of the direction points and degrees.

The second group studies a community map to locate their homes, school, churches, and other points of interest. Have each Scout spend time in both groups.

Persons responsible _____

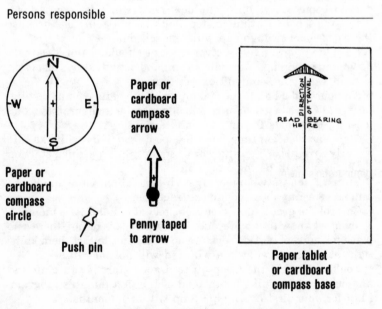

Paper or cardboard compass circle

Paper or cardboard compass arrow

Push pin

Penny taped to arrow

Paper tablet or cardboard compass base

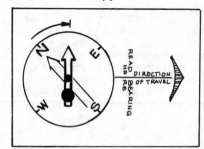

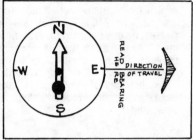

Attach the paper compass circle and paper compass arrow to the compass base with a push pin. Hold the paper tablet practice compass on edge and the penny's weight will make the arrow point straight up to "north." Lay the compass flat and hold the arrow in that position while you turn the compass circle until it lines up with the compass arrow. Read the bearing opposite the direction-of-travel line.
Compass is pointing east.

OPENING. A boy leader has the troop form a straight line. All come to attention and make the Scout sign. All repeat the Scout Oath or Promise.

Person responsible _____

ON MY HONOR I WILL DO MY BEST
TO DO MY DUTY TO GOD AND MY COUNTRY
AND TO OBEY THE SCOUT LAW;
TO HELP OTHER PEOPLE AT ALL TIMES;
TO KEEP MYSELF PHYSICALLY STRONG,
MENTALLY AWAKE, AND MORALLY STRAIGHT.

SKILLS DEVELOPMENT. Gather Scouts in a circle and seated on the floor. Have ready a list of interesting places in or near your community. The list should include such things as historic places, museums, scenic areas, government buildings, recreation areas, business or industrial sites, zoos, parks, homes of well-known persons, etc. All items on the list should be within 3 miles from your troop's meeting place.

Help boys plan the route of a 5-mile hike the troop will take at the end of this month. Plan the hike route to include a number of points of interest from the list.

Also talk about places where the troop can stop to eat a packed meal, and money needed for transportation, sight-seeing, or refreshments. Have a member of the patrol leaders' council take notes.

Person responsible _____

GAME. Play over and under relay. Form teams of five to eight boys each (patrols perhaps) in single files. The front player has a ball that he passes over his head, using both hands, to the player behind him, and so on down the line. When the last player gets the ball he runs to the front of the line and passes the ball between his legs back down the line. As each new lead player starts the ball down the line, the method switches from overhead to between the legs. The ball must not be thrown. The first team to play through until they are back in their original order of players is the winner.

Another way of playing is to have the first player pass the ball over his head, the second through his legs, and so forth down the line—over, under, over, under.

Person responsible _____

PATROL MEETING. Each patrol gathers at its own part of the troop meeting room. The patrol scribe collects dues and records attendance. He gives it to the troop scribe or Scoutmaster.

Patrols discuss things to take on a hike. They talk about personal items and patrol items. Each member makes a copy of what he should bring. Each patrol leader appoints a hikemaster to lead the patrol's participation in the troop's hike this month.

ANNOUNCEMENTS. Have the senior patrol leader regroup the Scouts in a half-circle and seated on the floor. Have him make the following announcements:

- Each Scout should read pages 175-176 in *The Official Boy Scout Handbook.*
- Select a service patrol for next week's meeting. They should arrive before anyone else and arrange the room. They also put the room back in order when the meeting ends.
- Scouts wishing to be tested or helped on skill awards may come to each troop meeting early. A leader will be on hand for that purpose each week.
- All Scouts who have compasses should bring them to next week's meeting. The troop may have some compasses, too.
- A meeting of the patrol leaders' council will take place after the troop meeting ends tonight.

A Scout leads the troop in singing the "Hiking Song." The tune is the "Artillery (or Caisson) Song."

> Over hill, over dale, we will hit the Greenwood trail,
> As our Scout troop goes hiking along.
> All around, in and out, gee it's great to be a Scout,
> As our Scout troop goes hiking along.
> And it's Hi! Hi! Hee! the BSA for me
> Shout out our name and shout it strong!
> Where'er we go, you will always know
> That our Scout troop goes hiking along!

Person responsible _____

SCOUTMASTER'S MINUTE. While Scouts are seated, read or say in your own words the following:

This month, many of the things we'll do and talk about will be about hiking. When the pioneers were opening the wilderness, hiking was about the only way to get where they wanted to go. They had to hike through thick brush and woodlands, over mountains and across plains. These hikers had to learn the habits of wild animals and know about plants in order to survive.

Today, you can hike wilderness areas and other kinds of trails, too. These may be unfamiliar to you and you'll need to learn how to find your way. You'll also have to learn how to take care of yourself under various conditions, and in any kind of weather.

You're going to learn things and see things you've never known before. And you'll enjoy every minute of it, too! Not all of hiking is easy, but you'll be proud when you've gotten through a tough section of trail— just like the pioneers of old!

CLOSING. After the troop has been formed in a straight line, a Scout reads the following:

• **THE OUTDOOR CODE** •

AS AN AMERICAN,
I WILL DO MY BEST TO —
BE CLEAN IN MY OUTDOOR MANNERS,
BE CAREFUL WITH FIRE,
BE CONSIDERATE IN THE OUTDOORS, AND
BE CONSERVATION-MINDED.

Person responsible _____

Dismiss the troop.

AFTER THE MEETING. The patrol leaders' council meets. Together they go over the program for next week's troop meeting. Assignments are made to obtain different kinds of maps for the instruction period. (Get maps from gas stations, stores, tourist departments, or chambers of commerce.) Gather information about places of interest discussed tonight.

Meeting No. 2

MATERIALS NEEDED. *The Official Boy Scout Handbook* and samples of different kinds of maps; compass; large practice compass; tape measure or yardstick; badges for recognition (if required); U.S. flag; chalk.

Person responsible _____

PREOPENING. The service patrol arrives early to clear the meeting room for troop activities. Skill award testing and help is provided by a leader for Scouts who want it.

As other Scouts arrive, other leaders show how to measure the length of steps and gauge distance.

Person responsible _____

OPENING. Scouts line up and face the U.S. flag. All salute while a Scout reads or sings the third verse of "America."

> Let music swell the breeze,
> And ring from all the trees,
> Sweet freedom's song;
> Let mortal tongues awake,
> Let all that breathe partake,
> Let rocks their silence break,
> The sound prolong.

Person responsible _____

SKILLS DEVELOPMENT. Show Scouts the different kinds of maps on display.

- Point out the difference between maps used to show bus routes or hiking trails, and road maps issued by petroleum companies.
- Tell how topographic maps show how land is shaped, and how they are helpful to hikers.
- Pass the maps around so each Scout can see the differences in each kind of map.
- Show how to measure distances along roads on a map by using the mileage scale. Point out some samples of map symbols.

Person responsible _____

Next, display the large practice compass used in last week's troop meeting.

- Have a leader show the eight principal points of the compass.
- Explain how to read the degree numbers.
- Show the Scouts a real compass. Show that the needle always points north.
- Have each Scout show how to turn the compass so the needle points to north. Don't rush this demonstration. Some boys may have some trouble at first. Take time to help them understand.

Person responsible _____

GAME. Let's test your Scouts' new knowledge in a compass game. Draw a large circle on the floor with a piece of chalk. (Pieces of masking tape will do if chalk can't be used.) Scouts stand on the circle line, facing inward. Each represents a compass point, except "it" who stands in the center. "It" calls out two compass points. (Example: north and west). The Scouts representing these points try to change position, while "it" tries to take the place of one of them. The Scout left without a place in the circle becomes "it." This game can also be played outdoors.

Person responsible _____

PATROL MEETING. Patrols meet in their usual places. While the patrol scribe collects dues and marks attendance, the patrol leader starts a discussion about designing a patrol flag, and making up a patrol yell. Let everyone in the patrol come up with an idea for each.

ANNOUNCEMENTS. A boy leader gathers Scouts together, seated on the floor. He makes the following announcements:

- Select next week's service patrol.
- At the beginning of each troop meeting Scouts interested in skill award requirements can get help.
- All Scouts should read pages 177-87 in *The Official Boy Scout Handbook*. It's a good idea to mark the pages in case the page numbers are forgotten.
- Introduce the patrol leaders' council member who found more information about places of interest to be seen on the hike. He tells what he was able to find out.
- Remind troop members that the hike will take the place of the regular troop meeting 3 weeks from tonight.
- A brief patrol leaders' council meeting will be held after the troop meeting ends tonight.

If anyone in the troop has qualified for a skill award belt loop, merit badge, or badge of rank, this is the time for awards presentation. Make sure the awards ceremony is dignified, yet simple.

SCOUTMASTER'S MINUTE. Read the following or say it in your own words:

The ship's compass is a valuable item of equipment that has been used by sailors for several hundred years. Men of the sea have put their complete trust in the compass, and for good reason: they knew they could believe in the direction their compass indicated. It's interesting that the compass needle point traditionally has been made in the shape of a fleur-de-lis, which the Scout badge is patterned after.

The Scout Oath and the Scout Law act as a sort of compass for you and me. We pledge to follow the direction each sets for us every time we raise our Scout sign and repeat the words. Learn to trust those words and they'll steer a great course for your lives.

CLOSING. Scouts form a circle with everyone facing in. Each crosses his arms and holds the hand of the person to either side. The leader stands in the circle's center and makes the Scout sign. He says: "Scouts, be prepared!" The Scouts answer, "We are prepared!"

Person responsible _____

Dismiss the troop.

AFTER THE MEETING. The patrol leaders' council meets to go over the program for next week's troop meeting. Each patrol leader is asked to get together with his patrol members during the week to create a patrol yell. This is a kind of cheer for the patrol.

Also, each patrol leader chooses another assignment for the instruction session of next week's troop meeting, from the following list:

- Making homemade canteens from plastic *food* bottles, *only.*
- Making a hiker's snack mix (sometimes called "birdseed"). See page 178 of the *Handbook.*
- Instructing Scouts on equipment and clothing to be used on both winter and summer hikes. (See troop meeting No. 3 program.)

Take a look at the maps to plan the hike route your troop will take in 3 weeks.

Meeting No. 3

MATERIALS NEEDED. *The Official Boy Scout Handbook* and lists of summer hike items and winter hike items; badges for recognition period (if required); cards for game; chalk.

Person responsible _____

PREOPENING. Service patrol gets to the meeting room early to get the room ready. Leaders are on hand to help Scouts with skill award requirements.

As other Scouts arrive they are each given a card which has a compass direction written on it. Each is told to place his card at the correct place on a circle drawn on the floor with chalk. Mark "north" on the circle to start them off.

Person responsible _____

OPENING. A boy leader forms troop in a straight line. Scouts are grouped by patrols. He calls each patrol forward in turn to demonstrate its patrol yell.

Person responsible _____

SKILLS DEVELOPMENT. Scouts sit on the floor in a horseshoe formation. The leader reminds them that the hike being planned will be a lot of fun, but much more fun if good hiking skills are used. Tonight, the subject of what to wear and bring will be demonstrated in three parts:

- Clothing and personal gear by the_____ Patrol.
- Homemade canteens by the _____ Patrol.
- Hike snacks by the _____ Patrol.

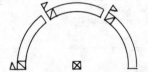

Horseshoe or half circle formation

Canteens. If a Scout doesn't have a factory-made canteen, he can make his own by washing out a plastic bottle that some kind of food came in. (Maple syrup, cooking oil bottles are good! But *do not* use nonfood bottles!) Make sure the bottle is washed out well. Tie a rope sling to the bottle so that it can be carried on the hike.

Person responsible _____

Nuts and Bolts. Mix together equal parts of raisins, peanuts, sugar-coated chocolate candies, pretzels, and wheat, rice, or corn cereal squares. Pack in a plastic bag.

Honey Bars. You'll need a half cup of each of the following: raisins, figs, dried apricots, and peanuts. Chop up fruit and nuts and mix together. Add a half teaspoon of lemon juice and enough honey to bind the fruit and nuts together. Shape into bars and wrap in aluminum foil. Ummm, boy!

Person responsible _____

GAME. Scouts form a large circle. One is chosen to be the *"sleeping sentry,"* who sits at the center, blindfolded. In front of him is an object. (A book, ball, or block of wood will do.) Scouts are to creep quietly up and remove the object without being heard by the "sentry." If the sentry hears an oncoming Scout, he quickly points at him. If he points correctly, that Scout must return to starting place for another try. The Scout getting the object, unnoticed by the sentry, scores a point. Repeat as often as time allows.

Person responsible _____

PATROL MEETING. Each patrol meets in its usual place. Dues are collected and attendance recorded by the patrol scribe.

The patrol discusses things needed for the troop hike. The patrol leader helps newer members plan how to get the things they need.

Work continues on designing and making a patrol flag.

ANNOUNCEMENTS. Scouts sit on the floor and in a circle. A Scout leads the following song to the tune of "Yankee Doodle."

Oh, soldiers march because they're told,
And chickens, they tread lightly,
But, we're like all the Scouts of old
And hike each new trail sprightly.
Chorus
See new sights and meet new friends.
Learn from ev'ry outing.
Pushing on 'til each trail ends,
We're on the road with Scouting.

Person responsible _____

A boy leader makes the following announcements:

• The service patrol for next week is_____ .

• Each patrol's flag is to be done in time for the troop hike 2 weeks from tonight.

Patrol flag ideas are in The Official Patrol Leader Handbook.

• All Scout should mark pages 188-97 in the *Handbook* and read before next week's troop meeting.

• As usual, Scouts may come to troop meeting early to be coached or tested on skill award requirements.

• Scouts who have earned a skill award belt loop should be recognized at this point of tonight's troop meeting program.

• Announce a brief patrol leaders' council meeting after tonight's meeting.

SCOUTMASTER'S MINUTE. The leader should either read the following or say it in his own words:

Here we are, only 2 weeks from the troop hike. You have been working hard to get ready for it. For some of you this hike will be the first Scout activity outside our weekly troop meetings.

Some people will say, "What's the big deal? A hike is nothing more than a walk!" Not so! A hike is a walk with a purpose. Think of all the things you've learned so far as you've been getting ready—planning where you're going to go, what you will see, what you will do. You've learned the kinds of food to eat on a hike and the proper way to dress comfortably. And you'll learn more, too! Hike safety, hike first aid, and perhaps a little bit about nature are a few things.

All that is much more than just going for a walk. Scout hiking is fun with good friends—and it's a walk with a purpose!

CLOSING. All Scouts form a circle with everyone facing the center. All fold their arms and bow their heads. The senior patrol leader stands in the center and recites the Scout benediction:

> May the Great Master of all Scouts
> Be with us till we meet again.

Person responsible _____

Dismiss the troop.

AFTER THE MEETING. The patrol leaders' council looks over next week's troop meeting. Assignments are made to prepare for games and demonstrations. Go over the hike route together and settle all questions.

Meeting No. 4

MATERIALS NEEDED. *The Official Boy Scout Handbook* and maps of the hike route; map signs for game; badges to be awarded (if any); pencils and paper, do's and don'ts quiz.

Person responsible _____

PREOPENING. The service patrol clears the room for tonight's meeting. Leaders are on hand to counsel Scouts on Hiking skill award requirements.
  As troop members enter the room they are each given a piece of paper and a pencil. They are then told to look around the meeting room for things whose name begins with a letter of the word "Scout." For example: Scoutmaster, Chairs, Overcoat, Uniforms, Table. Papers are collected just before the opening ceremony. Winners to be announced during the announcement period.

Person responsible _____

OPENING. Scouts form a straight line. A patrol leader reads the following:

The fifth part of the Scout Law is "courteous." A Scout is polite to everyone regardless of age or position. He knows good manners make it easier for people to get along together. People expect more from us because we're Scouts. So we've got to keep trying harder. (He makes the Scout sign.) Repeat after me: "A Scout is courteous."

Person responsible _____

SKILLS DEVELOPMENT. The senior patrol leader asks the troop to sit on the floor in a half-circle formation. He shows a map with the route of the troop's hike drawn on it. Several pieces of hike information need to be covered:

- Where troop members should meet.
- When they should meet.
- What each person should bring.
- How long the hike should take and about when the troop will return.
- Discuss proper care of the feet (socks, shoes, and how to treat a blister).
- Some tips on proper hiking methods and precautions. As an introduction, write the following questions (not the answers) on a chalkboard or large piece of paper that everyone can see. Have the group answer and talk about each question.

Person responsible _____

True False

_____ _____ 1. Most times, water from a stream is safe to drink.

_____ _____ 2. For safety reasons it is always a good idea to hike in groups of three or more.

_____ _____ 3. Stand under trees during a storm to protect yourself from the rain.

_____ _____ 4. Walking along railroad tracks is a good hiking practice.

_____ _____ 5. Don't take up the whole sidewalk. It's not safe or courteous.

_____ _____ 6. Wear something white on your arms and legs when walking on a road at night.

_____ _____ 7. Don't swim in unfamiliar water.

_____ _____ 8. If ice will support two people, it will hold your whole patrol.

_____ _____ 9. Where there are no sidewalks, always walk on the left side of the road, facing traffic.

_____ _____ 10. Don't use spray paint to mark walls and trees so you won't get lost.

Answers: 1. false; 2. true; 3. false, trees may be struck by lightning; 4. false; 5. true; 6. true; 7. true; 8. false; 9. true; 10. true.

GAME. Before tonight's meeting have someone prepare 12 drawings of map symbols on separate 3 x 5 cards. Place the cards on a table and cover with a cloth. Gather the troop members around the table and remove the cover.

Everyone studies the cards *in silence.* After 1 minute, the cover is replaced and Scouts regroup at their regular patrol meeting locations. Each patrol makes a list of the symbols they remember seeing. The senior patrol leader collects the lists at the end of a 10-minute period.

Here are some ideas for your map symbol cards:

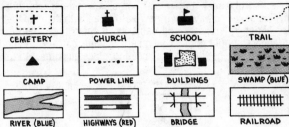

Person responsible _____

PATROL MEETING. Patrols remain in their meeting places. The patrol scribe marks attendance and collects dues. The patrol leader makes a final check of those planning to go on the troop hike next week. If time allows, practice compass directions together.

ANNOUNCEMENTS. All Scouts gather together. A leader announces the following:

• Mark pages 198-201 in the *Handbook* and read before the hike next week.

• Scouts can get help and testing on the Hiking skill award during the hike.

• Repeat meeting time and place for the hike.

• Those who have earned belt loops will receive them on the hike.

• Announce winners of the preopening game and the map symbol game.

• A brief patrol leaders' council meeting follows tonight's troop meeting.

Person responsible _____

SCOUTMASTER'S MINUTE. Read the following or say it in your own words:

(Hold up a crumpled piece of paper.) This paper is a form of litter. There are those who mar the beauty of the countryside by thoughtlessly scattering litter wherever they go.

Just walk down any street or take a bus ride and you'll see evidence of this all around you—on the street, in parks and camping areas, and especially on vacant lots.

We, as Scouts, can help to stop this if we decide never to be litterbugs ourselves. We can do our part by setting a good example and by asking that our friends and family do the same.

I'd like you to remember this while on our troop hike next week. The outdoors is for us to use and enjoy. It's also our duty to preserve its use and enjoyment for others.

CLOSING. Troop lines up by patrols. The senior patrol leader calls everyone to attention. Dismiss the game-winning patrol first. Then the second place patrol, and so on.

AFTER THE MEETING. The patrol leaders' council meets to go over final plans for the hike. Patrol leaders turn in up-to-date lists of those who will take part. Each patrol is asked to have their new patrol flag with them on the hike, skill books for hiking references, and cameras, if they have them.

Patrol leaders should contact members of their patrol to remind them of things to bring and getting to the meeting place on time.

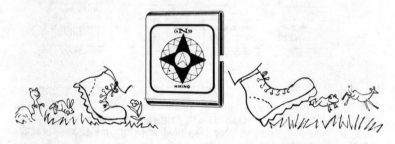

Meeting No. 5—The Hike

MATERIALS NEEDED. *The Official Boy Scout Handbook* and complete participation roster; badges for recognition; pencils and paper; personal drinking water, food, and equipment.

Person responsible _____

PREOPENING. Each patrol leader checks with his patrol to make sure everyone has proper footgear, a lunch, hiking snacks, water, telephone change, and raingear.

Patrol leaders report to the senior patrol leader when all Scouts have arrived and have been checked.

OPENING. The senior patrol leader gives final instructions for the hike. He leads the troop in saying the Scout Law. All make the Scout sign.

THE HIKE BEGINS! During any hike you should be prepared with games, stunts, and songs for Scouts to do. Even though the hike plan may have the group stopping at places along the way, it's good to keep generating spirit as you go. The hike will be more fun for everyone and it will make the time (and miles) pass more rapidly!

Here are some ideas for hike sparklers:

Walking "Buzz." The first Scout in line shouts "one," the next Scout shouts "two," and so on until the seventh Scout who says, "buzz." Each time the count comes to a number containing a seven (7, 17, 27, etc.), that Scout says "buzz." Each time "buzz" is said the direction of the count is reversed. (When the seventh Scout says "buzz," the sixth Scout says "eight" and the count moves to the head of the line until another "buzz" occurs: 17). If a Scout doesn't say the correct number, or "buzz," he takes a position at the rear of the hike line.

Person responsible _____

Trucking the Alphabet. The entire troop is a team in this game. As truck pass, Scouts read the lettering on them. Scouts call out letters beginning with "A" and work their way through the alphabet in order to "Z."
The same game can be played using license plates.

Person responsible _____

Pony Express Message. As Scouts hike in a file the last in line gives a message to the Scout walking in front of him. The message is passed up the line to the first Scout who drops to the rear and repeats the message to the Scout who started it. The chances are good that the message will have changed a great deal. Repeat the process beginning with the new last person in line.

Person responsible _____

Nature Hunt. As Scouts move along the hike route each must collect 10 samples of nature—leaves, stones, flowers, bugs, seeds, feathers; egg shells, moss, etc. Discuss and identify each sample by patrol groups during rest periods.

Person responsible _____

Songs. Any song whose beat can be adapted to a hiker's step can be sung while moving along. We've learned two hiking songs this month: "The Hiking Song" and "On the Road With Scouting."

Person responsible _____

ANNOUNCEMENTS. At the end of the hike, gather all Scouts together long enough to make the following quick announcements:
- Selection of next week's service patrol.
- Ask each patrol to choose a Scout to give a brief report of hike highlights at next week's meeting.
- Announce the time and place of a patrol leaders' council meeting to be held before next week's troop meeting.
- Award Hiking skill award belt loops to Scouts who earned them.
- Dismiss the troop.

The troop committee is your board of directors.

Getting Started With the Committee

You will be working closely with the troop committee. It is important to work out a basic understanding of who will do what. Generally, you will guide all activities in which boys are directly involved, and the committee will provide back-up support.

Be specific in asking for committee help. If it is in locating a campsite, selecting equipment, fixing up the troop meeting room, or providing transportation, tell just what you and the troop need and when.

It is important to note that the committee is responsible for troop leadership. If they did their job, they probably recruited you. They are also responsible for helping you secure an assistant Scoutmaster or two. And, if there are no assistants, they are responsible for leading the troop in your absence.

The troop committee can take a great deal of the recordkeeping and so-called "red tape" off your hands. Let them do it. It will free you to do more important jobs.

Some troop committees don't function. Often this happens because the Scoutmaster really doesn't let them help. He handles everything himself, and later on, when he really needs the committee, he finds that they have disappeared. You can avoid this problem by involving them in the troop from the start.

Another problem is the reverse—helping too much. You are lucky if your committee is made up of interested and aggressive members, but they must be led by a chairman who spells out exactly what their job is. Explain exactly what you want and don't want from the committee and count on the chairman to guide the members to give you the cooperation you want and need.

The committee should meet at least monthly. You should attend these meetings, to keep the committee advised of the needs of the troop and to be specific in your requests for help.

Getting Started With an Assistant Scoutmaster

If you are in luck, you will start the troop with an assistant Scoutmaster. Involve him in the planning. He will have good ideas to contribute, and the two of you will do a better job together. If he shares in the planning, he will also know what he is expected to do.

Divide responsibility specifically. You soon will learn what he does best. Then ask him to take on assignments and responsibilties that match his interests and abilities.

Don't expect every assistant to be on hand for every activity. If you have more than one assistant, you can divide responsibilities so that they are only involved in those meetings and activities where they have a direct part.

Share your ideas with your assistant.

Getting Started With the
Patrol Leaders' Council

After your first couple of meetings you will want to formally organize patrols. Use patrol-size groups (5 to 10 boys) temporarily at the start, but don't call them patrols until they actually are organized. The boys elect their patrol leaders.

Your senior patrol leader is a key boy leader. In a new troop you might nominate two or three boys for the position and then have the troop vote for the senior patrol leader from your selections.

The patrol leaders and senior patrol leader become your patrol leaders' council through and with whom you lead the troop.

We will talk more about this later in the next chapter.

Work through the boy leaders in a new or old troop.

TAKING OVER AN OLD TROOP

It is quite different to become the new Scoutmaster of an old troop. If you haven't had experience as a Scoutmaster, get some training right away to find out the best ways to run a troop. Or, next best, carefully read this *Scoutmaster Handbook.*

Find out whether the troop you will lead has been good, fairly good, average, or poor. Check up on how the former Scoutmaster operated and whether the patrols were functioning or just paper groups. Find out about the boy leadership. Is it good, bad, or indifferent? How about adults on the troop committee? Is there troop equipment? What is there and where is it stored? How about the troop treasury? Is there any money? Where is it kept and who is responsible for it? In other words, find out everything you can about the troop. Before you have a troop meeting, meet with the existing boy leaders, the senior patrol leader, patrol leaders, and junior assistant Scoutmaster. Have them tell you about their activities, what they think of the boys in their patrols, how well the patrol leaders' council has been functioning, and a little about the traditions of the troop.

If it appears that the boy leaders know what they are doing, encourage them to plan the troop meetings for the next month. If they don't seem qualified, you may have to do most of this for them.

Set the date for the first meeting and ask each patrol leader to call each boy in his patrol personally to let him know about the meeting date and time. Tell the leaders that you'll be in touch with them before the meeting for a report on prospective attendance.

The First Troop Meeting

Ideally, the chairman of the troop committee or someone else familiar to the boys will introduce you to the Scouts. If not, you'll have to introduce yourself. At some point in the meeting tell the Scouts of your enthusiasm for the things the troop is going to do and encourage every Scout to do his share to make it a great troop.

After the meeting, try to meet and talk with as many boys as you can.

Making Changes

Unless the troop is in bad shape, don't try to change things all at once. Be loyal to the old Scoutmaster. Don't listen to gossip about him from the Scouts, and don't criticize his work.

You may find that organization is nonexistent—patrols not functioning and leaders just names on paper. In this case, the troop must be reorganized. Call a meeting of the leaders. Ask them to agree to resign from their offices to permit free and open reorganization of patrols and election of officers. Point out that they will be eligible for reelection. Operate about the same way the Scoutmaster of a new troop would and get things going right.

The pattern of leadership you set during the first few months will determine troop operation for the whole time you are Scoutmaster.

Chapter 3

Troop Organization and the Patrol Leaders' Council

Scouting belongs to your chartered organization.

YOUR troop is an official unit of the Boy Scouts of America and like all such units it is owned and operated by a chartered organization. There are big troops and small troops and each may make use of the job titles and structure that the Boy Scouts of America has developed over the last 70 years.

CHARTERED ORGANIZATION

The organization responsible for your troop will appoint one person as Scouting coordinator. That person is the go-between for the pack, troop, and post and also represents you and your organization on the district committee and local council. The organization also will have many members—former Scouts, fathers of Scouts, former leaders, or other men and women who have some special leaning toward Scouting. Some of them might not be inclined to help just any troop, but will quickly join in to help "our" troop.

The members of your chartered organization can be recruited on a "permanent" basis to serve on the committee and as adult

CHARTERED ORGANIZATION

Scouting Coordinator

Troop Committee Chairman
Troop Committee Members

Cub Scout Pack

Your chartered organization works through a Scouting coordinator and a committee.

leaders or merit badge counselors. But you can also count on them for "spot" jobs—to help with a money-earning effort, a court of honor, or a camping experience.

Consider the members of your chartered organization very much on your side. If they're not doing much for the troop right now, it may be because nobody has asked them.

Your Troop Committee

Your most immediate resource is your troop committee. There are no fewer than three members on it, and most troops have many more. They have specific jobs as outlined in the *Troop Committee Guidebook*. You will get the greatest support from them if these jobs are carefully reviewed from time to time. You need to know what they're supposed to do. So do they. That will tend to eliminate any gray area that turns out to be nobody's job.

Once you and your committee each understand your jobs, you get your help by working through the chairman. You and he need to see eye to eye and have common objectives. You need to work closely and confer frequently.

Here are the general responsibilities of your troop committee:

1. Providing and supporting competent adult leadership for the troop.

2. Helping with the acquisition and maintenance of troop equipment.

3. Assisting with financing and records.

4. Supporting the advancement program of the troop.

5. Helping the troop recruit new boys and pack members.

6. Supporting the outdoor program.

7. Keep Boy Scouts and parents informed.

For most committees it is not practical for the whole committee to take on all these responsibilities. A typical committee has a member for advancement, another for finance, another for camping and another for the outdoors. Larger troops need subcommittees for some of these functions.

Exactly how responsibilities are shared among adult leaders, boy leaders, and committee members, is for each troop to work out. No one can tell you just how you should do it. In general, the committee supports the troop program but does not operate it. Its duties are in the area of administration. The Scoutmaster directs the program.

Parents of Scouts and members of the chartered organization are a good resource. There are thousands of troops whose rosters of committee members and leaders include only parents of registered Scouts.

At the same time, the potential of Scout parents is often not fully used. Scouts should have their parents complete a copy of the Troop Resource Survey, No. 4437. This sheet will help you identify many talented parents. There is no end to what parents can do to support the program.

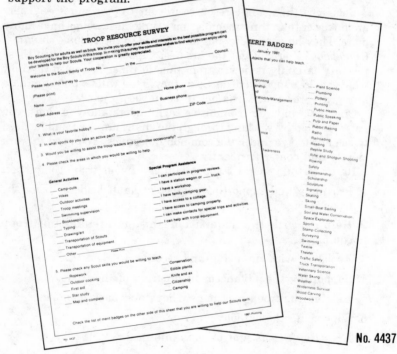

No. 4437

TROOP OFFICERS AND ORGANIZATION

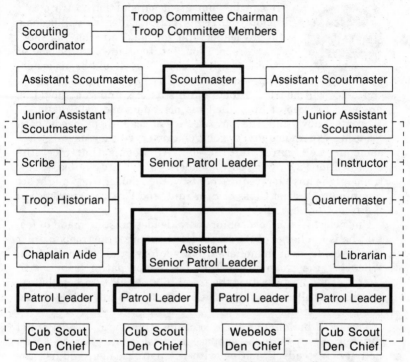

The patrol leaders' council appears within the heavy lines.

LEADERSHIP POSITIONS

You will find that there is a lot of flexibility in troop organization. For example, some troops momentarily short on assistant Scoutmasters will have troop committee members pitch in instead. An established troop may find it has little need for many assistant Scoutmasters because it has "grown its own" junior assistant Scoutmasters.

Some of the troop leadership positions are so natural that they explain themselves. The troop needs a qualified adult to run it: that's the Scoutmaster. It needs a qualified boy leader to direct the patrol leaders, chair the patrol leaders' council, and lead the troop in its activities: that's the senior patrol leader. If a troop owns any equipment, it needs somebody in charge of it: that's the quartermaster. If it keeps any records, it needs a scribe.

Elected Boy Scout Leaders

It can be your great satisfaction to train and develop your senior patrol leader. He will become your boy leader, and you make him the "big shot" of the troop. Your attitude toward the senior patrol leader is the key. You should be his coach, friend, and leader. Your senior patrol leader's character will be tried throughout his tenure, and you should be prepared to support him when his personal road gets rough.

Scouts know that the boy elected to lead them needs both Scouting experience and a good character, so they usually elect someone well suited for the job. All Scouts that meet the qualifications set by the patrol leaders' council are eligible. A new troop might have few requirements while an older troop might set a minimum of First Class or Star rank and 1 year's experience in the troop for eligibility.

Once elected, the new senior patrol leader must be made to feel that he is in charge of the troop. He should call the troop to order and preside over membership inventory and/or inspection. Whenever the troop is together the senior patrol leader is in charge. He may turn over the troop to an adult or a boy, but he retains overall leadership of the assembled troop. He should dismiss the troop.

The art of building up the role of the senior patrol leader is not difficult. As an example, suppose a patrol is late to arrive for an activity. Instead of visiting with the patrol leader, you ask the senior patrol leader to investigate. He is responsible to you for the action of the patrols. Use him.

You must build up the role of the senior patrol leader if the patrol method is to work. Giving real control of the troop to him means that he can then delegate it to the patrol leaders and other boys. If you run things yourself the leadership of the senior patrol leader constantly will be "short-circuited" and the boy will never feel the pressure or accomplishment of leading others.

Remember, the senior patrol leader is your funnel to the boys in the troop. Some of his usual duties are to:

- Chair board of review for Scouts of Tenderfoot, Second Class, and First Class ranks.

- Preside at all troop meetings, events, and activities.

- Chair the patrol leaders' council.

- Serve as leader of the troop's leadership corps.

- Name appointed boy leaders with the advice and consent of the Scoutmaster.
- Assign duties and responsibilities to other leaders.

Scouting, done properly, attracts boys of high caliber. Most any troop has several Scouts who could be capable senior patrol leaders. Your responsibility is to help a boy make the most of his valuable tenure as senior patrol leader.

 The patrol leader is elected from the membership of the patrol by its members. He must meet the requirements set by the troop leadership with regard to age, rank, tenure in the troop, performance, or whatever requirements that are established by the patrol leaders' council. The suggested term of office is 6 months. At the end of this time, the patrol must elect or reelect their patrol leader.

THE PATROL LEADER'S JOB DESCRIPTION

- Participate in junior leader training.
- Plan patrol meetings and activities.
- Lead patrol meetings and activities.
- Keep patrol members informed.
- Share leadership by giving each patrol member a job and replace dropouts.
- Instruct patrol members in Scoutcraft skills.
- Represent the patrol at the annual program planning conference and the patrol leaders' council meetings.
- Understand the needs of the patrol.
- Prepare patrol to take part in all troop activities.
- Develop patrol spirit and control.
- Work with other troop leaders to make the troop run well.
- Know what patrol members and other leaders can do.
- Set the example:
    Earn advancements.
    Live by the Scout Oath and Law.
    Wear the uniform correctly.

Appointed Boy Scout Leaders

There are eight boy leader positions which are filled by appointment by a senior patrol leader with your advice and consent. These leaders report to him after their appointment. Except for the assistant senior patrol leader, they remain in their patrols after their appointment.

- Trains and guides patrol leaders.
- Helps with leading meetings and activities.
- Serves as chairman of the Scout board of review when requested by the senior patrol leader.
- Takes over troop leadership in the absence of the senior patrol leader.
- Serves as leader of troop's leadership corps at request of senior patrol leader.

- In the den: the den chief assists the den leader with the meetings, helps Cub Scouts earn achievements, helps Cub Scouts be leaders, sets good example.
- For the troop: the den chief is the recruiting officer, bringing Cub Scouts into the troop, and promotes joint activities.
- Looks to assistant senior patrol leader or Webelos den resource person for guidance.

- Keeps records of patrol and troop equipment.
- Keeps equipment in good repair.
- Checks out equipment and sees that it is returned in good order.
- Suggests new or replacement items needed to senior patrol leader or patrol leaders' council.

Guidance may be given the quartermaster by the Scoutmaster, an assistant Scoutmaster, or a troop committee member with a responsibility for property.

- Keeps a log of patrol leaders' council decisions.
- Records attendance and dues payments.
- Records advancement in troop records.

- Gathers pictures and facts about past activities of the troop and keeps these in permanent forms such as scrapbooks, wall displays, or information files.
- Takes care of troop trophies and keepsakes.
- Keeps information about troop alumni and their doings.
- Helps the chartered organization and the troop leadership in making use of troop historical material.

- Keeps records on literature owned by the troop.
- Advises senior patrol leader or Scoutmaster of new or replacement items needed.
- Has literature available for borrowing at troop meetings.
- Keeps system to check literature in and out.
- Follows up on late returns.
- Keeps the merit badge counselor list.

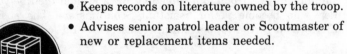

- A troop may have one or more instructors according to its needs. They instruct in advancement skills according to their abilities.

- Helps in troop program planning to consider religious holidays in planning and include religious observances in activities.
- Assists chaplain in planning and carrying out religious services at troop activities.
- Tells troop members about religious emblem program of their faith and how to earn one.
- Encourages troop members to live up to the ideals of the Scout Oath, Law, and slogan.

The assistant patrol leader is appointed by the patrol leader.

- Leads the patrol when the patrol leader is not present.

- Helps with patrol business.

Upon his 16th birthday, a qualified Scout may be appointed junior assistant Scoutmaster by the Scoutmaster with approval of the troop committee. There may be more than one junior assistant Scoutmaster in a troop.

Such junior assistant Scoutmasters really function as assistant Scoutmasters, though they will not reach the minimum age for that position until age 18. It is a great compliment to a troop to be able to grow and hold the fine young men who become junior assistant Scoutmasters. The position offers them further opportunities for service and leadership.

- Supervises and helps the support staff of the troop including scribe, quartermaster, librarian, troop historian, instructors, and chaplain aide.

- Works with Cub Scout and Webelos den chiefs.

THE PATROL LEADERS' COUNCIL

The purposes of the patrol leaders' council are to plan and run the troop's activities and to train the patrol leaders. Both of these purposes are important and both may be agcomplished by a well-run patrol leaders' council.

The patrol leaders' council runs the troop through democratic representation of the patrols. Every patrol has a voice in the running of the troop through its patrol leader. The senior patrol leader is a member and is the chairman of the council. The assistant senior patrol leader(s) is also a member. If there is a leadership corps, it is represented by an elected member or an assistant senior patrol leader. The Webelos Scout den chief should be invited when joint activities are to be discussed. Others may be invited to sit in, but they are not voting members of the patrol leaders' council.

Your patrol leaders' council plans the troop program.

Order of Business

The patrol leaders' council is charged with the responsibility of deciding what the troop wants to do, planning it, and carrying it out. In order to accomplish its task, the council must be chaired effectively, run in an orderly fashion, and its decisions must be recorded faithfully in its logbook.

Let's look at a typical patrol leaders' council meeting. This is a suggested order of business:

Patrol Leaders' Council Meeting

1. Call to order
2. Reading of logbook
3. Unfinished business
4. Patrol leaders' reports
5. New business
6. Advancement review
7. Next month's program
8. Season program check
9. Scoutmaster's minute
10. Adjournment

The meeting flows in a logical order. The senior patrol leader calls the council to order (preferably on time). The logbook is read. The troop scribe may be used as log keeper. If so, he is only an observer. "Unfinished business" is a follow-up on tasks that were previously assigned and a time to bring up items previously tabled. During the "patrol leaders' reports," each patrol leader reports the activities of his patrol for the previous month. He may share achievements, Good Turns, his general impression of the progress of his patrol, and he may discuss his concerns or problems. During "new business," matters that have come up during the month are discussed. This could be patrol problems, program problems, opportunities for Good Turns, or the like. The "advancement review" consists of reviewing the advancement of candidates for Star, Life, and Eagle for recommendations to the troop committee. During the "next month's program" part of the meeting the details of the activities of the next 4 weeks are hammered out. Specific jobs are assigned and agreements are made. During the "season's program check," the yearly program is compared with the accomplishments of the last month. If they square—fine. If not—why not? During the "Scoutmaster's minute" you may give the Scouts a pat on the back for a job well done, congratulate them on an achievement, suggest a program item, or inspire them to future service with a personal sharing. The senior patrol leader adjourns the meeting on time.

The senior patrol leader keeps the meeting on track. He "keeps the ball rolling" by guiding the discussion to the subject that the council is discussing (not the hometown football team or Jimmy's sister). The art of chairing a meeting is learned with practice and the senior patrol leader will need time and coaching to do it well.

The Yearly Program Plan

The most important planning meeting is the one held for the yearly program plan. You, as the Scoutmaster, are responsible for presenting the options to the patrol leaders' council. It's a good move to attend the district or council program planning conference in late summer. Then the troop will be able to enter district and council activities and dovetail the troop's program with the district and council.

It's a good idea to get a yearly calendar and mark off district and council activities. If a district camporee is going to be held in April, your Scouts are going to want to be there. That would serve as your troop activity for April. Other troop activities could be planned to prepare for the camporee.

Troop tradition, the vacation time of the adult leaders, and the desire of the Scouts all have a legitimate part to play in yearly planning. Let's examine an ideal situation.

The patrol leaders' council has been notified in advance that the yearly planning session is going to be held the second Tuesday of August in your home. They have discussed possible options at patrol leaders' council meetings. You have a copy of the yearly Troop Planning Worksheet, No. 26-005, and two yearly calendars. The *Boy Scout Leader Program Notebook,* No. 26-002, is ideal—it runs from September of one year to August of the next. The worksheet and calendars or notebook have district and council events marked in them. You have notes from the troop's camping chairman that present several long-term summer camping options. *Boys' Life* and *Scouting* magazines are on the table.

The patrol leaders' council is called to order. The patrol leaders talk about the past year—what worked, what didn't. They discuss what they would like to do again and what they'd like to try for the first time. You can share program ideas that you've picked up at roundtables or from Boy Scout literature.

The *Boy Scout Program Helps* from *Scouting* magazine and the *Boy Scout Leader Program Notebook* are particularly useful at this time. Using the program theme each month as presented in Boy Scout literature, the patrol leaders' council decides on the program for each month. As an example, a monthly theme of "being strong" is about hiking and biking and would include activities such as map and compass reading, orienteering, check out of bikes and a bike hike, and a wilderness scavenger hunt. The program highlight could be an orienteering hike held on a Saturday during the monthly campout.

The weekly meetings should "groove" with the theme. Troop meetings should include map and compass skill games, distance judging skill games, a cycling safety presentation and check, and similar activities. Each month is planned by the Scouts. Individual troop meeting activities may be suggested but the program details should be left until the month before.

Long-term summer camp options should have been presented to the patrol leaders' council some time ago. They should be narrowed down to those options that are possible and have the support of the troop committee. The final decision, if it still has not been made, should be made now. Superactivity possibilities also should have been reviewed with the council several months earlier. Those plans are finalized at this meeting.

At the close of the yearly program planning patrol leaders' council all of the major events in the life of the troop for the coming year should be known. Now take the plan to your troop committee for their support. Superactivities, long-term summer camp, and other major activities already should have been reviewed by the committee, so the group is shown what the patrol leaders' council has decided to do. Individual responsibilities for camp reservations, transportation, leadership, and finances are delegated by the chairman of the troop committee.

Monthly Planning

When the patrol leaders' council meets each month it reviews the yearly plan and fills in the details of the month's progress. The council prepares a Troop Meeting Plan for each troop meeting. It is the responsibility of the patrol leaders' council to follow up on their individual responsibilities.

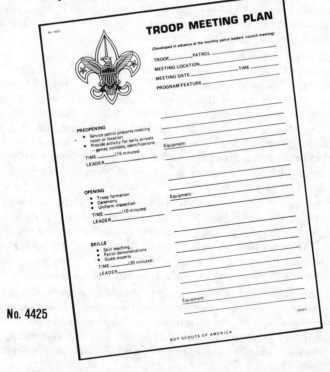

No. 4425

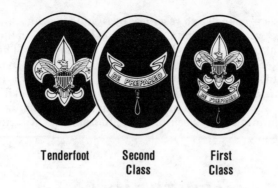

| Tenderfoot | Second Class | First Class |

The Board of Review

All or part of the patrol leaders' council (appointed by the senior patrol leader) comprises the board of review for the Tenderfoot, Second Class, and First Class ranks.

The review has three purposes:

1. To make sure the Scout has done what he was supposed to do for the rank.

2. To see how good an experience the Scout is having in the troop.

3. To encourage the Scout to progress further.

The reviewing group consists of not fewer than three nor more than five members. The troop's advancement chairman, committee member, or another adult sits in on the review. That person may or may not take part in the questioning, but does discuss the qualification of the candidate with the board during the time the candidate is not present and then a recommendation is made.

Appearing before the board of review can be a sensitive time for the Scout being reviewed. It is the responsibility of the board to ensure that the Scout has done what he is supposed to have done, not to retest the Scout on his skills. The adult adviser should be alert to maintain fair, orderly reviews.

The Scoutmaster's Role

The Scoutmaster is the adult leader responsible for the actions of the troop. He has been appointed by the chartered organization and the troop committee. Because of his position and responsibility for the troop, the Scoutmaster is the adviser to the patrol leaders' council and reserves the right to veto anything that he believes would be harmful to the troop or contrary to the Rules and Regulations of the Boy Scouts of America. The wise Scoutmaster, however, will never have to exercise this authority. He should guide the patrol leaders' council with careful suggestions and mature insights. In this way the council will be trained to appreciate good judgment in activities and program, as well as planning and executing the program that it creates.

ADULT LEADERS
AND THE COMMITTEE

The troop committee supports the leadership and program of the troop. Yet the committee is more than just a support, because of its responsibility for recruiting the Scoutmaster and assistant Scoutmasters. It is the committee's job to select and recruit the best leaders available and then give those men unending support.

The Scoutmaster should have a hand in the selection of assistant Scoutmasters. He has to work with them, and he should have compatible men. If he is dissatisfied with the amount or caliber of adult leadership, he should make clear to the committee that he needs and expects more. Scoutmasters must be conscious of the fact that assistant Scoutmasters, just like boy leaders, expect to be used constructively. No one will serve for long in such a position unless he has honest work to do and a contribution to make.

How should assistant Scoutmaster jobs be assigned? It depends on the work to be done and the qualifications and interests of the assistants. If there is a sizable job in equipment and physical arrangements and there is a man ready and able to do it, then break up the work that way. If the Scoutmaster is strong on camping and weak on meetings, he can put a better qualified assistant in charge of planning and operation meetings. If the Scoutmaster is a good counselor but a poor skill instructor, he can delegate this task.

In short, there is no single way to divide the work of troop leadership among Scoutmaster and assistants. There are probably hundreds of ways, and if the best qualified men are doing the job, that's the right way.

Assistant Scoutmasters are important for two reasons. They provide the two-deep manpower that ensures continuous, effective leadership for the troop and a trained replacement, if necessary. He will already be acquainted with the Scouts—available to step into the top spot.

Since the Scoutmaster works closely with the assistants, his wishes should be a major consideration in their assigned selection.

The assistant Scoutmasters should be assigned a job. This will depend on the work to be done, the qualifications and interests of the assistants, and the strengths of the Scoutmaster. The example below illustrates how well-run troops can utilize assistant Scoutmasters' skills.

First Assistant Scoutmaster (Activities)

- Serves as the troop leader in the absence of the Scoutmaster.
- Is responsible to the Scoutmster for program and activities of the troop.
- Works with the assistant senior patrol leader in administering troop operations.
- Coordinates troop/Webelos Scout den activities.
- Is responsible for the troop's participation in district and council activities.
- Participates in training.

Second Assistant Scoutmaster (Physical Arrangements)

- Is responsible to the Scoutmaster for troop physical arrangements.
- Works with the troop quartermaster and troop committee member (equipment and facilities).
- Is responsible for the care and neat appearance of all equipment.
- Is responsible for health and safety in all troop affairs.
- Participates in training.

The troop chaplain may or may not be the head of the religious body chartered to use the Scouting program. If he is the head of the chartered organization, he may volunteer to serve on the committee as troop chaplain. If not, the troop chairman, after consulting with the Scouting coordinator and/or head of the organization, may select a chaplain for the troop from the local clergy.

The troop chaplain

• Provides a spiritual tone for troop meetings and activities.

• Gives guidance to chaplain aide.

• Gives spiritual counseling service when needed or requested.

• Encourages Boy Scouts to earn their appropriate religious emblem.

• Provides opportunities for Boy Scouts to grow in their relationship to God and their fellow Scouts.

Webelos Resource Person

Your troop can benefit greatly from a relationship with a Webelos den and Cub Scout pack and can have a continuing source of fine new Scouts. By designating a Webelos resource person to coordinate the relationship with the pack you take a big step to making things happen. This person, who can be an assistant Scoutmaster or committee member, works closely with the Webelos den leader, helps arrange joint activities and troop visitations, aids the pack in outdoor activities and outdoor requirements, represents the troop in pack ceremonies, and represents a troop presence in the pack. He or she also aids in recruiting, training, and using den chiefs.

This responsibility can be an excellent job for a parent of a new Scout who last year was a Webelos Scout.

This responsibility can be an excellent job for a parent of a new Scout who last year was a Webelos Scout.

THE LEADERSHIP CORPS

The troop leadership corps is an optional part of the Scouting program. It offers older boys in your troop a chance to learn and practice leadership and to have group activities of their own, thus holding their interest in Scouting.

If you have several 14- and 15-year-olds in your troop, they can be a valuable source of leadership. Many young men of this age are capable of handling jobs now being done by you and the other adult leaders.

Their continuing service in the troop will not only give you a new leadership resource, but it will also help them grow as leaders. For these reasons, it is recommended that the troop consider forming a leadership corps.

Members must be—

- 14 or 15 years old.

- First Class Scouts or higher.

- Potential leaders, as shown by active participation in patrol and troop activities.

- Willing to take leadership development training from your adult leaders and through the district and council.

You must have at least three such boys in the troop to form a leadership corps. As a rule of thumb, not more than one-fourth of your troop's registered membership should be in the leadership corps. This means that in a troop with only 12 Scouts, not more than three would be leadership corps members; in a troop of 60, about 12 could be corps members.

It is recommended that a leadership corps start with a few capable young men and, if the troop is large, gradually expand. The Scoutmaster should select the first members and work closely with them until the leadership corps can function on its own.

Adult Leadership for the Corps

The man who advises the troop leadership corps must remember he is a coach and adviser—not a man directly involved in leading the older Scouts. He is not the patrol leader of a "superpatrol."

How the Leadership Corps Serves

The leadership corps should be a prime resource for the troop. Since it is composed of older, experienced Scouts, it should provide Scout skill instructors, temporary patrol leadership, advisers to new patrol leaders, and a service corps for camps and campouts.

The big guys in the troop can provide good
examples for younger Scouts.

Service as a den chief will help the pack and the troop.

Scoutmasters whose troops have formed leadership corps have been enthusiastic about the potential. Not every member of your leadership corps will be transformed immediately into an outstanding leader the moment he joins. But he should get sufficient exposure to leadership responsibilities so that he has a chance to progress as a leader. A special opportunity for leadership corps members could be service as den chiefs.

The leadership corps should have values for both the troop and the boy. Your troop should be improved by holding these older Scouts' interests and experience. Most importantly, the leadership corps should help its members grow into capable, effective, participating citizens.

Special Activities

The leadership corps, working with its own leader and adult adviser, can go for high-adventure activities, social activities with and without their girl-friends, athletic events with other groups, or just about anything else that might occur to them. They can go on a moving camp or tour, visit a foreign country, have a canoe trip, go to Philmont, hunt, fish, water-ski, do service projects or attend the Super Bowl.

Chapter 4

The Patrol Method

When you build patrol spirit, you have it made!

VALUES of belonging to a working patrol for a Boy Scout have to do with being important in a small group. The patrol permits experiences that a troop-size group will deny a Scout because he is just one of many.

THE PATROL IN THE TROOP

A patrol works best with other patrols. No one wants to belong to a football team that never meets an opponent. Likewise, a patrol-size group that is isolated from other patrol-size groups will have lost some of its reason for being a team.

The troop provides support services that a patrol could not have on its own—equipment, meeting place, adult counseling and guidance, etc. Most patrols would find it hard to develop this kind of support.

The troop's relationship to the patrols is not unlike that of councils and districts to the troops. They create conditions under which the troop unit can succeed.

In the process of using the patrol method, the troop gains, too. The principal gain is that the otherwise overwhelming task of planning, teaching, directing, supervising, controlling, etc., is delegated to Scouts. To put it more bluntly, it becomes possible to run a good troop with the patrol method. The task, without it, may be insurmountable.

Further, the patrol method is the only way of assuring that the troop program will be run by Scouts. If the program is operated on a troop basis, it is almost certain that it will become the primary responsibility of men.

We use the patrol method in Scouting because it is geared to the way boys are. Here, boys can have the kinds of experiences that lead to the aims of the Scouting movement. It is a method essential to Boy Scouting. Giving it up means giving up many of the reasons for the existence of the program.

SETTING UP AND MAINTAINING PATROLS

A troop is *composed of* patrols, which seems to suggest that the patrols are what count and the troop is nothing without them. Thus it is reasonable that a troop with only eight Scouts should be composed of two patrols—even though they are small.

Setting Up Patrols

Let these principles guide your setting up of patrols:

Friendship. If Scouts were allowed total freedom to organize patrols, they would naturally choose to belong to groups of Scouts they already know. Each boy wants to be accepted, and he is more likely to be accepted by acquaintances than by strangers. In most situations, Scouts will function best if they choose to be together in a patrol.

Growth. The size that patrols should be when formed depends on your plans for growth.

The point is, you have to plan for at least some additional Scouts when you set up patrols. The membership of the troop is constantly shifting, and you need some flexibility. Twenty-four Scouts are probably better formed into patrols of six or even five. Notice, too, that patrols don't have to be the same size.

Allow for Leadership. Scouts' choices should be observed, but each patrol should have at least one potential leader.

Ignore Age. Patrols should generally not be organized by age: All 12-year-olds, for example. They can be whatever mixture is dictated by their members. Chances are, it will not come out on an age basis. A Webelos den, however, may join the troop and ask to be a patrol.

Get Scouts' Choices. Forming (or re-forming) patrols is a big occasion. Take the Scouts into your confidence. Tell them what's going on. They need to know how patrols will be working and why forming (or re-forming) is necessary. They need to understand that they will be working and playing together as patrols and that they need to be compatible.

You will have to make some compromises, but eventually you can put together the right number of patrols with greatest weight being given to boys' own choices.

JOHN'S LIST

Bill
Jose
Dick
Al
Mel

	JOHN	BILL	JOSE	DICK	AL	MEL
JOHN		X	X	X	X	X
BILL	X		X			X
JOSE	X			X		X
DICK	X		X		X	
AL	X		X	X		
MEL	X		X			

Let each boy make a list of the Scouts he would like to have in his patrol. Gather the lists and make a chart like this one. In doing so, you'll spot the leaders and be able to make some wise choices.

Maintaining Patrols

Once formed, a patrol should live as long as it can function. Some patrols live for years, often after the original members have grown up. This can happen when new members join the patrol to replace old members who leave.

A patrol should exist as a patrol for as long as possible. But we are looking for more than just existence; we seek a lively, loyal, functioning patrol.

It should be clear that boys should not be placed in positions of conflicting loyalties. Once a member of a patrol, a Scout should not be expected to temporarily "fill out" another patrol that is short a man or to be part of some combination of patrols. Small patrols can compete in most contests, although they will be handicapped. In relay events, one or more Scouts will run more than once.

Every possible aspect of the troop program should be set up and run so as to encourage patrols and strengthen them. Here are the principles involved.

1. *Every patrol must be given continuing, maximum responsibility.* This will include planning all troop functions and carrying them out. Patrols must put on ceremonies, prepare and clean up the meeting room, run games, give demonstrations, camp, cook, and hike together. An occasional responsibility as a patrol is not enough; it must be continuous.

2. *Patrols must compete.* They can compete on an informal, short-term basis in games, Scoutcraft events, etc. They can compete on a more formal, long-term basis in contests that include all sorts of performance—attendance, advancement, wearing the uniform, assisting with troop meetings, etc. Competition, like responsibility, must be almost continuous; the patrols must be forever vying with one another.

3. *Patrols must be active.* They must do things as patrols, both as part of the troop and separately. Group loyalty and enthusiasm arise out of doing things. If a patrol is to be more than "the group that stands over there," it must do things as a patrol. The patrol that does nothing is nothing.

Where the troop runs its program on the patrol method, the patrols thrive, prosper, and last. No special efforts are needed to keep active, busy, constructive patrols alive. They keep themselves alive. The troop's job is to support and not to interfere.

Baden-Powell gave full responsibility to his
patrol leaders for their patrols.

Patrol Organization

The name and traditions of a patrol should be rigidly
maintained. But the organization of a patrol should be flexible.
In that way, the patrol can adapt to changing needs.

The patrol has one leader. He is the patrol leader, elected by
the membership of the patrol, from the patrol. He must meet the
qualifications for age, rank, tenure in the troop, or whatever
requirements are established by you, the troop, and your troop
committee and installed into office. In a new troop, these
qualifications would have to be low or no one could qualify. As
the troop becomes experienced, the qualifications can be raised.
The minimum term of office for patrol leader should be 6
months.

The patrol leader assigns jobs in the patrol as needed. He
gives Scouts in his patrol special responsibilities for single
events.

The advantages of this system are flexibility and training.
Jobs are reassigned as needed to give everyone a chance at
accepting responsibility and contributing to the patrol.

PATROL MEETINGS AND ACTIVITIES

As noted earlier, patrols succeed because they do things as patrols. In the early life of the patrol, it will do things mostly as part of the troop. As it becomes experienced and competent, it will be able to function apart from the troop. It will plan and carry out activities in which the troop is not involved at all.

Patrol Meetings

A patrol can meet as a patrol during a troop meeting or separate from it in its own patrol meeting place. Patrol meetings are made necessary by troop program or other patrol activity. So a patrol meets because it has businesss to attend to.

A patrol might have to:

- Plan a menu.
- Plan its part in a troop activity.
- Make or repair some equipment.
- Practice for some competition or show.

In an active troop that places emphasis on the importance of patrol activity, patrols will have lots of need to meet both at the troop meeting and at their own separate patrol meeting places.

Patrols can meet by themselves.

Patrol Hikes and Camps

These activities are encouraged for those patrols that have trained, competent leadership. What the patrol does is determined by what's available, what the patrol elects to do, and the ability of its leader.

Scoutmaster's approval is always required for patrol hikes and camps. You can base your decision to approve or disapprove on the recent history of the patrol in accepting and carrying out responsibility. If you feel you must disapprove because the patrol leader isn't competent, you can help the patrol to secure an adult to accompany it.

The *Official Patrol Leader Handbook* has a great deal of information on this subject.

Your troop might develop a tradition around its own "Campbell Souper Bowl."

PATROL RECOGNITION

Recognition is a reward. It may come about in all sorts of ways. For example, the honor of winning is usually rewarding. Possessing a rotating trophy of some kind—until losing it to another patrol—is rewarding. Winning a special trip may be rewarding.

In general, patrols that are busy and active, competing regularly, generate their own rewards. They do not need special incentives to run well.

Occasionally, a troop may wish to set up some kind of recognition system for patrols that extends for a specified time. It will involve some kind of rating plan, the winner of which is treated to some kind of special honor, activity, trip, etc.

1. *Rewards are better than punishments.* Concentrate on rewards for positive activity rather than on demerits. Reward the performance you want rather than punish the performance you don't want.

2. *Interest in rewards slacks off over a long period.* The longer the period of the contest, the more likely interest is to slack off.

3. *The monetary value of rewards is not what counts.* A patrol might very well work harder to possess a painted tin can used as a trophy than to win $50 worth of merchandise.

4. *If the intention is to recognize a patrol, then give the reward to the patrol.* It is self-defeating to motivate a patrol to function as a patrol and then distribute winnings or honors to individuals. The patrol should—as a patrol—share the winnings. That's why a special trip or adventure is many times better than—for example—money for each member.

Setting Up a Recognition Plan

1. *Keep the length short.* Three months is probably the effective maximum. Or you can say that the contest will end "after 3 months or when one patrol gets 1,000 points, whichever is earlier."

2. *Include only items you want to promote.* Examples might be advancement, game winning, demonstrations, attendance, dues payment, Scouts signed up for summer camp, uniform worn, etc.

3. *Weight the contest items according to their relative value to the troop.* For example, your contest might include eight items. Each would be worth a basic 10 points. But certain items could be weighted with a multiple. For example, a merit badge earned could be 20.

4. *Keep the rules simple and understandable.* If it takes a professor of mathematics to figure out how the contest works, it will generate arguments and lead to confusion.

5. *Keep a visible scoreboard.* Post the patrol standings weekly where all can see.

B P TROOP CHART PATROLS ▶	BISON			PINETREE			STAG			VIKING		
MONTHS	1	2	3	1	2	3	1	2	3	1	2	3
ON TIME FOR TROOP MEETING	◍◍◍◍	◍◍◍◍		◍◍◍◍	◍◍◍◍		●◍◍◍	●◍◍◍		◍◍◍◍	◍◍◍◍	
INTER-PATROL ACTIVITY	◍◍◍◍	◍◍◍◍		◍◍◍◍	◍◍◍◍		●◍◍○	◍◍◍◍		◍◍◍◍	◍◍◍◍	
UNIFORM AT TROOP MEETING	◍◍◍	◍◍◍		◍◍◍	◍◍◍		●◍◍	◍◍◍		◍◍◍	◍◍◍	
DUES PAID	◍◍◍	◍◍◍		◍◍◍	◍◍◍		●◍◍	◍◍◍		◍◍◍	◍◍◍	
ON TIME FOR OUTING	◍	◍		◍	◍		◍	◍		◍	◍	
GOOD TURNS	◍	◍		○	○		◍	◍		◍	○	
ADVANCEMENT	◍	◍		◍	○		●	◍		●	◍	

● RED—GET GOING	◍ GREEN—KEEP GOING	○ GOLD—GOOD GOING

This visible scoreboard promotes the national Baden-Powell patrol rating system over a 3-month period.

The Baden-Powell Patrol

Patrols are encouraged to meet certain standards to become Baden-Powell patrols. Patrols earning this recognition receive an embroidered star to be worn beneath the patrol medallion.

There are eight requirements and the record is kept in the *Patrol Record Book,* No. 6516, or in a patrol logbook.

Challenge your Scouts to earn this star.

Baden-Powell Patrol Requirements

1. *Spirit.* Have a patrol flag and rally around it. Put your patrol design on equipment. Use your yell or cheer and patrol call. Keep patrol records up to date for 3 months.

2. *Patrol meetings.* Hold two patrol meetings each month for 3 months.

3. *Hikes, outdoor activities, and other events.* Take part in one of these within 3 months.

4. *Good Turns or service projects.* Do two patrol leaders' council-approved Good Turns or service projects within 3 months.

5. *Advancement.* Help two patrol members advance one rank during 3 months.

6. *Membership.* Build patrol to full strength (eight Scouts).

7. *Uniform.* Wear the uniform correctly (at least six Scouts).

8. *Patrol leaders' council.* Represent the patrol during three patrol leaders' council meetings within 3 months.

SUMMARY

Baden-Powell said the patrol method was not a way to operate a Boy Scout troop, it was the only way. Unless the patrol method is in operation you don't really have a Boy Scout troop.

Chapter 5

Troop Meetings

Meetings can be held anywhere.

EETINGS provide the most *contacts* a Scout has with his troop, so it is important that they be both constructive and fun.

You should recognize—if you haven't already—that good meetings are a very important part of your program. But good meetings don't make a complete troop program, although no troop program could be complete without them.

HOW OFTEN?

Let's start with this principle: there should be some Boy Scout activity for every Scout—or nearly every Scout—every week, year round. Notice the word *activity*. A weekend campout is an activity. A day hike is an activity. Summer camp is an activity. In the weeks that such activities happen, you don't need a troop meeting. You *may* have one, but you should not feel that the sky will fall if you don't. In planning your year-round program, you need to plan for one activity a week. The activity may or may not be a meeting.

Suppose your troop schedules one outdoor activity or special event per month. The troop may then decide not to have troop meetings during the weeks of these activities. This "event week" is a good time to hold patrol leaders' council meetings.

You might also plan a program that calls for one planned patrol activity per month separate from the troop. The troop could decide that during the weeks of the patrol activities there would be no troop meetings.

The object is not to shrink or expand the number of meetings, but to hold the meetings necessary to carrying out your troop's planned program. What you need more than anything is a Scout activity a week year round. How many of those are meetings of the troop, and how many other kinds of get-togethers, must be decided by you and your patrol leaders' council.

Most troops meet weekly. Some manage very well once a month. Some choose to meet on alternate weeks.

The more irregular your meeting pattern, the more important it becomes to be sure everyone involved knows the meeting dates. In particular, a written copy of the meeting schedule for the year is needed by: the Scouts in the troop and the organization that grants the use of meeting space. If there are changes, both must be notified promptly.

Check your calendar.

PURPOSES

Bring the Troop Together. The troop meeting brings all the boys in the troop together for a common purpose. The troop learns and grows together, strengthening troop unity.

Build Strong Patrols. Patrols are strengthened during the meeting as they learn and share together. Patrols also help run the meeting. Each patrol should contribute to the meeting. Each should work as a patrol during the meeting. Each should be a stronger patrol at the end than it was at the beginning.

Learn and Practice Skills and Pass Tests. This does not mean that every single troop meeting should have an "advancement" period. It does mean that a Scout should look to troop meetings as places where he can learn some of what he wants to learn, and pass requirements.

Promote Patrol Spirit Through Competition. One good reason for having troop meetings is to do things that can't be done separately by patrols. One such thing is competitive events. Win or lose, patrols learn to work together and cheer for their Scouts when they compete.

Provide Chances To Practice Leadership. Every troop meeting should be "engineered" to provide as many chances as possible for as many Scouts as possible to use leadership skills.

Get a lot of activity into a troop meeting.

Scouts need a little extra windup to get them started on advancement to First Class.

Motivate

They should encourage Scouts to remain active, to advance, to improve themselves, to take part in other activities, to follow Scouting ideals. Every boy should leave every meeting feeling more like a Scout than he did when he came. The action and excitement of this kind of meeting spells F-U-N.

Certainly not every troop meeting will serve each of these purposes. It is not reasonable to try. But a year's assortment of meetings should, taken together, meet all of them. Any one meeting can be reviewed—both before and after it happens—with the purposes in the forefront. You and your patrol leaders' council should ask questions like these:

Just what practice of the patrol method does (or did) this provide for?

What did (or will) Scouts get a chance to learn? What chances were there to complete requirements?

What was done for (or against) patrol spirit?

Who—and how many—got a chance to lead others?

Such evaluation will help you to strengthen troop meetings. Never stop asking questions like these, or believing that your meetings can be better. After you have a real blockbuster of a meeting, take the time to find out what was so good about it and why. Then you can have another like it.

GENERAL SUGGESTIONS
FOR GOOD MEETINGS

Start on time. Expect Scouts to be on time. Don't teach bad attendance habits. If the troop meeting is held at a "bad time," then change the time.

Close on time. Don't make it late. If Scouts walk, parents should know when to expect them. If they are driven to and from meetings, parents don't want to wait outside for the meeting to end.

Plan more, not less, than you can actually do. It is easy to leave something to another time. It is a real blow to discover you have run out of program and there are 15 minutes to go.

In general, keep the length of one activity down to a maximum of 20 minutes. Stop activities when they are still fun.

Avoid wearing out good things. A game that makes a big hit should be retired for some weeks before coming out again.

Gaps during which nothing happens invite trouble. Pace the program fast so no one will get bored and make his own amusement.

Try not to have any more adults on hand than are needed. If there is a gallery of visitors, try to keep them out of the middle of things. If you have several adult assistants, arrange to have them attend on a staggered basis as needed.

Every meeting must have *action.* Boy Scouting is not a spectator sport. Boys are not good at sitting still. Get them up and doing things. Alternate sitting activities with active things.

Keep a file of troop meeting programs. The good ones can be used again after a period of time.

Every meeting must have *variety.* Every meeting should be different from other meetings. The parts of any one meeting should also provide variety.

Every meeting must have *purpose.* Boys can sense better than anyone when a meeting has been thrown together without any real purpose. A troop meeting should accomplish something, and all who are there will know whether it does.

Good meetings are constructive and fun. Recent studies tell us that boys leave Scouting because Scoutmasters talk too much and the meetings are boring.

TROOP-MEETING INGREDIENTS

A good troop meeting is like a good meal. It consists of a nice mixture of several different things. Just bread or just peas won't make a good meal. Just games or just skills development won't make a good troop meeting. There must be a mixture of ingredients.

The best guide to these ingredients is the Troop Meeting Plan form. If you have a copy available, keep it handy for reference in this chapter. If not, one is reproduced here for your guidance. But, be

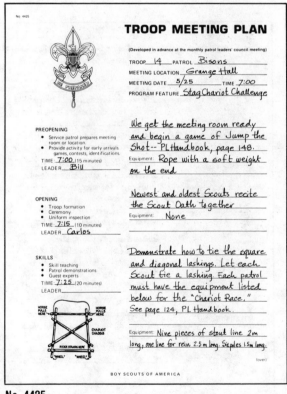

No. 4425

sure to get a supply as soon as you can. You will use several to plan each meeting (because patrol leaders and others use them, too), so get a good supply.

Let's take each ingredient on that planning sheet and examine it in detail.

Preopening

Troop meetings begin before they start. If a troop meeting is scheduled for 7 p.m., the first boy probably arrives at about 6:45 p.m. That's when the meeting really starts. Just how good a meeting it is depends in part on what happens between 6:45 and 7 p.m. Here's what should be happening.

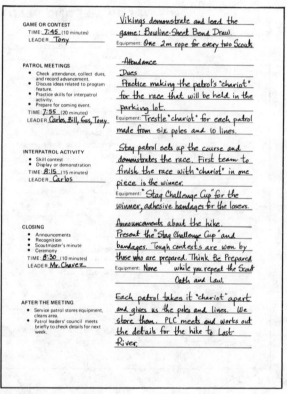

GAME OR CONTEST
TIME: 7:45 (10 minutes)
LEADER: Tony

Vikings demonstrate and lead the game: Bowline-Sheet Bend Draw.
Equipment: One 2m rope for every two Scouts

PATROL MEETINGS
- Check attendance, collect dues, and record advancement.
- Discuss ideas related to program feature.
- Practice skills for interpatrol activity.
- Prepare for coming event.
TIME: 7:55 (20 minutes)
LEADER: Carlos, Bill, Gus, Tony

Attendance
Dues
Practice making the patrol's "chariot" for the race that will be held in the parking lot.
Equipment: Trestle "chariot" for each patrol made from six poles and 10 lines.

INTERPATROL ACTIVITY
- Skill contest
- Display or demonstration
TIME: 8:15 (15 minutes)
LEADER: Carlos

Stag patrol sets up the course and demonstrates the race. First team to finish the race with "chariot" in one piece is the winner.
Equipment: "Stag Challenge Cup" for the winner, adhesive bandages for the losers.

CLOSING
- Announcements
- Recognition
- Scoutmaster's minute
- Ceremony
TIME: 8:30 (10 minutes)
LEADER: Mr. Chavez

Announcements about the hike.
Present the "Stag Challenge Cup" and bandages. Tough contests are won by those who are prepared. Think Be Prepared
Equipment: None while you repeat the Scout Oath and Law.

AFTER THE MEETING
- Service patrol stores equipment, cleans area.
- Patrol leaders' council meets briefly to check details for next week.

Each patrol takes it "chariot" apart and gives us the poles and lines. We store them. PLC meets and works out the details for the hike to Lost River.

No. 4425, reverse side.

The Scoutmaster is on hand to unlock the door and make sure things get under way. He can delegate this responsibility to another leader. But it is best if he is there to talk to individual boys who may not be able to stay after the meeting.

The service patrol—appointed at the monthly planning meeting—is there to set up the meeting room, get necessary equipment from the quartermaster, and make all last-minute physical arrangements.

The quartermaster is there to check equipment out and in.

If patrol leaders have patrol business to do, Scouts can report directly to their patrol leader on arrival. If not, then there should be some central activity as a preopening. Such activity is planned at the monthly patrol leaders' council meeting and assigned to one or more specific leaders. Here are samples of such activities.

Games. The only suitable games are those that more can join as they arrive. Informal softball, volleyball, Jump the Shot, and Steal the Bacon are examples. These games should not become formal or highly competitive, or the players will be reluctant to break them up when the meeting starts.

Contests. As Scouts arrive they can try their hand at skills requiring little time. They can pair off for informal dual contests or demonstrate what they can do with knots and hitches, tie a bandage, or otherwise qualify or earn a score.

Identifications. Samples of unidentified materials can be laid out or hung up and numbered. Each incoming Scout takes a piece of paper and a pencil and writes the name of each. You can use merit badges, conifer needles, leaves, soil types, corporation symbols, and many other unlabeled things.

Opening

The meeting needs to have a formal opening to mark its official beginning. This always should be exactly on time, even though not everyone is present.

The troop should use a formation for the opening. It is not necessary to use the same formation.

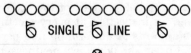

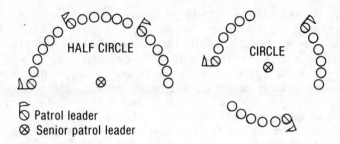

HALF CIRCLE

CIRCLE

🔵 Patrol leader
⊗ Senior patrol leader

Some troops begin with reports of attendance from patrol leaders to the senior patrol leader. These are received formally and briskly, thus:

SPL: Hawk Patrol

PL: Hawk Patrol, one absent, sir.

SPL: Apache Patrol

Most troops have some kind of ceremony to mark the start of the meeting. It may be patriotic, religious (in church-chartered troops), or rooted in troop or Scouting tradition. It is recommended that there be variety in ceremonies as well as in parts of the meeting.

The Scout Law itself is 12 separate ceremonies. One cermony could devote itself to the first part, plus a reading of the explanation. For example:

TROOP: A Scout is trustworthy.

LEADER: A Scout tells the truth. He keeps his promises....

Eleven meetings later, the subject of the ceremony would be "A Scout is reverent."

Likewise there are many varieties in patriotic ceremonies. In addition to saluting the flag and pledging allegiance, a good singing troop can sing a verse of any of several patriotic songs. Or a reader can read from the writings of any number of authors and poets who have helped us to understand what it means to love one's country. A single patriotic ceremony, no matter how good, is bound to lose some of its meaning by endless repetition. If a ceremony of any kind has lost its meaning to those involved, it is not worth doing.

Inspections often are held as part of the opening period. Most troops do not hold an inspection at every meeting, but do often enough to keep standards of uniforming and personal grooming high. A Boy Scout troop should expect neatness, cleanliness, and proper placement of insignia. Inspections help to ensure this.

Skills Development

Interpret the words "skills" and "development" broadly. Boy Scouting is a broad program. A presentation by a forest ranger, a discussion of citizenship and its meaning, or a well-chosen film on waterskiing safety all qualify as skills development.

Consider this also. There need be no suggestion that every member of the troop must take part in every skills development period. Here are some ways in which the troop may be together or separate during this period of the meeting.

1. **Whole Troop Presentation.** A state conservation spokesman will show slides and discuss with Scouts the problems involved in cleaning up the river that runs through town. Since he is a special guest and since what he has to say and show affects all members, this period will involve all members of the troop, regardless of age or rank.

2. **Divided Participation.** Scouts are interested in learning basic wrestling and gymnastics. It is not practical to teach the whole troop at once. Further, some boys aren't interested in both. So in this situation, the instruction will be offered to two separate groups for four meetings in a row. Each boy elects which group he wants to join. The instruction groups will meet at the same time and have the same length of time for their programs.

3. **Skill Groups.** Scouts are always at different points in earning skill awards. Since each boy moves at his own speed and elects those things that interest him, the troop does not advance as a group. Nevertheless, group instruction is possible by groups, for this period, those interested in particular skills. The number of instruction groups that can be operated at one time is limited only by the number of instructors and the size and nature of the meeting place.

4. **Teaching Stations.** Something must be taught to the troop, but it cannot be taught effectively to everyone at once. So stations are set up, and each patrol goes to one station. Each instruction station may be teaching the same thing or a part of the whole. For example, you could have multiple tent-pitching instruction stations operating at once. Or you could have multiple first aid stations, one teaching burns, another shock, etc.

Instruction and practice also take place in patrol meetings.

Games or Contests

The games and contests that happen in troop meetings have as much method in them as any other part. They are not just "for fun."

1. They give patrols a chance to operate as patrols (if it's that kind of game).

2. They give Scouts chances to practice skills (if skills are involved, as they usually are).

3. They promote patrol spirit (if the patrol plays the game as a patrol.)

4. They offer one or more Scouts a chance to lead.

5. They may very well motivate Scouts to learn more and do better.

6. They do provide fun. By a pleasant coincidence, the part of the meeting that is usually a highlight to boys is also a whale of a way to accomplish the purpose of having a troop meeting in the first place.

As to contests, there is scarcely a skill of any kind that cannot be used as the basis of a contest. Once patrols learn to chop a log in two, there can be a contest to see which can do it in the fewest strokes. When they learn to do some first aid, there can be contests with similar "victims" for each patrol. Once they learn to tie a knot, they can compete to see who can tie the greatest number correctly in the least time.

Contests can be run at least three ways: (1) to produce an individual winner, second place, etc., (2) to produce a patrol winner, second place, etc., and (3) to qualify any and all who meet a standard. The second and third types do most to strengthen patrols, because they promote patrol teamwork and spirit. Individual contests are good to have, but they serve the patrols less.

A file of troop meeting plans from the past will provide you with a record of the good games and contests held in the troop. This in turn should help you to know what will work and what won't.

Ideally, every troop should have a large supply of games and contests. Favorite games should not be replayed week after week or they soon will be worn out.

Patrol Meetings

This is a time for patrols to conduct their formal business such as taking attendance and collecting dues. It's also a time for planning, preparing menus, and so on.

If the next activity in the meeting requires patrol preparation, this is the time to prepare.

Instruction and practice of advancement skills are often part of a patrol meeting, so if the patrol needs to practice certain skills, this is the time to practice them.

The length of these patrol meetings is flexible. There may have been patrol meetings during the week, and so the patrols need only 5 minutes for routine business. The patrols could, however, have lots of preparation or practice for a coming event and use up to 20 minutes for their meetings. (More if a variety of activities is involved. Campout preparations, for example, take longer.)

Cut off this part of the meeting when one or more patrols have finished doing what they started to do. You invite discipline problems if the period drags on when the business has been completed.

Take care of patrol business in the patrol meetings.

Interpatrol Activity

The most common activities that occur at this point are patrol demonstrations of Scoutcraft or contests in Scouting skill. In either case, one or more patrols—preferably all—are featured and function as patrols with the patrol leaders in charge.

You can see that this part of the troop meeting is closely related to at least one other part. If a patrol is demonstrating, then they will have used their patrol meeting to prepare the final parts of what they demonstrate.

If a Scoutcraft skill contest is held, it is usually based on skills taught or practiced earlier in the same meeting.

Closing

As every meeting needs a formal opening, so does it need a closing.

Troops frequently use an artificial campfire for their closing period. This sets a good tone, putting Scouts in the proper mood for the inspiration that should come at this point in the meeting.

Announcements. These are reminders about the next meeting, where to assemble for the hike, what to bring to the Scouting show, etc. They must be kept brief, and there must not be too many, since Scouts will not remember a lot of details. If you can get access to any kind of duplicating equipment, put announcements into print and hand them out. If you need a list of announcements in order to remember them, the Scouts also will need a list to recall later what you said. Announcements should be made by the person most deeply involved. The quartermaster, for example, would make an announcement about equipment.

Recognition. This is the time of the meeting to make any immediate recognitions that are appropriate. Examples would be: installing a new patrol leader, investing new Scouts, presenting skill awards, merit badges, or badges of rank. Distinguish this from the court of honor, a special recognition occasion held infrequently, during which every Scout who has advanced during the period since the last court of honor is recognized. But badges of office, skill awards, merit badges, and badges of rank should be presented immediately after a boy has become entitled to them.

Scoutmaster's Minute. This is an occasion for a brief story with a moral, a few well-chosen remarks, a little lift of some kind from you to the Scouts. It is serious, short, and makes a single point.

Ceremony. The end of the meeting is more serious and less lively than the beginning. The recognition and Scoutmaster's minute will have slowed the tone of the meeting from high spirits to quiet contemplation. The meeting begins with exuberance; it ends more calmly. Thus, the closing ceremony is quiet and permits individual thought about one's self and the point of the ceremony. The playing (well or not at all, please!) of "Taps," the singing of a quiet song, and the Scout benediction (May the Great Master of all Scouts be with us till we meet again) are all traditional to this period. There are many other possibilities. They are at their best when they offer even a few brief moments for Scouts to reflect on themselves. The mood and thus the influence of a closing ceremony are destroyed by giggling, missed cues, bad bugling, or a forgotten announcement that is boomed out just when the mood begins to work.

If there is even a trace of showmanship in your soul, put it to work on your closing ceremonies. If that kind of thing is not your specialty, there is probably someone in the troop—man or boy—who can do it well. Let that be his job. Potentially these 60 seconds are worth a sack of diamonds, and it is worth a lot of effort to make use of them.

If you have a good bugler, he can help close the meeting.

After the Meeting

As troop meetings begin before they start, they end after they finish. The closing moments signal the official ending of the meeting. Most of the Scouts grab their personal gear and leave after that. Some don't.

The service patrol puts the room back in perfect order, exactly as prescribed by the organization that has been kind enough to let you use it. The leader of the service patrol should report to the senior patrol leader for an inspection of the premises before he dismisses his patrol.

The patrol leaders' council meets briefly to review the meeting and pick up any loose ends about the next meeting.

Scouts will have individual business with the scribe, quartermaster, Scoutmaster, and other leaders. Equipment and books will be checked in or out. Appointments will be made for other meetings.

The service patrol puts the room in order, and you check on next week's activity.

SOME UNANSWERED QUESTIONS

What you have just read is the story of troop meetings. There probably are some questions left in your mind, and this section will try to answer some of them.

Where Is the Scoutmaster?

Observing. Watching to see how leaders perform, how Scouts respond, how things go in general. Noticing individual behavior. Thinking how to improve meetings.

Conferring. Both boys and adults often will want to get your ear for a while. It ought to be available to them.

Meeting New Boys. New arrivals need a private conference with you. Tell them about the troop, how to join, and answer their questions about it.

Coaching. Boy leaders can learn a lot from you if you're available. Get them aside and help them.

You can't do these if you are tied up in direct leadership. Your proper role is to see that others play theirs. You are the director of the play, not the star.

What Are the Other Leaders Doing?

Your assistant Scoutmasters should be concerned with their specific areas of responsibility, such as physical arrangements and activities, etc. The physical arrangements assistant would have responsibility for the preparation of the meeting area, equipment, and other physical arrangements. The assistant for activities would be directly involved with the smooth operating of the entire meeting. The assistant Scoutmasters may also serve as "experts" in training or presenting if the situation calls for it, but remember, boys should be given a major responsibility within the troop.

The senior patrol leader, as the boy leader of the troop and your liaison with the patrol leaders, runs the troop meeting. He calls the Scouts to order, leads the opening, and moves the Scouts from activity to activity. He also closes the meeting.

The assistant senior patrol leader will be working with a new patrol leader during the troop meeting, or may be doing a job assigned to him by the senior patrol leader.

The junior assistant Scoutmasters should be given a specific responsibility just like the assistant Scoutmasters. Junior assistant Scoutmasters have served admirably in training other boy leaders, assisted in program planning, and organized troop Good Turns. The important thing is to make sure that every leader has a specific ongoing responsibility. But remember that all are under your direction.

How Formal Is a Troop Meeting?

The answer is it is partly formal and partly informal. It is undesirable for Scouts to operate in fear of their terrible-tempered Scoutmaster, almost afraid to breathe. It is equally undesirable for discourtesy to reign.

The troop should be able to form into almost any formation with the silent signals shown here. No leader should ever need a whistle to gain attention. The Scout sign raised high is all that is necessary.

There is no reason to spend a lot of time on military drill and rigid formations, but the troop should be able to organize itself physically in a short time without a lot of confusion.

Saluting leaders is not the only way to build a cooperative relationship between leaders and boys. Scouts should be taught to address adult leaders politely. Most troops still expect boys to call their Scoutmaster "Mr." but there may be some situations where the first name can be used more effectively.

Courtesy is a mutual matter, however. You and the other adults must show respect for Scouts as persons. They need the right to express their thoughts, to disagree, and to have a say in the troop operation.

The silent signal for ATTENTION is the Scout sign, held up high.

SILENT SIGNALS

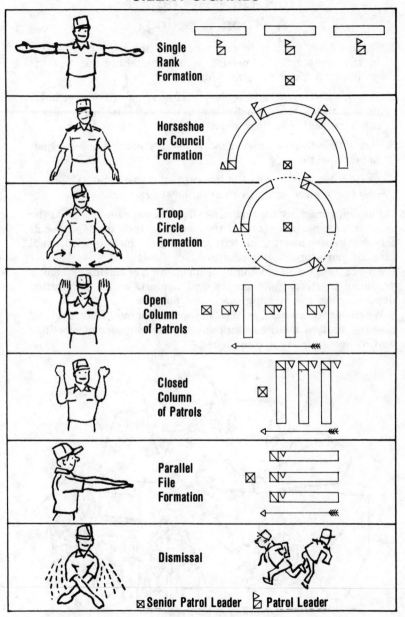

Single Rank Formation

Horseshoe or Council Formation

Troop Circle Formation

Open Column of Patrols

Closed Column of Patrols

Parallel File Formation

Dismissal

⊠ Senior Patrol Leader   ⧄ Patrol Leader

How Do I Recognize
A Good Meeting?

1. Review every meeting by comparing it with the purposes stated in this chapter. If a meeting is accomplishing some of the purposes, it has a lot going for it.

2. Watch attendance records closely. If meeting attendance holds up to a high percent, meetings must be good. If it slips or runs at a low percent, meetings must not be so good.

3. Review meetings with your patrol leaders' council and get their honest reactions.

4. Call in somebody whose judgment you respect and ask him to observe a meeting or two and offer suggestions.

Finally, remember that meetings don't always have to be at the regular meeting place, and if they are not, they probably won't follow the same meeting pattern as the regular meeting. The usual meeting parts probably would not be followed.

There might not, for example, be an opening or closing ceremony or patrol meetings, and games and contests might be omitted depending on the meeting place and purpose.

Wherever the meeting is held, however, it should fit into a total meeting pattern for the month so that the purposes of meetings and of Scouting are accomplished.

Call in an observer.

TROOP MEETINGS

Pattern 1	Troop meeting place	Some other time and place
1st week	Troop meeting	Patrol meeting or activity
2d week	Troop meeting	
3d week	Troop meeting	
4th week	Patrol leaders' council	Troop outdoor activity

Pattern 2	Troop meeting place	Some other time and place
1st week	Troop meeting	
2d week	Board of review	Patrol meeting or activity
3d week	Troop meeting	
4th week	Patrol leaders' council	Troop outdoor activity

Troop Good Turns

Troop Good Turns often are spontaneous. Someone is stalled in the parking lot, or stuck in the mud or a snowdrift. The troop meeting comes to a halt and everyone goes to the rescue. When they return, the Scouts radiate the enthusiasm of having been needed.

Being a knight in shining armor is a wonderful feeling, so encourage departures from planned activity whenever the opportunity to be helpful presents itself.

Good Turns on a troop basis can also be planned. For that reason, space is provided to jot down a Good Turn idea for each month on your Troop Program Planning Sheet. Some of the ideas may extend over several months. For example, building a trail and maintaining it may be a long-term Good Turn project for your troop. Long-term or short, the Good Turn idea is the happiest thought anyone can have. Just keep this in mind: "How can we be helpful and how can I make it an adventure for the Scouts?" Some surprisingly good answers will occur to you!

Part 2

HELPING THE BOY

WHEN you have been in Scouting for a while you'll need more information than that fitted into a preparation kit. Part I of this book can get you started; now you need the what, the why, and the how of Scouting. Part 1 dealt with the troop; these next four chapters deal with the boy.

Chapter 6

Aims
and
Methods

Scouting can become a powerful influence in support
of the family, school, and religious community.

THE purpose of the Boy Scouts of America is to help boys
become honorable men. No one would suggest that Boy
Scouting alone will bring boys into manhood with qualities
of decency. The man is the product of many influences. Your troop
is not the property of the Boy Scouts of America. It belongs to your
chartered organization which may be a church or synagogue, a
school, or civic organization.

Boy Scouting works best when it is used by and becomes a part
of the home, school, and religious community. Boy Scouting adds
to them. It may even substitute for one or another of them as well.
Not every Boy Scout in your troop comes from a home that
provides all the right influences. Not all schools are able to meet
the demands on them. Not every boy is influenced by a church or
synagogue. In the lives of such boys as these, Boy Scouting is even
more important as an influence.

THE AIMS

Every Boy Scout activity and design strives toward the three aims of Boy Scouting: (1) building character, (2) fostering citizenship, and (3) developing mental, moral, and physical fitness.

Character

By this we mean what the boy is himself: his personal qualities, his values, his outlook. Here are some signs to look for:

- The boy is confident in himself, but not conceited.
- He is honest with himself and others.
- His personal appearance—grooming and neatness—shows that he respects himself.
- He has developed special skills or hobbies that absorb his energies and develop his competence and confidence.
- He can take care of himself in emergencies.
- He can plan and use logic to meet unfamiliar situations.
- He is courageous in difficult situations.
- He is responsible to the commitments he makes to himself and others.
- He believes in some religious concept and practices his belief in his daily life.
- He respects other people's beliefs when they are different from his own.

It is not reasonable to expect every boy to meet these standards. Nor will a boy do well consistently.

Look for the good qualities in boys.

Cheerful citizens make America beautiful.

Citizenship

The boy learns his obligations to other people, to the society he lives in, and to the government that presides over that society.

Our objective in Boy Scouting is to develop in boys the feeling of people's interdependence. They enter the program at the end of a quite self-centered period of their lives. As they grow out of this stage, they need clear direction and useful experience. It is here that we use the program to draw them into relationships with other young people and with adults. They learn citizenship "from the inside out." In camping, for example, they learn to live with a group, the patrol, with rules based on the common good.

If you are making progress in citizenship training, you will observe behaviors like these:

- The boy knows something of his heritage as an American and is proud of it.

- He understands to some degree American social, economic, and governmental systems.

- He understands and can use leadership skills to lead a group to a successful outcome.

- He demonstrates concern for and interest in others.

- He has some knowledge of cultures and social groups other than his own and is able to understand something of what it is like to belong to another such group.

- He is aware of community organizations and what they do.

- He understands and respects the ethnic and social relationships of his community.

- He contributes in some way to the improvement of the environment in which he lives.

- He wisely uses property belonging to himself and others.

- He resists the urging of his peers to experiment with smoking, drugs, and alcohol.

- He explores career and hobby possibilities for himself.

Fitness

There are four aspects of fitness: fitness of the body (well-tuned and healthy), fitness of the mind (able to think and solve problems), fitness of the "moral fiber" (as demonstrated by courage, respect for others, etc.), and fitness of the emotions (self-control and self-respect).

Physical Fitness. It is fairly easy to observe progress toward these outcomes. Scouting contains a lot of vigorous activity, both indoors and out, and boys' ability to cope with it reveals their physical fitness.

Here are some of the ways you can judge physical fitness:

- The boy has good health habits. He eats properly, exercises daily, and gets enough sleep.

- His physical fitness is shown by strength, muscle tone, and endurance.

- His coordination is reasonably good.

- He keeps his weight within reasonable limits.

Beating past performances in push-ups takes determination and a little encouragement.

Mental Fitness. We are talking here about the brain, not the emotions—about using mental ability. A brilliant boy may waste his brainpower. A retarded boy may achieve far beyond his apparent ability.

One who is mentally fit is able to make good use of the intelligence he has. This may show as:

- Being alert (mentally awake!).

- Being able to give and receive information.

- Using good judgment, thinking logically, making sound decisions.

- Solving problems creatively.

- Using a questioning approach to problems.

Being mentally fit isn't just for geniuses; everyone can "Be Prepared."

Moral Fitness. Morality is a somewhat more difficult area than the others because of the moral contradictions we all encounter. What you consider moral or immoral depends on your upbringing and background.

Moral questions often fail to come out nice and neat. The town's chief industry employs hundreds, but pollutes the air and the river. A young man who marches in a picket line is immoral to some. If you don't march, you are immoral to others.

Despite the moral contradictions, we cannot let boys go unprepared to face the assorted moral crises that will confront them. They must go prepared—but with what?

As evidence of a boy's ability to act correctly when faced with a moral decision you might look for:

- Courage about what he believes. Being called "chicken" doesn't divert him from doing what he believes is right—or not doing what he believes is wrong. For example, he resists the urging of his peers to experiment with smoking, drugs, and alcohol.
- Respecting the rights of others.
- Compassion for others' feelings and needs.
- Acting as if the rights of others matter to him.
- Accepting others as equal in worth and dignity.

Emotional Fitness. Boy Scouting helps boys to understand themselves and to maintain emotional balance. It helps prepare them to withstand the emotional crises they will face later. Evidence of their preparedness will show as:

- Adaptability—being able to adjust to new or changing situations.
- Self-discipline—having self-control.
- Respect for self.
- Constructive and enthusiastic attitudes.

The accomplishment of these three aims takes time. No single hike, game, or meeting can improve character, citizenship, and fitness all at once. Yet these aims should underlie all Boy Scout activities.

Helping boys face up to tough situations with courage is one of the gifts of Scouting.

THE METHODS

The purpose of a Boy Scout troop is to provide opportunities for boys to grow as they reach to achieve the aims of the movement. The Scoutmaster's *objective* is to help his Scouts to achieve these aims. The Scoutmaster's *job* is to use the methods of Scouting in troop operation and activities.

Boy Scout programs and activities are developed to utilize the methods of Scouting. Of course, all of them may not be used at every meeting, but if over a period of time each method is evident, then the troop program will be successful.

We have considered the aims of Scouting and some of the evidence of achieving them. There are eight methods we use to accomplish these aims. They are not listed in order of importance because they are all of equal importance.

Ideals

The ideals of Scouting are spelled out in the Scout Oath, the Scout Law, motto, and slogan. The Scout measures himself against these ideals and as he reaches for them he has some control over what he becomes.

The rules and regulations, or "bylaws" of a Scout troop are the Scout Oath and Law, and all matters of conduct are measured against them.

Throughout history boys have been attracted to codes of conduct to use as guides in their growth into manhood. The ideals of Scouting provide a proven code for living.

If you believe in the ideals of Scouting it will mean more to your Scouts.

The patrol is a Scout's "family circle" within the troop community.

Patrol Method

"The Patrol System is the one essential feature in which Scout training differs from that of all other organisations, and where the System is properly applied, it is absolutely bound to bring success. It cannot help itself!

"The formation of the boys into Patrols of from six to eight and training them as separate units each under its own responsible leader is the key to a good Troop.

"The patrol is the unit of Scouting always, whether for work or for play, for discipline or for duty."—B-P

Outdoors

The Boy Scout program is designed to take place outdoors. It is in the outdoors that Scouts share the responsibilities and learn to live with each other. It is here that the skills and activities practiced at troop meetings come alive with purpose. Being close to nature helps Scouts gain an appreciation for God's handiwork and mankind's place in it. The outdoors is the laboratory for Scouts to learn ecology and practice conservation of nature's resources.

Scouting is outing—boys join Scouting to go camping.

Most boys join a troop with the expectancy of outdoor adventure. The *Official Boy Scout Handbook* promises exciting outdoor activities, and is a handbook for outdoor living. It can be assumed that a main purpose of troop meetings is to learn skills needed for outdoor adventure. As a general rule there should be an outdoor experience for the troop at least once a month.

Advancement

Scouting provides a series of surmountable obstacles and steps to overcome them through the advancement method. The Scout plans his advancement and progresses at his own pace as he overcomes each challenge. The Scout is rewarded for each achievement, which helps him gain self-confidence. The steps in the advancement system help a boy grow in self-reliance and the ability to help others.

Scouting provides a system of education that allows boys to learn while they're having fun. Advancement can be likened to getting a suntan. It happens while you're having fun in the right climate. The Scoutmaster and troop committee have the responsibility of providing the right climate. Scout skills provide learning experiences that are good wholesome fun.

A Scout can set his own pace and go as far as he likes on the trail to Eagle.

Believe it or not, you are a hero to individual boys in the troop.

Adult Male Association

Boys learn from the example of their adult leaders. In his quest for manhood, every boy needs contact with men he can copy. The Scoutmaster and his assistants provide a masculine image of the Boy Scout program. Providing good examples of manhood is one of the methods of Scouting.

Boys tend to copy whatever models are available to them, and some may not be really good models. As Scoutmaster, you provide an example of what a man should be like. Your role as a friend, coach, and leader to Scouts is a most important part of Scouting.

Uniform

The uniform makes the Boy Scout troop visible as a force for good and creates a positive youth image in the community. Scouting is an action program, and wearing the uniform is an action that shows each Scout's commitment to the aims of Scouting. The uniform gives the Scout international identity in a world brotherhood of youth who believe in the same ideals. The uniform is practical attire for Scout activities, and provides a way for Scouts to wear the badges that show what they have accomplished.

Just as it identifies the wearer as a Scout, the uniform reminds him that he is a Scout and influences his actions. The Scout uniform is also a leveler. Whatever a boy's background, when he puts on the uniform he shares equally in the program.

Leadership Training

The Boy Scout program encourages boys to learn and practice leadership skills. Every Scout has the opportunity to participate in both shared and total leadership situations. Understanding the concepts of leadership helps a boy accept the leadership role of others and guides him toward the citizenship aim of Scouting.

Leadership is action. It is doing things rather than holding a title. Troop and patrol activities allow boys to lead no matter what their positions in the troop structure. The Scoutmaster watches to see that every boy has opportunities to practice leadership successfully.

Personal Growth

As Scouts plan their activity, and progress toward their goals they experience personal growth. The Good Turn concept is a major part of the personal growth method of Scouting. Boys grow as they participate in community service projects and do Good Turns for others. There probably is no device so successful in developing a basis for personal growth as the daily Good Turn. The religious emblems program is also a large part of the personal growth method. Frequent personal conferences with his Scoutmaster help each Scout to determine his growth toward Scouting's aims.

Growth in moral strength and character is an outcome of the Scout program. Personal growth is also a method since a conscious effort is made to see that it happens. As you, the Scoutmaster, guide your troop in planning program and activities, you help boys grow by involving them in service to others and stretching to reach their goals.

Doing thoughtful, little things for others is the Good Turn habit that is always appreciated.

Imagination is the secret program ingredient.

OTHER PROGRAM ELEMENTS

We have considered those parts of Scouting that are so essential to the success of the program that we call them methods. There are, of course, other features and elements—some unique to Scouting, some not. Each contributes its own flavor to the total program.

We note some of these other program elements here, in no special order.

Adventure

Adventure is something out of the ordinary. It is a happening that somehow amounted to more than the participants expected. It is something a boy looks forward to.

As Scoutmaster, you must never lose sight of adventure as a necessary ingredient in the program. Boys are unable to speak clearly about their quest for adventure, but when they say, "same old stuff" or "no fun" you will know that they looked for adventure but didn't find it.

Adventure is a canoe trip instead of a hike. Adventure is going to a new campground. Adventure is paddling 3 miles down the lake to get the food for dinner. Adventure is anticipating a new experience.

Competition and Sports

Our society encourages men and boys to be competitive. Any boys' program that denies competition and sports is making a serious error. However, sports and competiton can also be overemphasized and escalated to extremes.

Boy Scouts should participate in sports and compete against Boy Scouts, patrols against patrols, troops against troops.

But Scouts or leaders shouldn't engage in cutthroat competition, concentrate totally on winning contests, or develop a few superstars who compete while all the others watch.

To win a Scouting contest is a fine experience when the rules are right and everyone goes by them.

If we believe that competition is a game, then we will keep it a game and not let it become a life-and-death struggle. If we believe that competition is good for boys, then we will keep it at their level and not let anyone inflate it into a spectacle. We will see that those who participate are recognized and those who try are praised for trying. In Scouting, every boy is given an equal opportunity to compete. No boy is left on the sidelines even if he is a bit clumsy. Quiet boys are encouraged to join in the competition and to do their best.

Sports and competition, therefore, should be a part of the troop program and take advantage of the program resources in the sports-oriented merit badges.

Competition in the Troop. Competition is to be encouraged as a regular part of the troop program. "Competitive activities shall be used as a vital learning process and a means of enhancing the growth and development of boys. The activity, whether it is group competition with overall winners, group competition to a standard, or individual competition, must be so planned and run that it results in positive character and attitude outcomes."

Team Sports Policy

One of the methods of meeting boys' interest in competition will be by the use of team sports on an informal basis and as a natural part of troop activities. Contact sports that involve heavy physical contact as part of the regular play should not be used in this program. Such sports cannot be safely conducted without proper equipment, special fields, constant conditioning, special facilities, and trained coaches.

Activities Among
Troops, Packs, and Posts

Most local councils and/or their districts conduct camporees once or twice a year. Here dozens or even hundreds of troops camp together for a weekend. Usually highlighted by contests and other special events, camporees and see'n'dos provide a fine chance for both Scouts and leaders to meet others and to see other troops in action.

Scouting shows are often held on a council or district basis. Together with the Cub Scout packs and Explorer posts of the area, troops take part by demonstrating skills, and otherwise showing the public what Scouting is all about.

Summer camp is another chance for troops to join together, usually at the council's camp, each troop under its own leadership.

Some troops make a practice of joining informally with another on occasion. They may have a joint meeting or campout.

Whatever you do in Scouting, make it the best show in town!

Chapter 7

Leadership

You need to get behind the troop and move it along in the right direction.

BEING a leader is getting a group to do something. If your troop hasn't been very active, it's up to you to get it moving.

Start with ideas of things your troop can do. First use ideas that you can help three or four boys with; then involve the whole troop.

Until you have your patrols organized and your patrol leaders' council running smoothly, give jobs to do for each meeting to known boy leaders. Talk to each boy before the meeting. Tell him exactly what to do. After the meeting, give him a pat on the back, and if necessary, some ideas on how to do it better next time.

The Functions of Leadership

Every leader has just two functions: first, to get the job done, and second, to keep his group together. "The job" is whatever the group is organized to do. In your case it's giving boys Scouting. It doesn't have to be work: it might be a game or a contest. Sometimes a skilled leader can make a game out of work itself.

With good leadership a patrol leader will be able to get his patrol to clean up its campsite. With great leadership, the patrol will have fun doing it. The book that can help you accomplish that miracle is *The Official Patrol Leader Handbook.*

Styles of Leadership

There are five ways a leader can help his group get the job done. No one way is always right. You may find yourself using one or more of these ways or styles of leadership:

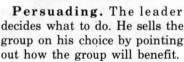

Telling. The leader checks the alternatives. He may or may not think about the group's feelings. He selects what he thinks is the best thing to do and tells the others.

Persuading. The leader decides what to do. He sells the group on his choice by pointing out how the group will benefit.

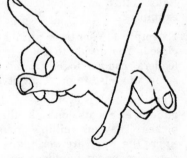

Delegating. The leader states the problem and the rules within which it is to be solved. He then turns the problem over to the group. He accepts and supports the group's solution, as long as it falls within the rules.

Consulting. The leader encourages group members to take part in the decisions, plans, and guidelines. He may make suggestions but is sensitive to the group's response.

While usually it isn't apparent, the leader still makes the decisions but they're popular because they reflect the consensus of the group.

Joining. The leader agrees in advance that he will abide by the group's decision. He takes part in the discussion as any other group member, but he never gives up his role as leader.

How They Work

In the beginning you will be telling your Scouts what to do. Later, other ways or styles will work better. Here are some examples:

Example 1. Your troop arrives at a museum only to find that it is closed. You decide to get a group decision. You call the patrol leaders' council together and explain the problem. They pick something else to do. That style of leadership is *joining*.

Example 2. It is evening and the troop is going to play an outdoor game. The Scouts don't like the game the senior patrol leader has picked. They are milling around, suggesting other games. You figure that they are working within the rules and that the senior patrol leader can handle it. So, you do nothing. Soon they agree on a game and begin playing it. That style of leadership is *delegating*.

Example 3. You find a Scout burning a kerosine lantern in his tent. There is a rule that flame lights in tents can't be used because of fire hazard. You order that the lantern be put out. It is a matter of safety, and you do not compromise. That style of leadership is back to *telling*.

Study the styles of leadership. Try different ways. Keep things going by telling, if you have to, but work toward delegating and joining. In that way you will develop boy leaders.

Skills of Leadership

Following are some skills of leadership that good leaders use in Scouting.

- **Communicating.** As a leader you both get and give information. You must be able to do both of these well. Teach Scouts to take notes when there is a lot of detail. Ask questions after giving instructions. Get feedback to make sure the message gets through. Discuss things that are going to happen. You measure your success in terms of the job getting done and the degree to which instructions were followed.

- **Knowing the Resources.** You depend on what members can do, as well as what you can do. To use these resources, you must first know what they are. Check the Scouts' advancement. Look at the records. Talk with your leaders. Watch the Scouts in action. You will know when you are using the group's resources; then others will lead, and the troop's program won't be just the result of your ideas.

- **Understanding the Needs.** Scouts come from different backgrounds. Each Scout has certain strengths and weaknesses. By understanding each boy's individual needs, everyone benefits. The patrol leaders' council helps apply this skill, because the purpose of the council is to plan and run a troop program that meets the needs and desires of the Scouts.

- **Representing the Group.** The patrol method uses this skill. Patrol leaders take their boys' ideas and problems to the patrol leaders' council and bring back to the patrol decisions of the council. You are succeeding in this area when everyone in your troop feels that he has a part in troop decisions.

- **Evaluating.** You do this both during and after everything your troop does. For this process to work you must have a goal for each activity. Scouting's aims and methods are your guidelines. For example, when you complete a camping trip, review it with your boy and adult leaders. Did you strengthen the patrols? Is there a stronger Scouting spirit? Did each boy grow in Scouting?

- **Planning.** The core of a successful program is planning. You must do it when no one else can, but don't do it for very long. As soon as possible, train your patrol leaders' council to do the planning. In that way boy leaders are involved in planning and carrying out the troop's program. With the patrol leaders' council doing its job, you'll find it easier to involve adult leaders.

- **Controlling the Group.** A controlled group can do its job and be happy while doing it. This means that the troop has good meetings, activities, and camping trips. Along the way, the members are in good spirits, become better Scouts, and are in stronger patrols. Sometimes controlling the group means stopping behavior that hurts the group. Use your patrol leaders' council to control the troop. Everyone is happier when the troop can control itself.

Imagination tempered with common sense makes a great Scoutmaster.

- **Counseling.** You must be able to counsel or coach Scouts in order to help them. Listen carefully to each Scout. Ask him what he hopes to be and do. Give him facts, but not advice. Help him think things through for himself.

- **Sharing Leadership.** With leadership goes trust. You can and must share your leader's role, but you cannot give up your responsibility for the welfare of the troop. The secret is to let others share in making decisions without giving up your trust.

- **Setting the Example.** What you are speaks louder than what you say. Wearing your uniform encourages Scouts to wear theirs. The way you act should be in harmony with Scout ideals. Boys need a model to copy and you might be the only good example they know.

- **Effective Teaching.** Scoutmasters have done this since 1910. Don't assume that boys have learned something just because you've done some teaching. The proof lies in what they can do. The trick is to put them in a spot where they see the need for the skill or knowledge you wish to teach. Then offer the help they need.

Recruiting Leadership

Your position as Scoutmaster gives you status from your chartered organization which owns and operates your troop. This combined with enthusiasm for the program may make you Mr. Scouting to your friends and associates. As such you will find it easy to invite others into Scouting through your chartered organization.

The secret of recruiting leaders is to match the job to be done with the people you know or have just met. As a matter of fact, parents of new Scouts are excellent prospects. That is especially so if they are new to the community, for Scouting is an outstanding way for them to become acquainted with and a part of their new community.

Chapter 8

Understanding the Boy

You don't need to be a brain surgeon to find out what makes boys tick.

SCOUTMASTER needs to understand boys. It helps to know individual boys if you begin with boys in general. There are no descriptions to explain all boys. Every boy is an individual. He develops at his own rate, has his own thoughts, and makes his own goals. Yet boys of a given age and background have much in common. If you understand some of these common characteristics, you can work more easily with boys. You'll have fewer surprises.

Our general observations about boys of Scout age have to be divided in terms of older and younger groups you deal with, because they differ greatly.

The divider between the "old" boys and the "young" boys is puberty, that radical change from boy to man. Physical, mental, emotional, and sexual changes at this period of a boy's life are drastic. They mark the end of the boy and the beginning of the man.

As we have divided up the boys for discussion here, we have placed puberty between age 13 and 14. Actually, of course, it occurs over a much wider age span. There are mature 12-year-olds and immature 15-year-olds. To understand any given boy, we have to slide up or down on the scale according to the speed with which he has matured.

Somewhere between the ages of 12 and 15 nearly all boys undergo a fairly rapid transition from child to adolescent. Physical growth is the most obvious and dramatic. Shoulders broaden, chest expands, voice changes, sexual maturation occurs, clothes are outgrown.

Some changes are quickly over and done. Others linger and shift about for years. The working out of difficulties occurring during this period, by the Scoutmaster and the Scout together, provides a real opportunity to influence a Scout's later beliefs and ideals.

It is obvious not only from these observations but from your own experience that adolescents are different from younger boys and cannot be treated the same. That does not mean that they cannot work together in the same troop. They can and do. But they are not alike.

Here are some suggestions:

1. By the time a boy is 14, he should be or have been a patrol leader. He is probably capable of making a larger contribution to the troop than he can as a patrol member.

2. A boy who is 14 and has been a patrol leader should probably not just be thrust back into the patrol. He, too, should be ready for a greater contribution.

3. Adolescent boys may want and should have some activities separate from the "younger set." Girls may be involved in some of these, by the boys' choice.

4. A well-matured adolescent may be *too old* to be an effective patrol leader. His interests are with those of his age. The gap between him and the 11-year-olds may be too great.

5. A troop that has grown its first teenagers (boys who started at 11, and are now 14 or more) should make its program more adventurous than when it started out. Some adventures can be limited to the older boys. Teenagers will stay on for several years if they can share new adventures. If they are limited to having the same year's experience five times, they will leave.

CHARACTERISTICS OF BOYS

	Physical	Mental
11-12-13	Good health, rarely sick. Active and somewhat accident-prone. Slow growth at ages 11 and early 12. Coordination improving. Needs sleep: 9 to 10 hours. Occasionally quite childish. Increasing sexual curiosity.	Curious, adventure-seeking, likes to experiment. Improving attention span. Better skill and patience at crafts. Confidence and courage increase with success (and decrease with failure). Turned off by nagging and criticism. Needs freedom to develop interests and abilities.
14 AND OLDER	Rapid physical growth and change. Awkwardness. Adult masculine features develop: facial features, beard, body contours, sexual maturity. Good health. Prodigious appetite. Inconsistency: powerful at times, puny at others. Continues to need plenty of sleep: 9 to 10 hours. Tends to overdo in physical sports.	Can think and talk about abstractions. Thinks more creatively and critically (and thus seems argumentative). Intelligence measures (at age 14) at adult levels. Daydreams. Memory good. Leadership ability shows itself in groups. Begins to think about vocations. Wants to make his own decisions.

CHARACTERISTICS OF BOYS

Social	Spiritual
More interested in approval of boys than of parents. Forms gangs and clubs. Looks sloppy. Unsure with girls. Controls his emotions except at home. Team play gradually replaces individual play. Some rebellion against authority. Feels some guilt as his loyalty shifts from parents to friends.	The spiritual side of boys' development is influenced by their families and their exposure—if any—to religious experiences. In this period, boys tend to grow in: Belief in fair play. Sensitivity to doing wrong. Appreciation of God. Acceptance of the Golden Rule in everyday living.
Self-conscious, especially with adults. Aware of the difference between the standards of his group and those of his parents. Wants to be treated like a man but feels treated like a child. Matures less rapidly than girls the same age. Dating begins. Maximum loyalty to his group. Can take more responsibility and wants it. More interested in personal grooming.	Begins to develop some kind of philosophy of life. Searches for values and standards. Concerned more with the needs of others. More interested in identifying right and wrong.

PROBLEM AREAS

As a Scoutmaster dealing with a group of other people's sons, you probably expect to have some behavior problems along the way. And indeed you will. Your troop, if it is like most, takes on whatever boys come to it, complete with their strengths and weaknesses.

You may be tempted to get rid of any boy who fails to meet the behavior standards. This is handy for the Scoutmaster, but quite opposite to the goals of the movement. The purpose of the program, of course, is to help boys and to prepare them for the life they have ahead. They must continue in the troop if they are to benefit from Scouting. Only when every reasonable effort has failed should a boy be dropped.

The opposite temptation is to overlook poor behavior.

Both temptations fail to deal with the problem. One approach puts it back out in the street for someone else to work on at some other time and place. The other leaves it right in the troop, untouched, laying the groundwork for more of the same, and worse. Neither is any kind of solution.

Whatever the solution is to dealing with problems of boy behavior, it seems to lie in the middle ground between overreaching and ignoring. But what, precisely, is it?

We must make clear that we are really dealing with two kinds of things here: the behavior of groups, and of individuals. One is a question of proper use of skills in handling groups. The other is handling individuals properly. Let's consider the group question first.

The Matter of Discipline

Ultimately, we want each boy to be responsible for his own behavior. We want a troop of Scouts that acts like a troop of Scouts. How do we get it?

Here are some of the building blocks of a self-controlled or disciplined troop.

The Leader Must Lead. We have noted that the beginning Scoutmaster must take command at once or he is lost; he does not continue commanding, but he must start there. The troop takes its shape from the Scoutmaster. He sets the kinds of behavior that are acceptable, and conveys this quickly to all other leaders.

The Program Must Move. A number of things are implied here. Among them are these: (1) There *is* a program, written down, and understood by those who are responsible for it. (2) The program is *paced properly;* that is, there are no dead spots with nothing to do. Activities are not allowed to run on past the point where interest lags. Things do not bog down waiting for some leader to get organized. (3) The program involves everyone. It is not a spectator sport, but a series of activities in which everyone takes part.

Limits Must Be Established. Discipline and control move down the line from Scoutmaster to boy leaders to Scouts. At the outset the Scoutmaster makes clear what is acceptable: "We don't do that here." "We do it this way here." The boy leaders pick this up. Control comes from them. In time, boys can control themselves in large measure: "I won't do that because it's not done here."

A Scout doesn't have to stand in the corner in order to get the message that his behavior is not acceptable.

There is a little wildness in everyone that needs to be tamed.

Boy Leaders Must Be Trained To Control. A boy does not necessarily know how to handle a group just because he was elected its leader. He needs to know—quickly—what to do and how to do it. He must understand the special power he has *because* he is a boy. He can get what he expects of his patrol.

Every leader must recognize that boys do not like and will not put up with an undisciplined troop. This may look like a conflict with the way boys produce instant chaos if left to their own devices. It is not. Boys create havoc because they don't know what else to do. But they will not remain long in a troop that never rises above the free-for-all. They expect to be controlled but will test until they find every limit.

Boys recognize the contrast between the ideals and what happens in the troop. What possible meaning has "A Scout is obedient" if anybody can do anything he wants? The Scout Law describes a community that every boy would earnestly like to live in. But he needs your help in developing it.

Behavior can be anticipated. If you camp near water, somebody will go swimming. If you camp near trees, somebody will hack one or cut it down. If you have patrol meetings during the troop meeting and there is nothing for the patrols to do, there will be trouble. Since none of these things comes as a surprise, you can prevent problems by anticipating them. Define the rules under which swimming will be done. Make clear that axes or other tools will not be misused and that trees will not be damaged.

LEADERSHIP AND UNDERSTANDING

- Use boys for control as much as possible. Get everybody used to the idea that they take their cues from boy leaders.

- Use the patrol leaders' council for serious infractions. They usually can decide how to handle a problem as well as or better than you. But they will need your guidance.

- Address them as "Scouts" rather than "boys." There's a difference, and they need to be reminded.

- Keep your voice down. Try to outshout them, and you will lose. Use silent signals. Avoid public discipline of individuals. They may welcome the attention they get, or they may be hurt by being made a spectacle. Talk to boys in private when there are problems.

- Give and demand respect for all leaders. Formality is in order for ceremonies and inspections. Don't keep boys standing in formation any longer than necessary and they will pay more attention to what leaders have to say.

- Treat boys equally. Any favoritism you show will be noticed.

- Avoid threats. They are easy to make when you are hot, but not so easy to carry out when you have cooled off. Beware of making threats that you don't intend to carry out.

- Don't be afraid to send home someone who is disrupting the program for others. Let him know he is welcome back when he is better able to cooperate. Call his parents and tell them why you sent him home.

- Recognize that every boy who does something disruptive is in some way trying to meet a need of his own: recognition, acceptance, or something else. Try to find better ways for boys to meet their needs.

INDIVIDUAL BEHAVIOR PROBLEMS

There are no neat rules for handling each behavior problem. In general, you should try to understand why such behavior occurs. Then you should try to find a way to keep it from happening again, or at least to cut down its frequency or importance. You will not solve all such problems, but you will be able to have a big influence on many boys.

Cheating

You may find cheating taking place in Scout games and contests. You may find it in Scout advancement.

In cheating at games and contests, you often will find that the rules for play were not clearly defined and understood. Boys are quick to notice any suggestion of cheating, and just as quick to point it out. In that sense, cheating is usually handled in the troop without adult interference. Much cheating, and charges of cheating, can be eliminated by making the rules clear.

Cheating in advancement is another matter. It is often the result of carelessness by adults. A leader signs a boy's record without demanding proof—"I know you can do that." A merit badge counselor is supposed to ask for demonstrations and evidence of ability, but may accept the boy's word that he has met certain requirements. A misguided father, eager to bask in the glory of his son's Eagle badge, may sign approval, demanding less than the boy's best.

These are things for you to handle. You can't ignore cheating. Get at the root of the problem. It may be parental pressure. It could be a need for recognition by a boy unable to get it any other way. Point out that there is no meaning to an unearned badge. Both boys and parents need to be reminded of this fact.

Help boys understand that cheating gets them into trouble.

"Somebody stole my book."

Stealing

Reports of stealing in your troop probably will outnumber actual thefts. Sometimes Scout-age boys are quite careless about taking care of their things. When a knife comes up missing, it is stolen— "I had it right here and now it's gone."

The first step when a theft is reported is a quiet check to make sure that something is missing. A good many searches will turn up the "stolen" property not far from where it was supposed to be.

The second step is to investigate—if something is indeed missing—whether something else could have happened to it. Did the owner lend it out? Might someone have borrowed it without permission? Could the owner have used it somewhere else and forgotten it?

If no good explanation can be made of why the property is missing, it may—tentatively at least—be considered taken without permission. Now what?

Ask the owner whether he has any idea who might have taken it. Make it clear that any investigation will be made by you and not by him, and that he is to accuse no one to his face or to another Scout. If he is able to name anyone, ask him what evidence he has to support his belief.

Scouts can exercise a good deal of control over stealing by making clear that they will not put up with it. Most boys will not indulge in behavior that is not tolerated by the group.

If guilt is established, the subsequent handling of the matter is between you and the guilty boy. The incident should be used to help him. Certainly, the property should be returned and justice meted out in the form of penalties or deprivation of privileges.

Lying

The circumstances of lies are more important than the lies themselves. The boy who lies, "My uncle is a big TV producer," is looking for recognition and needs some honest ways of getting it. The boy who lies to protect a friend is practicing a form of loyalty, and we must recognize it as such even though we do not condone the lie. The boy who lies to cover other offenses of his own ("Yes sir, the KP's all done!") is learning to lie his way out of the realities of life and has to be stopped.

A boy must understand that he cannot afford the reputation of being a liar. To be trusted is a supreme experience, and one that every boy must earn for himself by his devotion to truth.

As a leader there are things you can do to influence the use of the truth. You can encourage or discourage truth. For example, you can ask members of the patrol leaders' council for their reactions to some idea you have. If they react negatively you can thank them for their honest reaction and let the group vote on it. Thus they will learn that what you really want is their honest opinion and not just agreement.

If you respect truth as a noble and perishable idea, you will seek it out and let it flourish on every occasion. When your Scouts know that you honor truth above all else, they will, too.

Swearing

Public attitudes toward cursing and swearing have undergone radical change since most current Scoutmasters were boys. Against this background, it is not surprising that boys of Scout age swear. They hear it many places they go. Many hear it at home. This manner of speaking always has been mistaken by the young as a sign of maturity, of adulthood. It is even more easily taken that way today.

What should a Scoutmaster's attitude be?

First, he should not swear himself. If you cannot keep your own language under control, you may as well not try to control that used by Scouts.

Second, a Scoutmaster can discourage swearing by quietly identifying it for what it is. Some boys go for profanity because they think it marks them as adults—or almost, anyway. If they know you see it for what it is, they will find other ways to prove their manhood.

Smoking

Smoking, like swearing, is a way for youth to try to look grown-up. Almost every smoker began in his youth.

Today we all know the dangers of smoking. They have been well publicized. Warnings have been printed on packages. Thousands of doctors have quit smoking.

A boy may start to smoke in spite of the known dangers because he wants to conform with the group and be accepted by it. Being in with the guys—or girls—at his age is far more important than lung cancer at age 45. It is today that counts.

Yet for all the difficulties, you are not powerless as a Scoutmaster. You can probably do some good. Helping a boy to find his talents, to develop his strengths, to prove himself, will help him to meet his need to be accepted. Speaking from your personal experience may help whether you've never smoked, have quit, or still smoke.

You have limited powers to prevent boys from smoking. Yet you should not allow smoking at troop meetings and activities. Make it clear that smoking there will not be tolerated. Adult leaders should not smoke at troop activities.

Don't allow smoking at any Scout activity.

Drugs and Alcohol

Your Scouts are part of a nation of pill takers. If you count only the uses of coffee, alcohol, and aspirin among average people living average lives, you have identified several **multi-billion-dollar** industries. It is a rare Scout who does not have access, **in his home,** to at least a dozen varieties of pills and liquids that he sees used regularly. Most of it is bought openly and legally in ordinary retail stores. Most of it is widely advertised.

As Scoutmaster, you do not have many direct methods of preventing drug use or abuse by your Scouts. Yet, as in the case of smoking, you might very well have just what they need as a substitute.

Suppose, through counseling, you help a boy to find himself. He may have needed the adventure and the group acceptance that drugs provided. He knows what he can do. He accepts himself. You may have helped him to find a way around the terrible trap that drugs represent. This is accomplished by developing a substitute that he will accept, not by a lecture on the evils of drugs.

Your troop program should be a challenge and an adventure in itself. While such a dynamic program is no guarantee that boys who get it won't use drugs, it certainly holds promise that idleness and boredom don't.

You must, of course, be on guard that the troop itself does not become a place for drug use. Meetings and especially campouts easily might be so used without alert leadership. It is better to be aware that such things might happen than to assume that they could not.

Your use of alcohol or drugs will not provide an acceptable example for your troop to follow.

Be on guard so that the troop itself does not become a place for drug use.

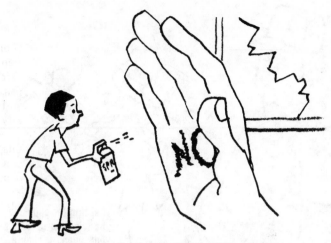

Help boys resist the urge to do willful mischief.

Vandalism

Scouting actively encourages far and wide adventure in the outdoors. It also uses regularly meeting places belonging to others.

It is obvious that Scouting can ill afford to leave in its wake defaced walls, broken furniture, carved-up trees, unburned garbage, or any of the other signs of vandal behavior that could remain behind.

The right to own and use property is fundamental to our system and society. Scouts must learn not to interfere with that right.

Your Scouts need to understand that your troop meeting place is only on loan to them. In most cases Scouts pay nothing for such places and have not legal—or other—rights to the place. As guests, they must treat that property with respect. They must always leave it in a better-than-they-found-it condition. They must report any accidental damage and pay for it. They must not intentionally damage anything.

Campsites, too, must be left spotless. Other people's messes must be cleaned up. Garbage must be burned or toted back home. Trees, ground cover, sod, water supplies must be left in their natural state or improved.

If vandalism takes place, determine the guilty parties and see that they pay for all damages. If guilt cannot be established, the whole troop should share in paying for the damage.

Razzing the opposition can be tolerated up to a point, but even it should have limitations.

Sportsmanship

Scouting is not really a sports program in the way that organized football and baseball are. But sportsmanship is called for throughout its activities, and especially where there is competition.

Boys will learn sportsmanship from you. If they hear you griping about the inept judges or the unfair rules or the cheating done by other troops, they will go that route, too.

If you understand your troop's purpose, then you will recognize that whether your troop wins or loses the contest is not important. You are out to build something in boys, and in the case of sportsmanship it must begin with you.

Where you have individual examples of poor sportsmanship, some direct and private counseling will help. Most boys want to be good sports and will appreciate your help in becoming so.

Hazing

Older Scouts sometimes feel that new Scouts should be "initiated" into the troop with a hazing activity. You should be alert to this desire of older boys and direct their efforts into meaningful initiation programs. Hazing has no place in Scouting, nor does running the gauntlet, belt line, or similar punishments.

Sex Curiosity

In the age span covered by the Scouting program, boys discover sex as one of the realities of living. They are naturally curious, and they may have limited opportunity to find out about it.

It seems to be general belief that boys should learn of sex and family life at home, from their parents. While there are few objections to this principle, it is not borne out in fact that this teaching actually occurs.

You must respect the right of parents to teach their sons about life. You must also recognize that many of them will not do this very well, and some won't do it at all. Some of their failings will come to light in your troop.

You may find magazines at practically any level of obscenity being circulated during a campout.

You may have boys asking you for information or advice about sexual matters.

You may overhear sex talk, both informed and uninformed, in the troop.

You may discover or hear about incidents of sexual experimentation among troop members.

How should you handle such matters?

Rule number 1. You do not undertake to instruct Scouts, in any formalized manner, in the subject of sex and family life. The reasons are that it is not construed to be Scouting's responsibility, and you may not be qualified to do this.

Rule number 2. If Scouts came to you to ask questions or to seek advice, you would give it within your competence. A boy who appears to be asking about sexual intercourse, however, may really only be worried about his pimples, so it is well to find out just what information is needed.

Rule number 3. You should refer boys with sexual problems to persons qualified to handle them. If the boy has a spiritual leader or a doctor who can deal with them, he should go there. If such persons are not available, you may have to help him meet with one. But don't try to play a highly professional role and avoid passing the buck.

And now how about some of the questions we raised?

Publications that you judge unacceptable should be removed from the scene, and those who brought them told that you don't want them around, and why.

Incidents of sexual experimentation that may occur in the troop could run from the innocent to the scandalous. They call for a private and thorough investigation, and frank discussion with those involved. It is important to distinguish between youthful acts of innocence, and the practices of a homosexual who may be using his Scouting association to make contacts. A boy of 15 or so cannot be assumed to be acting out of innocence. Assist him in securing professional help.

It is of greatest importance that such occasions be kept quiet. Avoid accusations and any loose talk. Avoid making a small and innocent act into a mammoth offense.

Discuss these problems with the Scout's parents, religious leader, and troop committee.

Inattention

It is typical of boys of the younger Boy Scouting years to be rather weak on paying attention. This suggests some rules for you and other leaders.

- Give the sign for attention (Scout sign held straight up) and wait for everyone to be quiet; then talk.

- Keep activities in meetings short. To guard against overrunning the attention span of younger boys, as a general rule, no activity should go beyond 20 minutes.

- Keep distractions out or at least down.

Never overestimate what you have to say or underestimate the power of bubble gum.

Homesickness

Whenever the troop is away from home for any extended period, you can expect to find some homesickness. Here are some tips that may help you deal with it.

- Most attacks occur in the first 2 days of camp.

- Homesickness is seldom announced as such by the victim. He has a stomachache, can't eat, has an asthma attack, or otherwise feels physically ill. He probably will say he wants to go home because of his illness. Be sure the boy isn't truly sick before you worry about homesickness.

- Rainy weather may bring more than an average number of cases of homesickness. This is in part a reflection of the gray weather, but more important, it reflects a curtailed program that needs special attention.

- It occurs mostly among your youngest Scouts.

- You often can predict homesickness. Look for boys who don't join in activities.

- If a boy goes home from camp early because he is homesick, you probably will not see him in Scouting again. He won't be able to face his friends. (But telling him this at camp will not dissuade him from wanting to go home.)

- Boys can cure homesickness better and faster than adults. What the homesick boy needs is to do something with a friend. Be sympathetic but get him going, doing things with another boy who *asks* him. (Get somebody to ask him!)

- If you suspect a boy is homesick, or might be, get him deeply involved in interesting activities right away.

PROBLEMS AT HOME

Some of your Scouts may not have either parent at home, and are being brought up by others. Some may have only one, having lost the other by death, divorce, or separation. Some boys live with alcoholism, infidelity, greed, stupidity, child abuse, and about any other kind of poor influence you may be able to think of. The home they come from usually shows, somehow, in what they are and do.

Little wonder then that delinquency, runaways, and suicides exist among Scout-age boys. A boy who comes from a troubled home is lonely and desperately needs someone to talk to, someone to be his friend. In this situation, Scouting offers some of what is missing at home. The Scouting influence rises to its fullest height when this happens, yet you may never know that it is happening until years later when a grown man tells you that something you did or said changed his life.

It is impossible even to speculate on the many ways in which the troop and its leaders may substitute for parental guidance. It may be a matter of table manners. It may be some of the problems we have noted earlier—drugs, swearing, smoking, etc. A boy without proper parental guidance may be handicapped in dozens of different ways.

Single-Parent Families

Being both father and mother to a Scout-age boy could be a full-time job. Unfortunately, single parents must earn a living and in the time left over take care of their homes and their children. Such parents welcome your leadership and the example you provide for their sons.

In addition to the support you already are giving in that way, you might encourage all Scouts to pitch in on household chores. The same jobs have to be done at home and in camp. Therefore, a good camper can and should be a help at home.

Encourage Scouts to do their share of the work at camp and at home.

SCOUTS WITH HANDICAPS

Your troop should accept boys with obvious handicaps as if no special problems will develop. Because probably none will. Nevertheless, it is important to "be prepared" in some respects when a boy with a serious handicap joins. These are various kinds of handicaps.

Physical Handicaps

They range from eyes or ears that don't work to impaired limbs, or perfectly healthy-looking arms or legs that won't do a thing. You can look at a boy with cerebral palsy as having a physical rather than a mental handicap. Boys who have physical handicaps are otherwise just as "normal" as any other, and want to get on with the game. Often the physical handicaps of one boy bring out the best in others. Boys are by nature compassionate and will rush to push a wheelchair, guide the blind, or pick up fallen crutches.

If sometimes there is a difficulty with a boy with a physical handicap, it may be in keeping him within his own limits. Such boys are often more anxious to succeed than those without handicaps, and may push themselves beyond their limits.

There are many disabling conditions that are not readily visible such as heart and circulation problems, diabetes and epilepsy to name only a few. Most communities have branches of national health agencies dealing with specific disabilities where information is easily obtained. Also, the boy's parents and doctor are usually willing to share necessary information concerning allergies and medication. Their suggestions will be most helpful for boys in hiking and camping situations.

Boys with physical handicaps must meet the regular advancement requirements within their physical abilities and substitute authorized different requirements only where necessary. They choose a route through the ranks that fits their abilities. Advancement does not set them aside as special, and their other participation in the troop need not either. Recognize their abilities for what they are. Praise them for accomplishments. Additional help can be found in *Scouting for the Physically Handicapped*, No. 3039; *Scouting for the Hearing Impaired*, No. 3061; and *Scouting for the Visually Handicapped*, No. 3063.*

Mental Handicaps

There are many kinds of mental handicaps. The largest group generally involves retardation which ranges from boys who are a little slower to a smaller number who are severely retarded. These boys may remain in the troop beyond the usual age and may continue advancement— *Rules and Regulations of the Boy Scouts of America*, Article XI, Section 3, Clause 19.

The boy who is severely retarded probably will be in an institution. Many boys who are just slow learners are active in regular troops. You need to protect these boys from the unthinking gibes of other Scouts.

Scouting has much to offer the handicapped boy. On the whole, it is far better that individual boys who are not institutionalized with handicaps be members of regular troops. If there are many, special leadership may be needed. Additional help can be found in *Scouting for the Mentally Retarded*, No. 3058,* which describes a special advancement program for moderately retarded Scouts.

Scout-age boys with various learning disability problems also require patience and understanding. But the results, as with all boys, are worth the effort. Teachers and parents can be helpful in explaining possible problems and offering ways to cope.

Then, there is a growing number of young people in our increasingly complicated society who have developed mental or emotional disabilities. Unless institutionalized (the most serious cases) these boys should join regular units and be given a chance. Additional help can be found in *Scouting for the Emotionally Disturbed*, No. 3008.*

---

*These pamphlets contain specific information on registration and advancement of Scouts over the age of 18 and who have severe physical handicaps or are severely retarded.

Alternate Eagle Award Merit Badges

Scouts should be challenged to meet the requirements for ranks that are stated in *The Official Boy Scout Handbook*. In some cases it is impossible for Scouts with severe physical or mental handicaps to complete merit badges required for the Eagle Award. In these special cases, the Boy Scouts of America authorizes the use of the Application for Alternative Eagle Award Merit Badges, No. 30-730. If a unit leader, after consultation with the Scout, his parents, and his physician, believes that the alternative merit badges should be considered, he may secure an application from his local council.

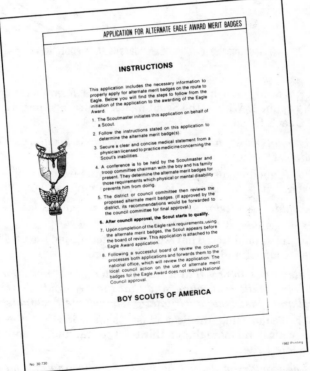

No. 30-730

Chapter 9

Counseling

A Scoutmaster can work wonders with friendly talks.

 OW do you help boys grow? Is there a formula that can be applied? Why is the Scoutmaster conference important for each Scout?

Q: By counseling, do you mean the Scoutmaster giving the boy advice?

A: No. A good counselor absolutely refrains from giving advice, even if it is asked for. He really acts more as a coach.

Q: Should a counselor use a counseling session to let the other person know "where he stands," so to speak?

A: No, he should not. That would be offering judgment. No one can counsel and judge at the same time.

Q: This seems to say that a Scoutmaster would not do a lot of talking while counseling, and that the boy would do the most talking. Just how much talking should the Scoutmaster do?

A: When counseling, the Scoutmaster should do very little—at the very most, no more than a third—of the talking. A tenth would be lots better.

Q: How would you define the kind of counseling you mean?

A: To counsel, as we mean it here, is to listen, and to support and encourage the boy being counseled to think out his needs and goals and solve his own problems.

When To Counsel

1. *You counsel when asked.* Any time a Boy Scout asks to talk to you, you may need to counsel. He may of course just be asking for information, and no counseling is necessary.

2. *You counsel when you see it's necessary.* The occasion might be a specific behavior problem. It might be to discuss a possible leadership job with a boy. You may discover that you haven't had a chat with a particular boy in a long time. Then you, not the Scout, initiate the counseling.

3. *You counsel in the Scoutmaster conference.* Every Scout rank includes the requirement that the Scout participate in a conference with the Scoutmaster. This conference has specific goals and is discussed in more detail later in this chapter.

Where To Counsel

Counseling can be done anywhere—in camp, in a car, in a place of worship, at home, walking along the street. What is important is that it be private. That is, not overheard or interrupted.

Every Scout in the troop should understand that you counsel often with individuals. Every Scout should be made to respect your need to deal with the individual boy privately.

A good place to get down to the serious business of helping a Scout is in the most relaxed place you can find.

Objectives for Counseling

When possible, you should have an objective for a counseling session before you begin. When it's not possible, you may have to put one together during the session. This may be hard at first, but it will get easier.

Try to think of one step in what might be a long process. If a counseling session can lead to commitment to just one step, and the boy takes that step, then you have done something. Don't deal in great big absolutes like "shape up or ship out." Use smaller, attainable pieces of achievement that can happen quickly and will demonstrate success.

Suppose, for example, the troublesome boy agrees to try to get through one troop meeting without talking out of turn. It is best if he comes up with the goal himself. He says he thinks he can do it. You agree that he can, and that you'll talk again after the next meeting.

The counseling session can be considered a great success if this much progress comes out of it. So a small objective is often better than a big one—not always, but usually.

We must also caution that you keep your objective to yourself. Essentially, it is a private little deal with yourself: "I'd be happy if he would get one skill award." But you don't say that; you merely say it to yourself so you will have some idea where the counseling should take you and the boy.

The point of an objective in counseling is to begin with a small attainable goal. This, of course, requires that you really think about the Scout's problem to find small steps in solving it.

Understanding Your Role

You wear a different hat when you counsel than when you direct. You can't counsel as authority or judge. You can't tell or advise or threaten.

Perhaps you wonder whether the Scout can accept your counseling role when he knows you also in your more aggressive leadership role. The answer is that most Scouts can understand that you work with one of them differently than you work with the whole troop.

The question is, *can you?* Can you put aside your other role and take your place as a counselor? You'll have to ask questions instead of give answers, listen instead of talk, draw boys out instead of cut them off.

Drawing the Boy Out

Your counseling role demands that you listen. This means that the boy must talk. But when you sit down to talk, most boys have nothing to say. So you will need to get the boy talking. You do this with questions.

The kinds of questions you ask determine the answers you get. We are not talking here about the *subject* of the questions, but the *form* of them.

The question form most of us use most of the time is a very restrictive type. It tends to limit the answer to a word or two. Many of them are just *yes* or *no* questions. Examples:

"Do you go to Edison School?"

These restrictive questions are good for getting information. But they are not good for getting people to open up and talk.

Here is a kind of question that is much better for that purpose. It is an *open-end* question. Examples:

"How do you like being a Scout?"

"What do you think the problem is?"

"What do you plan to do after you finish First Class?"

"How do you feel about that?"

Such questions do not restrict the other person's answers. He cannot dismiss them with a single word, because a word or two won't answer them. He must put some ideas together.

Learn to ask questions that lead somewhere.

Scoutmaster: How do you like being a Scout?

Scout: Oh it's OK I guess. But it's not—well, it's not what I thought it would be.

SM: What did you think it would be?

S: Well, I'm not sure. I guess I thought it would be more outdoor stuff. You know, camping out and things like that. I've been in the troop 3 months and I haven't been camping yet.

Thus, a couple of good questions get at the heart of the matter. The boy is disappointed because he's not getting what he thought he would.

Sometimes an open-end question will not get anything. When that happens, you can turn to a somewhat more restrictive question to close it up a bit. This we call a *choice* question.

Q: *What sports do you like? (Open-end)*
A: Oh, I like 'em all.

Q: *Which ones do you like best, the team sports like baseball and football, or the individual ones like golf and tennis? (Choice)*
A: I like the team sports better.

Another kind of question that is useful is a *problem* question. It is really an open-end question, but it is preceded by a statement of a real or a theoretical problem.

"Suppose you and John were both candidates for election as patrol leader. John might tell the patrol that they should elect him because he gets to all the meetings and activities and you don't. How do you think you would answer that?

Are you listening?

The difficulty in learning to use questions in counseling is that most people's background involves using questions to get information. In counseling, information is not the objective. Instead, questions are used to get the other person talking.

To get a boy talking in a counseling session, you have available a range of question types. They run from the open-end and problem questions (which are the best ones for this purpose) through the choice questions, to the restrictive, short-answer questions. Let's look at a fragment of a counseling session to see their use. In this case, the Scoutmaster is counseling a boy after the boy disrupted the troop meeting.

SM: What was the problem tonight? *(Open-end)*

S: I don't see why you're picking on me. There was a lot of guys goofin' around tonight.

SM: You feel I'm picking on you? *(Restrictive)*

S: Yeah, well you know. I'm not the only one.

SM: I understand. You think that tonight was mostly your fault, or mostly the other boys'? *(Choice)*

S: Well…Maybe about half and half, I guess.

SM: Tell me about your half. *(Open-end, though not really a question at all)*

As the Scoutmaster plays a variety of leadership styles, he uses a variety of question types in counseling. No one type will work all the time. The idea is to get the boy talking about the subject. If he's talking, the questions are right. If he's not, try some others.

How To Respond

Restate. From time to time, reflect his feelings or restate what you think he is saying. Examples:

"If I understand, you're telling me your parents want you to make Eagle but you don't care one way or the other," or "You feel I wasn't fair about that," or "You'd like to go to camp but you don't think you can get the money together?"

Each restatement assures the boy that you understand and are listening. If you don't understand what he is saying, he can correct you.

Mention Feelings. From time to time, show him that you understand his feelings by trying to state them simply. Examples:

"You must have been mad when that happened."

"I can see how you got confused."

"I'll bet that made you pretty happy."

Show You're Listening. Nod your head. Say, "mm-hmm" or "I see" or some such from time to time.

Summarize. From time to time, pull together what he is telling you. Make a brief summary: "So you feel you've been patrol leader as long as you want to be, but the patrol is insisting that you stay on, is that it?"

Give Information. Where information is called for, give it. Be sure it is not opinion or advice.

Get Alternate Solutions. If the boy has a problem, he is probably working one solution again and again, and recognizing that it won't work. Encourage him to consider other ways. Don't just *give* him alternatives, but lead him to come up with them.

A Summary of Counseling Techniques

You have seen that counseling is a process of aiding someone to set his own goals and solve his own problems. Essentially, that is the only way goals get set and problems get solved.

A Scout needs a climate in which he can solve his problems. Counseling provides this climate. It is friendly. It does not threaten. As counselor you will listen and encourge. But you don't take on his burden. Instead, you enable the Scout to see how he can cope with it himself.

It's great when someone takes an interest in you.

COUNSELING

THE SCOUTMASTER CONFERENCE

A Scout must take part in a Scoutmaster conference as a requirement for each rank. Thus, a boy who goes all the way to Eagle will have many such conferences with you along the way.

Of course, conferences don't have to be limited to those called for in the advancement plan. Indeed, it is desirable and natural that there be other opportunities. You are, however, obliged to conduct the Scoutmaster conferences *required* for advancement, which are more formal. The Scoutmaster of a large troop may assign some of the conferences to assistants or troop committee members.

The purpose of the Scoutmaster conferences is to help a Scout accept the responsibility for his growth in Scouting and to establish between the boy and the Scoutmaster a relationship that will make this possible. The boy is challenged and helped to set his own goals and to work toward their achievement. These goals should be specific, measurable, and attainable.

The appeal of Scouting is that it is based on boys' needs and interests. The Scoutmaster conference must also be based on boy needs and interests.

A boy who attains Eagle would have had at least seven Scoutmaster conferences. He would have one as soon as he joins as part of becoming a Boy Scout. Then he would have had one for each of the six ranks as he went from Tenderfoot to Eagle. As a boy leader, he would have conferences on a regular basis.

Conducting the Scoutmaster Conference

The first conference occurs when the boy joins the troop. The purpose is for you to get to know the boy, his family and friends, and his strengths and interests. In this conference you establish a good working relationship between the boy and yourself. Here you get the information you need to help him get the most from the troop program and activities. If the boy has been a Cub Scout, find out about his experience.

The first conference should be chatty and low-keyed. The aim is to get the boy to talk about himself. Don't pry, but encourage him to talk about himself. Talk just enough to get the boy started talking. Encourage him to talk about things he likes to do and the things he thinks he does well. Then, show him how he can use his strengths and interests in Scouting in his patrol, troop, and advancement program.

Out of this conference should come the establishment of a simple goal which the boy himself sets. This goal should relate to his own strengths and interests and should involve listing the thing he agrees that he will do utilizing his strengths. This could be a thing he agrees to do for the troop, patrol, his home, or even just for himself. His objectives will be to do things before his Scoutmaster conference with you before he goes to the board of review for Tenderfoot.

You also talk with him about the troop's expectations for being active, living as a Scout should live, and his advancement progress.

Because duty to God, or a supreme being, is an important Scouting ideal, a boy should be challenged to think about this aspect of his life. Does he attend religious services regularly? Is he involved in religious youth group activities? While it is not your role or responsibility to do religious counseling, you should encourage a boy to consult with his particular religious leader. One way for a boy to learn more about his religious duty is to participate in the religious emblem program of his particular faith. This might be a goal which is set at a Scoutmaster conference. A boy should not progress all the way to Eagle without ever thinking about his religious duty.

Additional Conferences

How about subsequent Scoutmaster conferences? For one thing, you check to be sure he met the goal he set for himself. It is quite meaningless to set goals and then forget them. By the second and third conference you will know the boy quite well, so instead of probing for his strengths and interests, you might better talk with him about his attitudes. How is he doing in non-Scouting activities? What does he see for himself as he looks ahead?

Look to the future.

COUNSELING

At each of these conferences, he sets new goals. They can be related to new interests, or he could set more advanced goals for himself in the same strengths he started with. Obviously, the goals should be progressively more difficult. The goals of an 11-year-old would be quite childish to a 13-year-old setting a goal for Star. Since you know more about the boy at each conference, you can be more helpful in counseling him as to the direction his goals might take, and even the difficulties with them. Watch out here that you don't tell him what his goals should be.

Examples

You are saying, "That's fine, but give me an example." Examples are dangerous since they often become the pattern that is cut to fit all boys. Any example really could fit only one boy, since each boy is different from all the others in Scouting. However, at the risk of setting a pattern, here's an example.

Suppose a boy told you when he joined that he was interested in using hand tools and making things. This appears to be one of his strengths that could be used to help him grow. His first goal might be to repair the furniture at a neighborhood day care center. Or, he might agree to make a new candle device for troop induction ceremonies. When he completes his projects, he should be encouraged by a word of public recognition at a troop meeting.

At his next conference, he might decide to help some of the fellows in his patrol to earn the Home Repairs merit badge, thus giving of himself to others. Or he could help a Webelos den with the Craftsman activity badge, or a den leader with a craft theme.

Still more advanced would be the development and supervision of a troop project to collect and repair old toys for a Christmas project.

Some boys will accept this process early and they will respond quickly to the idea. With another you will have to measure progress in terms of your improved relationship with the boy even though he may have trouble setting meaningful goals and working at them. The point is to develop, not a complicated or artificial process but rather, a way of communicating with each boy and helping him make the most of himself. He determines where he stands at any particular time and what he can do through Scouting activities to get where he would like to be.

Each conference also should have some time devoted to reviewing the requirements for the next rank, and the development by the boy of a plan to achieve it.

Part 3

TOOLS
TO DO
THE JOB

ACH chapter in this tool chest will
be used time and time again; but
unlike the first two parts of this
book, no one expects you to read it from
beginning to end. This tool chest and the
friendly advice of an experienced Scouter
will help you keep your troop running
smoothly.

Chapter 10

Program
Planning

Your troop is as good as its program.

TROOPS that succeed have planned, written programs. Troops that fail do not. There are other reasons for success or failure, of course, but a planned, written program is certainly one of the key items.

You can't expect to achieve the aims of the Boy Scout program without careful use of the methods of the Boy Scout program. You aren't apt to think of these methods in running an unplanned meeting.

Two Kinds of Planning

There is long-range planning and the short, detailed, monthly planning. The first can be sketchy—just major activities and dates. The latter must be detailed right down to a time schedule with responsibility assigned for each time segment.

152 PROGRAM PLANNING

Your Three Program Assistants

Your first silent assistant is the *Boy Scout Program Helps*, which comes in *Scouting* magazine. Extra copies may be available from your council or district. This publication has a wide choice of things you can use to fill out your program. It is intended to provide a base from which to operate.

Your second silent assistant is *Boys' Life*, a monthly magazine available through the troop at special rates. It is a fine source of skills, stories of activities of other troops, fiction, and ideas of things that can be done by individual boys, patrols, and troops. Best of all, it comes directly to the Scouts.

Ideas like these for the theme "Looking for Trouble" in the pages of Boy Scout Program Helps can be customized to fit your troop. Themes are a great way to dramatize the skills of Scouting.

2 Boys' Life magazine picks up the theme and features it in the issue that arrives in the Scout's home a month before it happens in the troop.

The Troop Planning Worksheet, No. 26-005, gives you a chance to put your troop's annual program up on a bulletin board.

TROOP PLA...

MONTH	PROGRAM THEME	PROGRAM HIGHLIGHT	TROOP AND PATROL MEETINGS	OUTDOOR EVENT	SPECIA... EVENT
February	Looking for Trouble	First Aid Rallies	February 12 February 19	Troop Search and Rescue February 28 <u>AM</u>	Court of H... at Church S... February 2... Anniversary of S...

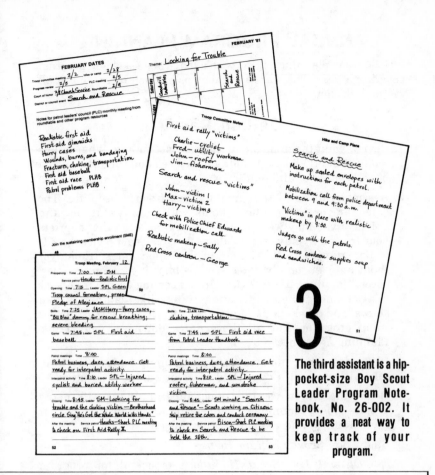

FEBRUARY '81

FEBRUARY DATES

Troop committee meeting 2/2   Hike or camp 2/28
Progress review 2/5   PLC meeting 2/5
Court of honor 2/9 Church Service   Roundtable 2/9
District or council event Search and Rescue

Notes for patrol leaders' council (PLC) monthly meeting from roundtable and other program resources

Realistic first aid
First aid gimmicks
Hurry cases
Wounds, burns, and bandaging
Fractures, choking, transportation
First aid. baseball
First aid race PLHB
Patrol problems PLHB

Join the sustaining membership enrollment (SME)

48

Theme: Looking for Trouble

Troop Committee Notes

First aid rally "victims"

Charlie – cyclist
Fred – utility workman
John – roofer
Jim – fisherman

Search and rescue "victims"

John – victim 1
Max – victim 2
Harry – victim 3

Check with Police Chief Edwards for mobilization call.

Realistic makeup – Sally
Red Cross canteen – George

Hike and Camp Plans

Search and Rescue

Make up sealed envelopes with instructions for each patrol.

Mobilization call from police department between 9 and 9:30 a.m.

"Victims" in place with realistic makeup by 9:30.

Judges go with the patrols.

Red Cross canteen supplies soup and sandwiches.

51

Troop Meeting, February 12

Preopening Time 7:00 Leader SM
Service patrol Hawks – Realistic first...

Opening Time 7:15 Leader SPL George
Troop council formation, present...
Pledge of Allegiance

Skills Time 7:25 Leader JASM Harry – Hurry cases,
"Bill Blow" dummy for rescue breathing;
severe bleeding

Game Time 7:45 Leader SPL First aid
baseball

50

Patrol meetings Time 8:00
Patrol business, dues, attendance. Get
ready for interpatrol activity.
Interpatrol activity Time 8:10 Leader SPL – Injured
cyclist and buried utility worker

Closing Time 8:45 Leader SM – Looking for
trouble and the choking victim – Brotherhood
circle. Sing "He's Got the Whole World in His Hands."
After the meeting   Service patrol Hawks – Shark PLC meeting
to check on First Aid Rally II.

52

Skills Time 7:45 Leader ...
choking, transportation

Game Time 7:45 Leader SPL First aid race
from Patrol Leader Handbook

Patrol meetings Time 8:00
Patrol business, dues, attendance. Get
ready for interpatrol activity.
Interpatrol activity Time 8:10 Leader SPL – Injured
roofer, fishermen, and sunstroke
victim

Closing Time 8:45 Leader SM minute "Search
and Rescue" – Scouts working on Citizenship retire the colors and conduct ceremony.
After the meeting   Service patrol Bison – Short PLC meeting
to check on Search and Rescue to be
held the 28th.

53

3

The third assistant is a hip-pocket-size Boy Scout Leader Program Note-book, No. 26-002. It provides a neat way to keep track of your program.

G WORKSHEET

DISTRICT OR COUNCIL EVENTS	COMMUNITY CALENDAR	TROOP GOOD TURN	BOARD OF REVIEW	LEADERS' MEETINGS		
				Patrol Leaders' Council	Troop Committee	District Roundtable
...strict Search ...d Rescue February 28 PM	Goodwill Industries Collection February 7	Collect items for Goodwill Industries	February 5	February 5	February 2	February 9

ANNUAL PROGRAM PLANNING

Good troop planning begins with a long-range skeleton program covering a year. There are several steps in this process, but it all starts with you.

Getting Ready

1. Review what the troop did in the year just ending. What things really paid off? What shouldn't have been done at all or should have been done differently?

2. Assemble all dates that might affect troop scheduling. The calendar for the public schools will show vacations and holidays you may want to use. The organization that charters your troop may have special dates to avoid. Your own schedule is important, too. What are your vacation dates? Holidays? What are your family dates such as birthdays, anniversaries, special family activities? Get dates of coming events from your district and council, including things like camporees, big shows, and other special activities that will add a plus to your troop program. Put all these dates down on your Troop Planning Worksheet.

3. Pick a date, time, and place for your planning conference. It will take at least half a day. Hold it in an attractive location.

4. Before the conference, talk about program plans with many people—troop committee members, unit commissioner, your council office, and assistant Scoutmasters.

5. Study *Boy Scout Program Helps.*

The Official Boy Scout Handbook is useful for program planning since it has all kinds of highly specific materials related to basic skills.

The *Fieldbook* is packed with advanced outdoor knowledge and skills.

The 12 Troop Leader Can-Do Kits featuring the *Skill Books* can be very helpful especially for new troops.

The Annual Planning Conference

This is for you, your assistant Scoutmasters, junior assistant Scoutmasters, and the members of the patrol leaders' council.

The senior patrol leader presides, and one of his first items of business is to call on you for a feasibility report. This is where you report on the research you have done. It isn't very "feasible" to schedule an overnight camp on your wedding anniversary, for example.

Get the dates to be avoided and the dates to aim at up where they can be seen—chalkboard, chart paper, or blank newsprint.

Review the program features that caught your attention in *Boy Scout Program Helps*, one at a time, and get a tentative acceptance or rejection of each from the patrol leaders' council. Put those approved on the calendar.

An important step is to date all special events such as hikes, overnight camps, parents' nights, boards of review, activites with Webelos den, and council and district events that appeal to the leaders.

Be sure that patrol leaders have a chance to express freely the wishes of their patrol members.

When you are finished with this conference, the troop will have a rough outline of what it will do in the months ahead. The details have not been worked out for any month or activity, but at least the items have been entered in the schedule. Details will remain for the monthly planning meeting.

Sharing Your Troop Program

The results of long-range planning are important to many people. For example:

1. The troop committee should be advised of the plan as soon as the planning conference is over. This group must agree to support the plan or tell you why they can't support it. If for any reason they cannot support some part of the plan, it should go back to the patrol leaders' council for reconsideration.

2. Every Scout and his family should receive a copy of the program showing all activities and their dates. Many troops also prepare a monthly newsletter for Scouts showing any changes from the original plan and announcing last-minute details.

3. Your chartered organization should have a copy of the program. If you meet there, all dates should be entered in the master calendar for the building.

4. Your commissioner will appreciate having copies of your program. It will help to keep him in touch with your troop, and who knows—your troop program might be a good example to show other troops.

5. Let the Webelos dens and Cub Scout packs you work with know your plans. Send a copy to the other Cub Scout packs in your area. They may have boys who want to join the troop.

MONTHLY PROGRAM PLANNING

The long-range program is just an outline. The monthly planning fills it out and makes it a real program.

Your patrol leaders' council meets monthly. The purpose of the meeting is to plan in detail the program for the next month. Thus, at the September meeting, the patrol leaders' council plans the October program.

Getting Ready

1. Review the long-range plan for the next month.

2. Attend the district Scout leaders' roundtable to get program ideas.

3. Check printed program sources—things like *Boy Scout Program Helps*—which probably suggested many of the ideas in your long-range plan.

4. Meet with the senior patrol leader and help him plan the agenda for the meeting. He will be running it, so he must know all that should happen.

5. Make sure all the leaders needed are invited. If a joint activity with a Webelos den is scheduled, make sure the Webelos den chief is present.

The Monthly Planning Meeting

The senior patrol leader presides. If you have prepared him well, you won't have much to do except to help him stay on the track.

Troop Meeting Plan sheets, illustrated on pages 59 and 81-82, should be in the hands of all patrol leaders, who should enter program items on their sheets as planning takes place.

The patrol leaders' council takes up each meeting and activity for the month ahead—one item at a time. Complete details are planned for each of these. This becomes the program for each event and, since all members of the patrol leaders' council helped plan it, all will know that responsibility they have for making things happen. Furthermore, each will feel an obligation to make it succeed.

The Weekly Review

Hold a short meeting of the patrol leaders' council after each meeting or activity. The purpose is to review the event just completed and to make sure everything is set for the next one. In the case of troop meetings, this patrol leaders' council review and planning meeting should take place the same night as the meeting. For other events, the review might happen following the next regular troop meeting or at the monthly planning meeting.

IN SUMMARY

The process of planning the troop program looks more complex than it really is. Any Scoutmaster and his patrol leaders' council can do it. The time used will be less than the time saved during the year. The results are so important to the success of the troop that it must not be skipped.

Planning together keeps everyone in step.

Chapter 11

The Outdoor Program

June is busting out all over! It's a grand beginning for a year-round adventure in the out-of-doors.

ACHIEVING the objectives of Scouting can best be accomplished through imaginative adventures in the out-of-doors. Boys want this kind of challenge and the outdoor setting is an ideal testing ground for their developing skills. For this reason, the outdoor program is a key method in gaining the objectives of Scouting; therefore, it's an absolute must in troop programming.

Having fun in the outdoors is one of the most significant reasons why a boy becomes a Scout. If every Scout were asked "Why did you join your troop?" Most would respond with reasons that are directly related to outdoor programs. A boy yearns for the enjoyment of participating in outdoor programs with a troop or patrol of his friends. The lure of hiking, camping, swimming, boating, canoeing, archery, rifle shooting, high-adventure activities, and tours is woven into Cub Scouting, Boy Scouting, and Exploring.

Cub Scouts participate in outdoor programs such as backyard projects, picnics, neighborhood explorations, day camp, and family outings. Webelos Scouts (10-year-old Cub Scouts) participate in outdoor activities that provide a gradual transition to becoming a Boy Scout. Outdoor programs such as father/son overnights are designed to give Webelos Scouts a taste of the fun and romance of Scouting camping, but not to duplicate the experiences of Boy Scout camp.

When a boy becomes a Boy Scout, hiking, campouts, and extended camping trips become an essential part of his experience. The outdoor program is one of the eight basic methods by which the objectives of Boy Scouting are achieved. However, a boy enjoys doing lots of things in the outdoors and only needs the thoughtful guidance of an adult or an older Scout to show him how to have fun in outdoor activities. Many outdoor events are related to advancement and become even more fun because boys enjoy being recognized for their achievements.

Learning by doing is natural and desirable, but young Boy Scouts need help in preparing for their first outings. If the first overnight camping experience is a disaster, a boy may never want to have anything to do with Scouting again.

Most troop and patrol meetings should be devoted to learning and acquiring knowledge and skills to help boys be successful in the outdoors. By addressing this need your troop meetings become more successful. Boys learn and acquire skills enthusiastically when preparing for hiking and camping. If meetings are oriented toward this end, they take on greater meaning and purpose. When boys understand why they need to acquire a skill, they become eager to learn in order to participate in exciting outdoor activities.

Successful outdoor activities should be in support of the aims of the Boy Scouts of America to encourage participating citizenship, to promote growth in moral strength and character, and to develop physical, mental, and emotional fitness. The adult example is important since most of these values are "caught" rather than taught. Baden-Powell said it well, "What the Scoutmaster does, his boys will do."

Outdoor programs focus on four fundamentals: woodcraft (including knowledge about the environment and conservation), campcraft (including all the knowledge and skills for living in the outdoors), aquatics (involving all water-related activities), and personal fitness (emphasizing physical skills).

Your role as a Scoutmaster is to make sure that your Scouts (1) attend summer camp, (2) have regular troop and patrol outings, and (3) camp at least 10 days and nights each year.

The need for environmental awareness and conservation has been stressed since the founding of the Boy Scouts of America. Today this need is greater than ever.

Scouts need to be encouraged to adopt an outdoor or conservation ethic (a set of values related to the environment) that they practice wherever they go. This ethic should encompass almost everything a Scout does. In different parts of the country and in differently populated communities, the ethic may differ, but the same general principles apply. It means being aware of the impact of our decisions upon our environment. It means using wisely what we have whether it be a natural resource or a product from a natural resource, such as a piece of paper. It means conducting ourselves in ways that minimize our impact on the environment. By not abusing what we have, it will be available for future generations. It means recognizing the obligations of a citizen to be conservation-minded and to take appropriate action to improve the environment, having a genuine concern for others and recognizing that everyone has a right to enjoy the outdoors. It means making others aware of the significance of their actions wherever they are, whether on a mountaintop or on a city street.

The Scouting idea of adventure has no limit. It can work as well in the city as it does in the country.

OUTDOOR PROGRAM OPPORTUNITIES

Outdoor program opportunities are as varied as boys' dreams. In Scouting we need to concentrate first on the basic outdoor skills. Boys are capable of learning and mastering these quickly through patient teaching, demonstration, and practice. When they become adept in the basics they are ready to reach out for a larger slice of adventure—for new outdoor challenges that require more learning and new skills. Outlined and briefly described here are some of the typical and special opportunities:

Long-Term Camping

Attending summer camp is long-term camping, but this also refers to any outdoor experience with at least 6 consecutive days of overnight camping.

Long-term camping is the highlight of the troop's annual program. Scouts can apply the skills they have been learning and dreaming about all year. With an hour of program each week the troop spends 52 hours a year, but 1 week of long-term camping may provide 60 or more hours of concentrated program. Summer camp is a year's worth of adventure compressed into 6 or more days.

Troops camp in many locations: the council camp, while touring, and at their own special places. The adequacy of troop equipment, the qualifications of your leaders, and the skill of your Scouts determine the options open to your troop. A completely self-sufficient troop can camp almost anywhere and successfully participate in many outdoor programs.

Camping should fit the needs and desires of the troop. It should provide a variety of long-term camping experiences. It should be forever pushing ahead from dependence to independence.

But when support is needed, your council and district are there to provide it. New or reorganized troops are helped to progress from dependence to independence. The camping program of your council has been designed to do just that.

USING COUNCIL SUPPORT. Councils are committed to promote and support Scout camping. Your council wants your troop to use its services and facilities. Here, briefly, is a summary of the kinds of things provided by your council.

Facilities. Most councils own and operate (or in exceptional cases lease) one or more Scout camps that can accommodate a few or a large number of troops. Camps equipped for long-term camping may be used year round if they are a reasonable distance from the council area.

Council camp facilities are developed according to how they are to be used. Some are primitive wilderness camps, and others may be highly developed with special facilities for training, Cub Scout day camping, or Explorer activities. Some offer facilities for family camping.

Your council has a system which permits your troop to reserve the campsite of its choice provided yours is the first request for that site and provided you have enough Scouts to use the site to full advantage. Your council will advise you on when and how to make a reservation.

Fees for using council campsites are low, and usually represent only a small part of the cost of operating the camp. Most councils have a range of fees that vary with the amount of service and equipment provided.

Personnel. Many council camps have a staff of specialists in woodcraft, aquatics, nature, field sports, and many other subject areas. They are available to help train your Scouts. Many serve as counselors for outdoor merit badge subjects. However, these specialists will not run your troop, but they do fill gaps in your troop's training abilities.

Equipment. Most council camps provide equipment to meet troop needs. A camp may provide everything for camping and include it in a fee or you may rent only the items needed.

Some councils provide rental equipment for camping off the council site. Thus, you may be able to rent canoes, paddles, tents, cooking gear, and whatever else you may need.

Your council camp represents a large investment in land, facilities, and equipment.

The time to begin planning next year's adventure is while you are enjoying this year's camp.

PLANNING FOR LONG-TERM CAMP. Planning for next year's camp begins during this year's camp. It's the natural time and place to begin exploring the question, "What shall we do next year?" You and the patrol leaders' council may not be able to pin it down for sure, but you'll certainly leave camp with some strong ideas of what you want for next summer. To reserve your favorite site, your troop may want to sign up for next year while at camp. And that's the beginning of planning.

Once back home, you will need to firm up your plans rapidly as to where you're going and what kind of experience it will be. If you need special equipment, you'll have to earn money, decide whether to buy or rent, and learn how to use it. You'll want to reserve your campsite as early as you can. You'll have to begin arranging for adult leadership. If you're planning a moving camp or tour, you'll have a lot of arrangements to make. Dates have to be set, and leaders will have to begin planning their vacation schedules.

Yes, it will take the best part of a year to plan a real highlight adventure and prepare to do it. These preparations affect your troop's program as you train and equip for long-term camp.

LEADERSHIP FOR LONG-TERM CAMP. When the troop goes camping, the Scoutmaster is in charge and is responsible for each Scout in the troop. Ideally, the Scoutmaster accompanies the troop to camp and remains with his Scouts. He really gets to know them and helps ensure the success of the troop's summer camp program since an objective of summer camp is to help the troop learn to operate on its own.

Yet the troop's program cannot be contingent on the availability of one man. If you, for whatever reason, are not available to lead the troop in long-term camp, it must take place anyway. This is far from ideal, but it is better than not going to camp at all. You and your troop committee are responsible for providing male leadership for the troop's camping program.

It's a lot more fun when there is another man to share the leadership.

Unless your troop is small, you should have at least two adult leaders in charge of the troop in camp. Substitute adult male leaders who accompany the troop to camp serve as Scoutmaster or assistant Scoutmaster. Additional adult leaders may be needed if the troop is larger than 30 Scouts. Check with the council to determine how many leaders may attend without charge.

The tendency to recruit leaders on the basis of availability rather than competence should be avoided. The object is not to provide a baby-sitter substitute but a strong leader who is qualified to be a year-round Scoutmaster.

The troop camp should include its regular, year-round boy leadership staff. Each patrol should operate with its regular patrol leader. If he is unable to attend, his place may be taken by an assistant.

Training. Most councils offer special precamp training for Scoutmasters and other adult troop leaders who will be coming to camp. This training emphasizes the need for Scoutmasters to provide adequate supervision for Scouts attending camp and the need to develop a program plan of activity for camp. In addition, many offer special precamp training for your senior patrol leader, your Scout aquatics specialists or your conservation specialists. These precamp training sessions are extremely valuable.

The troop is entitled to a well-organized camping experience. The adult is entitled to a satisfying experience. Neither of these reasonable expectations is likely to be met if the troop is in the hands of an untrained leader.

PROMOTING LONG-TERM CAMP. Since long-term summer camp is necessary to fulfill your troop's program, the troop committee and the Scoutmaster need to make it happen. Talk about it all year with the Scouts as if you expect everyone to be there. Talk about it to new Scouts and their parents as if they will be there, too. Make your plans early so family vacations can be scheduled around the troop camp. When summer comes around, you will not be surprised to find 80 to 95 percent of your Scouts in camp with you. The camp adventure should be part of the troop's year-round program automatically.

THE LONG-TERM CAMP PROGRAM. While attending long-term camp your troop can plan some things to do on your own as well as participating in organized camp programs. Take advantage of the special features offered by the camp and its environs, and the numerous opportunities to learn and practice. Skill awards and merit badges can be started and some can be completed before the troop returns home. Many of the requirements for any one of the first three badges of rank can be completed in camp.

If your troop goes to council camp, you will get help with program planning as needed. If not, you will be entirely on your own to plan and carry it out. There are values in having daily routines, and there are also values in shifting the routines. In general it is desirable to sleep and eat at regular times, and to have regular hours for swimming. Yet it is equally meaningful to a boy to get up early to fish or watch the sunrise, or to stay up late and study the stars. The program should be flexible to meet the needs and desires of boys.

RAINY DAYS. Rain may slow down or stop some planned activities. It may be too cold to swim, too stormy to canoe, too soggy to hike, and too drippy to do pioneering and woodcraft. But you can do handicrafts, have a songfest, practice first aid, and do lots of other things.

In general, it is a lot easier to be Scoutmaster under fair skies than in inclement weather. But both you and your Scouts can survive rainy weather and come out smiling if you work at it. The more adverse the weather, the harder you have to work, but the experience will remain longer as a great camp in the eyes of the boys.

When it rains, you supply the sunshine.

Troop and Patrol
Short-Term Camping

Since camping that lasts 6 days or longer is long-term camping, camping of fewer than 6 days, but at least overnight, is short-term camping.

LEADERSHIP FOR TROOP CAMPING. The troop must be led by an adult male, at least 21 years of age, at all times.

The senior patrol leader of the troop should play his normal role in the troop camp. If he can't attend, an acting senior patrol leader may be designated.

Each patrol should be under its elected or a designated acting patrol leader.

Where aquatics is part of the troop program, the Safe Swim Defense and/or Safety Afloat plan must be used.

PLANNING FOR SHORT-TERM CAMPING. Planning for a particular campout begins at the troop's annual planning conference when you set the dates. Choosing a site for your campout probably will be your next planning step. You need to line up your campsites well in advance. Your troop committee and friends of the troop will help you find new places to camp. Your council may have a list of good sites. (Send out a small advance party to check out unfamiliar sites to be sure they are satisfactory.)

Comfort in camp is knowing how to improvise.

Being prepared is taking advantage of training opportunities.

The final details will have to be planned during a patrol leaders' council meeting at least a month before the campout. The planning should concentrate on:

- The purpose of the camp
- Program
- Training
- Equipment
- Menus

Once the plans have been made by the patrol leaders' council, the other things can proceed: special training, transportation arrangements, menu planning by patrols, etc.

TRAINING FOR CAMPING. Many councils, recognizing the needs of new troops, have a plan to help.

After a new troop has had a few meetings, it may be invited to take part in an outdoor orientation experience at the council camp or other location. If the troop accepts the invitation, selected council or district Scouters provide lists of equipment and food types, a suggested patrol duty roster, a guide for securing or purchasing equipment, and instructions for cooking, dishwashing, and cleanup to help the troop prepare for the orientation.

While at camp, these same men—sometimes called a campmaster corps—give specific camping instruction and demonstrations. Both Scouts and leaders have a chance to learn good camping practices at the same time, but in no sense does the Scoutmaster turn over leadership of the troop; he is merely provided with expert guidance as needed. In many councils more than one troop at a time can be accommodated in this way.

Even if your council has no formal orientation program, it may be able to help you arrange for a similar experience, using council or district Scouters, or an experienced Scoutmaster to help your troop learn. Or your troop might team up with an experienced troop for its first campout. You and the other Scoutmaster agree on ways in which the other Scouts could teach yours.

Gaps in skills will be noted every time you camp. In turn, these gaps become the subject of subsequent training. If you have "experts" in these fields, put them in charge of the training. If you haven't, get some outside help.

MENUS, COOKING, AND CLEANUP. *The Official Boy Scout Handbook* section on Cooking can be a big help in this whole subject.

In Scout camping, cooking and eating are done by patrols. The patrol sets up a duty roster for fire care, cooking, and cleanup.

It is important for boys to learn how to cook if the meals on camping trips are to be tasty and edible. The quality of food eaten in camp is the result of skill in cooking rather than excellence in menu planning. Boys first have to learn how to cook; then they will become more interested in menu planning.

Try these steps to better cooking and eating on campouts:

1. Ask the parents to help their sons learn to cook at home in their own kitchens according to *The Official Boy Scout Handbook*. Then the Scouts will need only to make the transition from stove to outdoor fire.

2. Supervise menu planning closely until cooking skills are developed. Review all patrol menus and insist on dishes simple enough for the Scouts' skills. Feasts and exotic dishes can come later.

3. Control food costs. Allow only a stated amount of money per person for food purchases for each hike or campout.

4. Assign a troop leader to each patrol to eat as a guest. This will cause the patrols to become accustomed to eating and serving better than they might on their own. The guest should not cook or clean up, but should offer helpful advice if the patrol leader asks for it.

DUTY ROSTER			
DAY or MEAL	FUEL AND WATER	COOKING	CLEANUP
Friday • Lunch	John Sam	Julio Dick	Bob Bill
Saturday • Supper	Bob Bill	John Sam	Julio Dick
Sunday • Breakfast	Julio Dick	Bob Bill	John Sam
Monday • Lunch	Sam Julio	Dick Bill	Bob John
Tuesday • Supper	Bob John	Sam Julio	Dick Bill
Wednesday • Breakfast	Dick Bill	Bob John	Sam Julio
Thursday • Lunch	Dick John	Bob Sam	Julio Bill

When everyone has a job to do the work goes smoothly. Changing jobs gives each Scout a chance to learn something new.

5. Have contests for good cooking at campouts. Award prizes for the most unusual dish, best-tasting main course, most delicious dessert, etc.

As pride in cookery develops, the housekeeping aspects of cooking tend to become less of a problem. As Scouts learn to cook, they become more meticulous about sanitation and table manners. Encourage use of standards from *The Official Patrol Leader Handbook*.

One other part of cooking is eating. Encourage good table manners. Have patrols say grace before eating. Three graces are printed in *The Official Patrol Leader Handbook*, page 114.

MENU PLANNING. Good menu planning is essential for a successful outing, yet some troops assign it a low priority or simply buy food with little or no planning. Ideally your Scouts should have a hand in planning menus and buying food. This may be one of the most valuable skills they learn. They will need your guidance in how to proceed.

Menu planning depends greatly upon the type of outing the troop is planning. You would not take on a backpacking trek items suitable for a weekend picnic. It is important for boys to have a written menu first and then to develop a grocery list based on that menu.

Here are some major factors they need to consider:

1. Is the food purchased high in nutrition? Check labels to see what percentage of recommended daily allowances is contained in various foods. Usually the more processed the food product, the less nutritional value it has.

2. Plan well-balanced menus that contain all of the basic food groups. See page 103 of *The Official Boy Scout Handbook*.

3. Is the food planned appealing to Scouts? If your Scouts do the menu planning and buying, they will generally choose items they like. If someone else does it, care must be taken to select foods that the Scouts will eat, consistent with good nutrition. Also to be considered: Do any of the Scouts have special dietary needs (allergies to certain foods or religious dietary rules)?

4. How easy or how difficult should the food be to prepare? Have your Scouts done a lot of cooking or are they new to it? How much time will you have to prepare meals? One-pot menus make both food preparation and cleanup easier. If you need to get started early in the morning, a "no cook" breakfast may be advisable.

5. Will you have a means for keeping perishable foods cold or should you stick to canned, powdered, or freeze-dried varieties?

6. How much can the Scouts afford to pay for food? This often will be a limiting factor. Most convenience foods cost much more than food prepared from scratch. What is the price per serving?

7. Is weight or bulk a factor that needs to be considered? Will the food need to be carried on the outing? If the outing is several days in length, can you be resupplied midway?

8. Will you have difficulty in properly disposing of cans or bottles? Are the bottles likely to break en route?

9. What will you do with leftovers? Must they be destroyed? Are they packaged in a way that permits them to be stored and used at a future date, or should they be distributed to Scouts at the conclusion of the outing?

PROGRAM IN SHORT-TERM CAMPING. Good program includes camp housekeeping: setting up camp, cooking, cleaning up, etc. It also allows for sleep. But, what does the troop do the rest of the time? When there is too much program, Scouts are regimented and are continually on the run from one activity to another. When there is too little program, boys may become bored and engage in mischief.

Some troops have too little rather than too much program when they go camping. Their leaders somehow come to think that just being out there is sufficient program in itself—and of course it is not. Camping is more than sleeping and eating. Being out there affords a priceless opportunity to do many things that are impossible or only simulated in the troop meeting.

Let principles like these be your guide in planning and carrying out the program on camping trips:

• Have a written program, prepared by the patrol leaders' council.

• Put your emphasis upon nature and conservation, outdoor living, aquatics, physical fitness, and learning to live and work together. Teamwork is essential.

• Design the program to involve and strengthen the patrols. Have patrol activities and interpatrol competition.

• Give Scouts a chance to learn and practice skills required for advancement.

• Where aquatics is part of the troop program, the Safe Swim Defense and/or Safety Afloat plan(s) must be used.

- Ceremonies should be in harmony with the principles of Scouting.

- The daily schedule of activity should allow regular hours for meals and rest and provide for both formal and informal activity by individuals and patrols.

- The program need not be restricted to activities carried out by the whole troop.

- Permit no activity that destroys the personal dignity of an individual. This rules out hazing, initiations, and crude campfire stunts that make a "goat" out of a Scout. Scouts need to grow in character, and they can't do so if they do things to destroy the dignity of others.

Troop 24's Overnight Camp ♣ Friday, May 6

5:00 p.m.	Troop assembly at meeting place	
	Patrol leaders check patrols	
5:15	Start trip to campsite	
5:45	Arrival: Choose patrol campsites	PLs
	Camp making	
6:15	Start supper	
7:00	Supper and clean up	
8:15	Capture the flag	SPL
9:15	Campfire	Mike W.
10:15	To quarters	
10:45	Taps: Lights out : Quiet	

Saturday, May 7

7:30 a.m.	Get up, build fire, start breakfast	
8:15	Breakfast and cleanup	
9:00	Camp inspection	PLs
9:15	Scoutcraft and test passing	
10:45	Nature hike	Sam T.
12:30 p.m.	Lunch and cleanup	
1:30	Map reading race with 6 objectives	Juan H.
2:30	Spies in the woods game	Jim C.
3:15	Break camp — inspection	SPL&SM
3:45	Start for home	
5:00	Dismissal	SPL

Use this overnight camp schedule as a model to follow in planning your own troop overnight.

- Campfires and other group presentation programs should permit participation by Scouts and patrols and not be just spectator activities.

What, specifically, can and should the troop do while camping?

Do What's There. Take advantage of what the site and surrounding area have to offer. Swimming, boating, conservation projects, mountain climbing, rock hunting, fishing, and tracking and trailing are some activities that immediately come to mind. Each area will suggest others. The Scout advancement requirements will suggest more outdoor activity than you will be able to do on a hundred camping trips.

Have Some Contests. Let the patrols compete in just about anything that occurs to them.

Play a Wide Game. A wide game is one that is played over a large area of ground and involves a large number of participants. Weather and site permitting, choose a wide game from Scout literature or make up your own.

Improve the Campsite. With the owner's permission clean up a streambed, clear out an overgrown trail, make brush piles as a haven for wildlife, work on erosion control, plant seedlings.

SLEEPING IN CAMP. The first night in camp is not easy. Here are some tips to make it easier:

- Use two-boy tents.

A beautiful brook looks a mess when it is strewn with trash.

- Don't worry about 9-10 hours of sleep the first night. Put your hour for quiet rather late. The Scouts will not get to sleep early anyway.

- Before the troop retires for the night, make it clear that you expect everyone to be in his own bed by a stated hour, that everyone is to stay in his bed and not to visit other tents, and that no one is to rise or make noise before a stated hour.

- Make it clear that Scouts do not sleep in their clothes. If worn to bed, clothing absorbs body moisture, becoming cold and uncomfortable the next day.

- Be sure patrol leaders understand that it is their responsibility to get their Scouts into bed, and that they (the patrol leaders) are the last ones to retire.

- Allow a reasonable time (for example, half an hour) for getting in bed and settled. If you have a bugler, have "Taps" blown at the announced time. If you have no bugler, have boy leaders pass the word that the announced hour for quiet has come.

- Make a personal bed check to be sure all Scouts are accounted for and are warm and dry.

- Make the rounds of the patrols yourself a little after "Taps." Go first to the patrol leader and see that everything is OK. Then stop by each tent, in turn, to check and have a few words. Keep your own voice low; speaking in whispers is contagious.

The Official Scoutmaster Handbook can scarcely tell a Scoutmaster when and how to go to bed. If you are like boys and most men, you won't be ready to sleep very early the first night out. Meetings with adult or boy leaders, a few minutes around the fire, a hot beverage, and some time reviewing the events of the day may pass an hour or so until you're ready to retire.

A couple of gentle reminders: Don't let the adult fellowship disturb the Scouts. Keep alcohol out of the fellowship. There's no place in camp for alcohol or drugs.

While it is not necessary that all the adult leaders present during the day sleep out, it is absolutely essential that at least one qualified adult leader be on duty in camp at all times. And, two are better than one. They may sleep while on duty, to be sure, but are there and can be awakened in case of emergency. No thinking Scoutmaster ever leaves his troop without a qualified adult leader in the campsite. Note the word "qualified."

Scouts are a little more careful when they
know there will be an inspection.

CAMP INSPECTIONS. Essentially, there are three occasions in camping that require inspection: (1) after camp is set up, (2) after camp is taken down, and (3) periodically in between. Some of these inspections are of personnel, but not all need be. Mainly your interest in these inspections is to ensure a livable camp (or an unblemished site after you leave).

When you conduct an inspection (or someone else does), have the patrol leader accompany the inspector and make notes on conditions that require correction. Make it clear that the patrol leader is responsible for having his site brought up to standard.

SAMPLE INSPECTION CHECKLIST

Patrol Site Inspection After Setup

☐ Latrine:
- ☐ Done Right?
- ☐ Paper on hand?
- ☐ Everyone knows location?

☐ Tents:
- ☐ Pitched properly?
- ☐ Taut-line hitches used?
- ☐ Natural drainage?
- ☐ Pitched in line with prevailing wind?
- ☐ Entrance on leeward side?
- ☐ Tents pitched well away from fire lay?

☐ Beds and
☐ Personal
   Gear:
- ☐ Ground cloth used?
- ☐ Lumps removed?
- ☐ Adequate insulation from ground—foam pad or air matress?
- ☐ Personal gear neat and off the ground?

☐ Kitchen:
- ☐ Firesite cleared of combustibles?
- ☐ Fireplace adequate?
- ☐ Wood supply kept well away from fire?
- ☐ Waste water disposal properly done?
- ☐ Food supply properly stored?
- ☐ Dining fly set up?

☐ Area:
- ☐ No trash or equipment lying around?

Patrol Inspection During Camp

☐ Latrine: ☐ Being used properly?
☐ Tents: ☐ Neat, kept taut, bedding airing or folded or rolled neatly?
                     ☐ Personal gear picked up?
☐ Kitchen: ☐ Clean?
                     ☐ Food stored properly?
                     ☐ Eating area neat?
                     ☐ Utensils and dishes clean?
                     ☐ Cooks have clean hands?
☐ Scouts: ☐ Appropriately dressed for activity?
                     ☐ Reasonable personal cleanliness?
                     ☐ Health OK?

Patrol Inspection for Checkout

☐ Personal gear properly packed for return home?
☐ Trash packed for removal from site?
☐ Area free of any artificial litter: foil, plastic, paper, rope, string, etc.?
☐ Fires out and fireplaces (if improvised) left or removed in accordance with owner's wishes?
☐ Courtesy wood pile left for next campers in established sites?
☐ Latrine filled and sod replaced?
☐ Troop and patrol gear properly rolled, packed, stowed, etc., for return trip?
☐ Usable leftover food separate for distribution at home?
☐ Any holes or ditches filled and mounded?

Even the chipmunks object when we leave tin cans behind.

RETURNING HOME. Like a hike, a camp-out is hardest at the very end. Some are tired and ready to get home, clean up, and rest. Yet there are things to be attended to, and everyone must heave to and get them done.

Wet or damp canvas tents must be dried. Even nylon tents need to be dried to avoid mildew. If the troop's headquarters has no place to hang tents for drying, they will have to be distributed to homes and collected later.

Troop equipment other than tents must be put back where it belongs.

Any dirty gear must be cleaned before being stored.

Last-minute announcements made.

EVALUATING THE CAMPOUT. The campout, like a hike, should have a prompt though informal evaluation by you upon your return. The notes you make about the highs and the lows of the weekend will do a lot to make the next one better. Be sure to analyze the experience as it related to the personal growth and development of boys. A campout must be more than just fun if it is to be worthwhile. Remember, camping is one of the methods we use to accomplish our aims.

Cold-Weather Camping

Camping in cold weather is a true challenge for most troops. Some Scoutmasters and troop committee members may avoid it, but adequately trained and prepared Scouts are usually eager to go. Everyone on a cold-weather outing must keep reasonably warm and dry throughout the experience to enjoy it. A Scout who lies awake in his tent all night because his feet are cold and the breeze is whipping through the zipper on his sleeping bag may be so miserable that he will never go camping again. However, with proper preparation, a cold-weather outing can well be one of the most memorable experiences in a Scout's lifetime.

The key to successful cold-weather camping is to involve knowledgeable people and literature resources to help the troop prepare. The *Fieldbook* contains some great suggestions to help you begin. If your council has a campmaster corps, one of them may assist your troop. The Supply Division carries several authoritative books on the subject including *Winter Camping* by Bob Carey and a chapter on the subject in *Backpacking* by Bob Rethmel. Finally, your council may have literature containing winter camping and program ideas.

Camporees

Most councils or districts conduct one or more camporees annually. Camporees are usually held on a weekend and involve all troops of the district or council.

A camporee is a great opportunity for different troops to meet and learn from one another. It's a time for fellowship, learning, and fun. Programs may feature demonstrations, competitions, joint campfires, and other intertroop activities. Your troop will be able to demonstrate its outdoor knowledge and skills.

Special Events

In addition to the outings described above, many councils and districts offer opportunities for units or individual Scouts to participate in special activities. Usually these activities are oriented toward some special theme such as aquatics, conservation, riflery, archery, American history, survival, ecology, spelunking, rock climbing, world Scouting, or fishing. They may include opportunities for Scouts to work on merit badges or other advancement requirements.

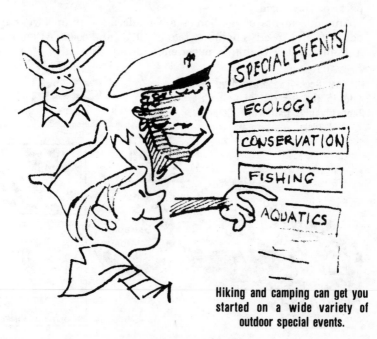

Hiking and camping can get you started on a wide variety of outdoor special events.

Family Camping

More and more councils are offering opportunities for family camping. Some councils offer sites for pitching tents, some have hookups for recreational vehicles, and others host families in cabins. *Introduction to Family Camping,* No. 3820, is available from Supply Division. A *Scouting Family Camping Directory* that lists more than 150 Scout camps with family camping facilities is available at your local Scouting service center. This directory indicates which facilities are available at each camp, date available for family camping, and addresses and phone numbers for making reservations. Each family with at least one registered adult member of the Boy Scouts of America is entitled to a free passport to Scouting family camping.

Jamborees

The national Scout jamboree (held every 4 years) is a gathering of Scouts from all parts of the nation to participate in outdoor skills and other events. World jamborees are also held every 4 years (in between national jamborees) including Scouts from all parts of the world.

Announcements of jamborees are made more than a year in advance and specify eligibility requirements and costs. Attending a jamboree is a highlight experience for any Scout.

National Scout jamborees have been held in the District of Columbia, Pennsylvania, California, Colorado, Idaho, and Virginia.

Expeditions

Some Scout troops plan extensive expeditions into remote backcountry and wilderness areas throughout the country. These treks generally require a tour permit, extensive planning, comprehensive training, and physical fitness routines to prepare Scouts. Usually they are the culmination of a series of lesser outdoor adventures.

Help to prepare for these adventures is available in *Tours and Expeditions,* No. 3734, the *Fieldbook*, No. 3201, and other literature available at your local Scouting service center or through the BSA Supply Division.

Expeditions that proficient, well-organized Scout troops undertake include: backpacking, canoeing, rafting, winter camping, cross-country skiing, horse trips, sailing, desert treks, mountain climbing, and bicycling.

High Adventure

Many high-adventure program opportunities exist for experienced Scouts, older Scouts, and Explorers. High adventure is the ultimate in outdoor experiences beyond the exciting, but lower-keyed program of Scout camp. Most high-adventure programs are an expedition with one or more purposes that involve a week or more in remote outdoor settings. Participants in high adventure should have mastered all of the basic outdoor skills and be ready for an outing that will offer new challenges. Considerable preparation is required for high adventure.

A new troop typically requires several years of training and outdoor experiences before undertaking one of these once-in-a-lifetime adventures.

HIGH ADVENTURE NEAR HOME. Many councils offer high-adventure program opportunities, including canoeing, backpacking, mountain climbing, trips on horseback, wilderness survival, rafting, sailing, and winter camping. Most councils offer their high-adventure programs and facilities to units from other councils as well as their own. Check with your Scouting service center to learn more about what is available in your area.

NATIONAL HIGH ADVENTURE. In addition to council high-adventure programs there are a number of national high-adventure expeditions. Participants must be 13 years old by January 1 of the year of attendance. Call your council service center for more information.

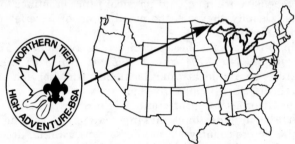

Northern Tier National High Adventure Programs. Located in northern Minnesota near the town of Ely, this base offers high adventure in the world's finest canoe country. Two outlying bases in Manitoba and Ontario, Canada, permit superb access to canoeing, fishing, and camping. Travel the historic fur trade routes of the early French voyagers.

A winter program is conducted from December through March in skiing, snowshoeing and snowcrafts, highlighted by sleeping in an igloo or thermal shelter. Backpacking is available in the fall and spring.

Satellite bases are located at Atikokan, Ontario; Bissett, Manitoba; and at the Northern Wisconsin National High Adventure Base.

Florida National High Adventure Sea Base. Choose year-round aquatics programs unique to Florida. A new sea base on Lower Matacumbe Key midway in the string of Florida Keys serves as the embarking point for an array of fascinating program features. Coral reef sailing, scuba diving, sailing the tall ships, deep-sea fishing, snorkeling, oceanography, and marine science are just a few of the programs available. Sailing brigs ply the Gulf of Mexico while smaller vessels negotiate the crystal-clear reefs of the Keys and the Bahamas. Set your compass for high adventure in Florida anytime of year.

Maine National High Adventure Area. Explore 6 million acres of forests, lakes and rivers in northern Maine with canoeing, backpacking, wilderness camping, and fishing. See the majestic moose. Climb Maine's highest mountain, Mount Katahdin. Enjoy float boating, canoe sailing, bushwhacking. Learn about the Maine woods' environment from a capable interpreter. Flexibility in operation permits freedom to choose your length of stay and choice of program.

Philmont Scout Ranch. Let's go to Philmont. Backpack through 137,000 acres of Sangre de Cristo Mountains that tower up to 12,500 feet. This challenge means rugged wilderness adventure in the tradition of the mountain man, the Indian, the trapper, the lumberjack, and the gold miner. Besides this, Philmont offers rock climbing, wilderness survival, western saddle horse riding, burro racing, search and rescue, archaeology, high-powered rifle shooting, and more. See the Santa Fe Trail, climb the mighty Tooth of Time, and fish for trout in gushing mountain streams. At Philmont you will go farther than you ever thought you could. Go to Philmont and see the high country. Check at your local Scouting service center to borrow a film about Philmont called "Coming on Strong."

Weeklong Scouter training conferences covering a variety of subjects are offered at the Philmont Volunteer Training Center. Scouters taking training are encouraged to bring their families. A special fun program is designed for each member of the family. Your council has information on all programs offered at Philmont.

Low-Impact Camping

Low-impact camping involves the skills, techniques, and attitudes that can give older Boy Scouts, Varsity Scouts, and Explorers a true wilderness experience. The goal is to give little evidence of their presence while in the area and leave no trace upon their departure. As a matter of law, designated wilderness and primitive areas often have strict limits on their use. Scouting groups must understand and respect these limits. Backcountry areas, not officially designated as wilderness or primitive, also deserve protection and care in how they are used.

Low-impact camping often is different from the type of camping normally found in established long- and short-term camps. The leader has a greater responsibility in controlling the group and providing minimum-impact programs and activities. The youth members will need training in the skills and attitudes associated with a true wilderness experience.

The booklet *Low-Impact Camping,* No. 20-126, is available from the Camping/Outdoor Division, Boy Scouts of America, 1325 Walnut Hill Lane, Irving, TX 75038-3096. It contains two training programs on low-impact camping.

Troop and Patrol Hiking

Hiking describes all sorts of outdoor activities that take up 1 day or part of a day. The emphasis might be on the things to see and do along the way—or it might be on what they do when they get there. A hike along an old canal towpath is one where the going might outshine the destination. A day trip to the beach would play down the travel and concentrate on the destination.

PLANNING FOR HIKING. Troop hikes are part of the troop's program and should be written in when the annual program is developed. Patrol hikes may also be scheduled in that way or organized later on as the wishes of the patrol dictate and in keeping with troop policy.

Hikes are usually more intriguing and exciting if they have some special purpose or theme.

A hike probably will be more interesting than an indoor meeting. Certain things will, of course, "just happen;" but to ensure a hike that achieves its purpose, planning must be as thorough as for any meeting.

Here's a sample of the kinds of things that might be planned into a troop hike:

PERIOD	ACTIVITY
Before the hike	Patrols assemble separately and travel to troop assembly place
Troop assembly	Patrols report; inspection; announcements and instructions
Out-trip	Games along the trail
	Competition
	Singing
	Observation
At destination	Scoutcraft instruction
	Fitness and Scoutcraft games
	Competition
	Advancement
	Campfire
	Cooking; eating; cleanup
Return trip	By patrols in the troop
Troop dismissal	Announcements and recognitions
	Dismissal

Generally, all hikes follow this pattern of operation with a planned activity for each one of the six periods.

Interesting destinations can be found by referring to local road maps and trail guides. Routes—if yours is a foot or bike hike— are best picked using a topographic map that shows contour lines.

Permission may be needed to cross certain lands, to build fires, or to engage in activities like swimming or skating.

Food and equipment planning will, of course, vary with the type of hike. If one of your main goals is to practice cooking for Scout tests, you will need careful planning for food and equipment. If eating and cooking are only incidental, you may plan a sandwich lunch.

Transportation is planned in detail the week of the hike, when patrol leaders can report for sure just how many are going.

ANNOUNCING THE HIKE. A troop hike should have been on the schedule for a month or more, so it doesn't come as a surprise. But when the time comes to announce the details, make it sound like the adventure you intend it to be. Make it a special kind of hike, and play that up when announcing it to the troop.

HARES AND HOUNDS ADVANCEMENT HIKE

Time	Activity	Leader
9:00 a.m.	Troop assembly at meeting place	SPL
	Patrol leaders check their patrols	PLs
9:15	Head out	SPL
	Game: Hares and Hounds	Wolf Patrol
10:45	Track of the "Hares" ends at camp	
	Games: Blind-fold Compass Course	Julio
	String burning	Greg
	Name It	Sam
11:45	Build patrol fires	PLs in charge
	Lunch: Kabob, baked potatoes, cookies	
1:30 p.m.	Cleanup and inspection	PLs
1:45	Scoutcraft test passing	PLs
3:00	Recheck the area for litter and cleanup, if necessary	SPL AND SM
3:15	Start return hike	
	Game: Wounded Spy	SPL
4:45	Back at meeting place	
	Recognize patrol and individual achievement	SM
	Dismiss the troop	SPL

This hike plan uses ideas from the Boy Scout Handbook, pages 128-29 and 256-57; the Patrol Leader Handbook, pages 105 and 122; and this handbook.

THE OUTDOOR PROGRAM

Parents, as well as Scouts, need to know the date of the hike, when and from where you will depart, and your estimated time of return.

HEALTH AND SAFETY ON THE HIKE. As soon as the troop leaves its safe indoor meeting place, hazards to health and safety multiply. Fortunately, most of the hazards can be avoided or reduced to small risks.

If there must be travel along a highway, observing simple rules will greatly reduce the risk:

- Walk on the left facing traffic.
- Walk single file by patrol, patrol leader in front, assistant patrol leader in back.
- No darting into the road or crossing it except on signal after check for traffic.
- At night, a white cloth is tied to everyone's lower right leg and lights are carried by those at each end of the column. (A safely planned hike will avoid night exposure on highways.)
- No hitchhiking.
- On the trail, anticipate physical hazards and give instructions.

Scouts should be in good health to go on hikes. The amount of exertion required should be tailored to their physical condition and prior practice in hiking. It is easy to overestimate what boys can take. Long hikes require short hikes to condition the hikers.

Footwear is an important part of hike clothing. Sturdy, broken-in shoes and wool socks that fit well will reduce the blister problem. Thin-soled or worn sneakers, tight or loose shoes, and brand-new or worn-out shoes cause the problems, and Scouts should be warned about them before the hike. Footwear should be appropriate for the weather and the terrain being hiked.

Drinking water from unknown sources is dangerous. Enough water must be brought from home unless pure sources can be counted on. You can boil or chemically purify water on location, but boys may be too impatient to take the necessary time.

Water may be purified using one of these methods:

1. Boiling it for 10 minutes.
2. Following the directions on the container of water purification tablets.
3. Adding two drops of liquid chlorine bleach per quart of water,

shaking or stirring it thoroughly, and letting it stand for 30 minutes.

4. Mixing four drops of tincture of iodine per quart of water and letting it stand for 30 minutes. *Do not use this mixture in an aluminum container because this may form a poisonous liquid.*

All measures except the first require 30 minutes of contact time with the chemical agent to eliminate impurities.

Take 5 minutes or so every half-hour rather than long rests infrequently. A hike that becomes a race may overtax weaker Scouts unnecessarily.

Unless there is adequate adult leadership, resist the temptation to "let the faster ones go on ahead." A split hiking group often leads to all kinds of otherwise easily avoidable trouble. Keep the group together.

HIKING COURTESY. The ideals of Scouting are just as important on a hike as anywhere else. Use the hike as a chance to practice what we all preach. Review *The Official Boy Scout Handbook,* pages 182-83, for hike courtesy suggestions.

ACTIVITIES ALONG THE WAY. Even though the big attraction may be at the destination, there's plenty of fun and learning to be done along the way:

• Practice finding directions with and without a compass.

Let the sun and your compass guide you!

- Practice reading and following a map.
- Stage an accident and practice first aid.
- Make plaster casts of animal tracks.
- Spot and identify bird species.
- Take photos.
- Identify and keep notes on all types of trees encountered.
- On a maintained trail, help with maintenance by clearing deadfalls across the trail, restoring trail markers, picking up litter, etc.

ACTIVITIES AT YOUR DESTINATION. Some destinatons, like beaches or museums, have the activity built in. But if your destination is "no special place," you will need carefully planned and supervised activities. Housekeeping takes some time. If there are no latrine facilities, you will need a temporary one. If you are there at mealtime, you'll be eating and possibly cooking. If you have planned cooking as a major activity, lunch may take 2 hours, from selection of fire sites to final cleanup. If you are eating sandwiches out of a bag, it will be more like 10 minutes. Beyond housekeeping chores, you will need some planned adventures that will make everyone glad he came. Here again are some samples for your suggestion box:

- Scoutcraft instruction, in keeping with the site, the weather, and what Scouts need to learn.
- Scoutcraft practice (doing things already learned but not adequately practiced).
- Wide games (or any other kind, for that matter).
- Contests.
- Adventure trail.
- Treasure or scavenger hunt.
- Campfire.
- Fishing.

The final activity at any hike site is to return the site to its original condition or better: fires out, any holes filled, all trash burned (where permitted) or bagged up to take home. (If you hike to a place such as a state park where trash receptacles are provided, they should be used as directed.)

RETURNING HOME. Troop members usually will return home together. Dismissal as a troop should be preceded by final announcements and instructions.

It takes real self-discipline for a leader to control the final hours or minutes of a hike or camp. Leaders, as well as Scouts, may be tired at the day's end. Yet here is where the best leadership is needed: to keep morale up, to get important things done, to send Scouts home with a feeling of having done something great. Use the challenge on page 119 of *The Official Patrol Leader Handbook* that begins: "When you get home...."

EVALUATING YOUR HIKE. Write down the high and low spots of your hike. What were the things that went especially well—so you can have more of that kind next time? What went badly, and how can you do it better next time? Did you accomplish the hike's purposes? Did you accomplish some of the purposes of Scouting? Did morale hold up? Did the Scouts enjoy themselves? Did you?

IDEAS FOR HIKES. Historical Hike. Have the patrol consult the library, schoolteachers, pastor, and the chamber of commerce for historical facts of the locality. Decide on a hike route which will include the greatest number of interesting spots.

Send out the patrols to investigate as many places as possible. At the hike destination each patrol reports on its findings.

Nature Hike. This may involve a hike to a certain habitat— marsh, lake, field, woods, etc.—to investigate all types of wildlife there. Or it may be a specific quest for one certain type of wildlife or plant: oak tree, primrose, chickadee, raccoon, etc. Each patrol brings a notebook to list its discoveries.

Various nature games may be played, such as a patrol nature "scavenger" hunt for about a dozen items—a piece of bark from a shagbark hickory, an acorn, a wild rose thorn—these items to be found within a certain length of time. Or have a tree identification game in which numbered tags are placed on several trees by the leader, after which the patrols try to find tags and make a list of the names of the trees to which they are attached.

Nature specimens may be collected: pressed flowers and tree leaves, smoke prints, plaster casts of tracks.

Star Hike. Make this a part of a later afternoon and evening hike. For beginners, a night lighted by a moon in its first quarter is best. At such time all smaller stars and the Milky Way disappear, thus emphasizing the stars which make up the constellations.

Use flashlight with a strong, narrow beam and use this for a pointer. Starting with the Big Dipper and the North Star, point out the main constellations in a natural, progressive manner. Have a contest to see which patrol can point out the greatest number of constellations. Then plot directions by the stars. Check the compass direction of the North Star against page 209 of *The Official Boy Scout Handbook.*

Long-Distance Hike. After some shorter hikes, take a 10-mile hike. Get the patrols and the individual boys interested in taking 10-mile hikes toward earning the Hiking merit badge.

Treasure Hunt. The treasure hunt activity with clues leading patrols from one station to another has been popular in Scouting for many years. The clues involve Scouting skills and the reasoning and observation abilities of competing patrols.

It is important that each clue be numbered and that Scouts finishing the search be required to present the message of each clue decoded, if necessary. This prevents the treasure hunt from becoming a game of follow the leader with patrols merely following the first patrol to figure out each clue. A sample of a treasure hunt follows. Scouts need pencils.

Clue No. 1
Get your Boy Scout Handbook; open it to page 356.

Clue No. 2

G O / O U T S I D E // G E T / N E X T /
C L U E / F R O M / P E R S O N /
1 8 / P A C E S / F R O M
T H E / D O O R. ///

The clues are written in Morse code. Scouts write the letters above the dots and dashes to decode the message. Have three or four troop committee members handing out clues at various distances from the meeting room door.

Clue No. 3

GIVE / THREE / SMALL /
STONES / TO / YOUR /
SCOUTMASTER. ///

A pace is a double step counting each time the right foot hits the ground. Pick an average-height Scout to help you establish the 18 paces. The person who stands here is the only one with the right clue, all the others have the false clue.

Clue No. 3*

THIS IS A FALSE CLUE. YOU
DID / NOT GO 18 PACES.

Clue No. 4

TREASURE / IS / UNDER /
CAR / WITH / LICENSE
_____ ///

Put in the license plate number on clue No. 4. If you wish, white out the letters above the dots and dashes and use these clues.

Caveman Hike. Train in cooking without utensils until each Scout can prepare a complete menu of primitive cooking. Then take a hike to use this utensil-less cooking skill.

Survival (Robinson Crusoe) Hike. A primitive cookery hike requires bringing foodstuffs but no utensils. For a survival hike it is the other way around. Here you bring utensils but gather the foodstuffs in the wild. Preliminary nature study is required to identify local edible plants, roots, berries, and fruits. Never eat anything you cannot positively identify.

Conservation Hike. Decide upon most appropriate places for brush piles for wildlife with the cooperation of local game experts. Assign definite jobs to the various patrols.

Tree and shrub planting, erosion control, clearing of brush, cutting of trails, and putting up birdhouses are in this class.

"Lost Child" Hike. "A child is lost. A search has been going on all night. The only place that has not been searched is a woodland, indicated on map sketch. Our help has been requested." Combine this with a troop mobilization.

Warn boys at previous troop meetings that they may be called out a certain day, but do not disclose the reason. The "child" is a life-size doll, made up of pillows and child's clothing, and placed in a spot that is not too conspicuous.

Following the mobilization, instructions are given and the patrols proceed with orders to meet at a given spot at a certain time when the search will end, whether or not the "child" has been found. Patrol locating "child" or otherwise showing most intelligent procedure is the winner.

Beeline Hike. This is a cross-country hike in a direct line, overcoming obstacles in the way. The route can be laid out on a topographic map as a single line from start to finish.

Patrols leave the starting point at 5-minute intervals, each following the compass bearing taken from the topographic map line.

A variation of this could be to follow a county line (shown on topographic maps) from one highway to another. These lines are marked at the highways where they cross, so accuracy can be checked.

Scoutcraft Obstacle Hike. Several troop committee members are required for judges at the various obstacles. The obstacles cover Scout requirements. The patrols are instructed in advance about what equipment to bring.

The patrols start off with 10- or 15-minute intervals. Obstacles may include (1) boy bitten by rattlesnake; (2) boy's bicycle broken down; (3) "Susie was frightened by a bear and climbed up in a tree. She must be lowered with a rope." ("Susie" is a life-size doll made of pillows, draped over a high branch.); (4) an unfinished bridge to be completed to cross an imaginary impassable marsh; and so on.

Sealed Orders (Mystery) Hike. Each patrol leader receives a series of numbered envelopes. Each envelope contains specific instructions covering a stage of the hike. The first may order the patrol to proceed to a certain crossroad by a certain route. The second, which is to be opened when the hikers reach the end of the first stage of the journey, gives the second part of the route, and so on. Each order should include specific instructions for observation, Scoutcraft, etc.

This method of giving instructions keeps the interest at a high pitch, especially as the final destination is not disclosed until the last sealed envelope is opened.

REMINDERS FOR OUTINGS

The Boy Scouts of America has an outstanding record in providing for the physical well-being of its members. Fitness is one of our key objectives. All Boy Scout outdoor activities must meet rigorous standards of health, safety, and program. Continued vigilance is necessary to ensure that Scouts have high-quality, outdoor experiences that do not expose them to unnecessary risks. On unit outings as Scoutmaster you assume responsibility for the health and safety for the members of your troop. Adequate supervision of each Scout in your troop through verbal and visual communication is essential.

These points are to remind you of some of the major needs to achieve high standards of health and safety. Many of these items should be assumed by your troop committee or delegated to your assistant Scoutmaster, your troop leadership corps, or even to individual Scouts as they become increasingly proficient in outdoor skills. When you, the other leaders, and your troop committee prepare for the next outing, review this list and decide who will be responsible for each item.

ONCE A YEAR

☐ **Person Responsible:** _____
1. Encourge each participant to have a current health history and a medical examination, BSA form No. 4412, (within 3 years) by a licensed physician. It is good troop policy to require each Scout to have a medical examination when he joins. Be aware of any special medical needs of anyone in your group and be prepared to deal with them.

☐ **Person Responsible:** _____
2. Each troop should have year-round accident insurance for troop activities. For long-term camp or council-sponsored activities, council accident and sickness insurance should be secured by the responsible council official. The council can provide much information on the various accident and sickness insurances available to your troop.

☐ **Person Responsible:** _____
3. Conduct survival training, including seven priorities—(1) will to live—keep calm, (2) shelter, (3) fire, (4) rest, (5) signaling device, (6) water, (7) food. Explain what to do if lost. Instruct the troop in how to use a compass and topographic maps. See the *Emergency Survival Handbook*, No. 3551.

☐ **Person Responsible:** _____
4. Instruct group on how to use and care for woods tools safely—knife, hand ax, ¾ ax. Always use the "contact method" for splitting wood.

BEFORE GOING

☐ **Person Responsible:** _____
5. Provide adequate adult leadership (age 21 or over) for the group considering the number of youth participants, their age, their training and experience for the type of outing being undertaken, and the degree of difficulty of the outing. Maintain a minimum ratio of 1 adult per 10 youths. Ideally, each group would have at least two adults.

☐ **Person Responsible:** _____
   6. Submit application for local, No. 4426, or national (500 miles or more), No. 4419, tour permit. Even if a national or local tour permit is not required, the provisions in these tour permits should be followed whenever possible.

☐ **Person Responsible:** _____
   7. Know the area, arrange to go with someone who does, or check the area out well in advance of outing.

☐ **Person Responsible:** _____
   8. Be sure someone in group has first aid training, especially for hypothermia, hyperthermia, dehydration, heat problems, blisters, frostbite, hyperventilation, altitude sickness, stings, and CPR.

☐ **Person Responsible:** _____
   9. Get written parental consent for each youth participant for adventurous outings that may involve a factor of risk. Be sure parents understand what the risks are and what precautions are being taken.

☐ **Person Responsible:** _____
   10. Devise a plan for outing geared to the abilities and experience of the group. See *The Official Boy Scout Handbook,* No. 3227, and the *Fieldbook,* No. 3201.

☐ **Person Responsible:** _____
   11. Check to be sure everyone is physically fit—no colds, serious allergy problems, etc. If trek is strenuous, conduct pretrek training to get everyone in shape.

☐ **Person Responsible:** _____
   12. Establish procedures for missing persons and severe weather emergencies—high winds, heavy snow, flooding. Search only the immediate area for missing persons—contact appropriate authorities if a more extensive search is needed.

☐ **Person Responsible:** _____
   13. Let parents know where you are going, when you will leave, where you will leave vehicles, when you expect to return, whom to contact for emergencies. Establish an emergency contact with a responsible adult in the unit's home community and specify times when an adult on the outing will check in.

☐ **Person Responsible:** _____
   14. Make sure every person is properly clothed, especially foot and headgear, for all possible conditions. The Scout uniform is designed to be worn outdoors and is appropriate for most outdoor activities.

☐ **Person Responsible:** _____
   15. Leave pets, chain saws, firearms, and fireworks at home.

☐ **Person Responsible:** _____
   16. Be alert to weather conditions. Develop an alternate plan for severe weather.

ON THE TRAIL

☐ **Person Responsible:** _____
   17. Always use the buddy system on the trail, while traveling, in boats or canoes, and especially for treks into remote areas and winter camping, to maintain alertness to potential medical problems, as well as to keep track of everyone. Hold periodic buddy checks.

☐ **Person Responsible:** _____
   18. Keep the group together on the outing. Use the rule of four—no fewer than four persons hike or canoe together. If one becomes seriously ill or injured, one administers first aid while two go for help.

☐ **Person Responsible:** _____
   19. Avoid hiking along highways, but if you must, hike against the traffic in single file well off the pavement. Wear highly visible clothing.

☐ **Person Responsible:** _____
   20. Recognize the difference between difficult and dangerous areas and bypass the dangerous entirely. Attempt activities involving a degree of risk (whitewater, rock climbing, etc.) only if equipment, ability, training, and accessibility of area are commensurate with degree of difficulty. Carefully check an entire whitewater course before attempting it. Portage canoes if unsure. Know the limits of your group and when to turn back.

☐ **Person Responsible:** _____
   21. See that everyone maintains an adequate intake of liquids to avoid dehydration and related medical problems.

☐ **Person Responsible:** _____
   22. Avoid lightning, swollen streams, rapids, traveling at night, etc. Stay away from peaks, ridges, and open fields when hiking or backpacking. Stay near the shoreline when boating or canoeing.

IN CAMP

☐ **Person Responsible:** _____
   23. Select campsites that are protected from high winds, lightning, flash floods, cliffs, falling rock, dead limbs or trees, etc., and that are free of poisonous plants, insects, etc. Take adequate measures to avoid problems from insects such as flies, ants, ticks, and mosquitoes.

☐ **Person Responsible:** _____
   24. Use treated water or purify untreated water. Water in stagnant pools or ponds or in heavily polluted streams must be avoided.

☐ **Person Responsible:** _____
   25. Permit no flame of any type to be used inside or near any type of tent whether flame resistant or not. Pitch tents at least 30 feet from any fire point.

☐ **Person Responsible:** _____
   26. All handling and use of liquid fuels must be supervised by a knowledgeable adult expeienced in their use and in use of the stove, lantern, or other equipment which they fuel.

☐ **Person Responsible:** _____
   27. Have a fire plan ready to use if a fire occurs. Appoint troop and patrol fire
       guards and rotate this duty daily. Never leave a fire unattended.

☐ **Person Responsible:** _____
   28. Provide a means for keeping perishable foods cold. Keep reconstituted milk
       cold. Once dehydrated milk is reconstituted, it can spoil just like fresh milk.

☐ **Person Responsible:** _____
   29. Stress that all pots, dishes, and utensils must be scraped clean, thoroughly
       washed in warm soapy water, rinsed in hot water with a sanitizing agent
       added, and then rinsed again.

☐ **Person Responsible:** _____
   30. Use cathole or straddle-trench latrine, located at least 200 feet from any
       water source—spring, lake, stream, etc. Cover fecal matter with dirt after
       each use and completely close hole before departing.

☐ **Person Responsible:** _____
   31. See that personal cleanliness is maintained by everyone. If showers are not
       available, participants should take a periodic sponge bath. Encourage
       everyone to brush his teeth at least once daily.

☐ **Person Responsible:** _____
   32. Plan activities to avoid horseplay—most injuries in camp are related to
       careless, unplanned activity. Report any serious accident to your council
       office. Schedule 9 to 10 hours of sleep between taps and reveille and see
       that quiet is maintained during this period.

☐ **Person Responsible:** _____
   33. Use the Safe Swim Defense for all swimming. Use Safety Afloat for all
       outings when watercraft are used.

☐ **Person Responsible:** _____
   34. Make sure fires are dead out. Sprinkle coals with water and stir them—
       repeat as many times as necessary. Use the "cold out" test by having
       someone run a bare hand through extinguished coals and ashes. Place
       crossed sticks over firelay to indicate that fire was left dead out.

AT CONCLUSION OF OUTING

☐ **Person Responsible:** _____
   35. Check in when returning—let contact person know you have returned.

☐ **Person Responsible:** _____
   36. Remove food packages from pack, especially opened ones.

☐ **Person Responsible:** _____
   37. Clean and/or dry equipment and store it properly.

☐ **Person Responsible:** _____
   38. Make sure every person has a way to get home.

☐ **Person Responsible:** _____
   39. Write thank-you to landowners and others who extended courtesies.

The wise outdoorsman wears layers of clothing that can trap body heat, and releases it by loosening or shedding the garments.

HYPOTHERMIA

Hypothermia is the lowering of the body's inner core temperature, and is a serious threat to those poorly prepared for the outdoors. Exposure to any combination of cold, wetness, wind, and fatigue may produce the condition. The cold need not be extreme, and the wetness can be from one's own perspiration. The insidious nature of hypothermia is its absence of warning to the victim, and the fact that, as its severity increases, chilling affects the brain, thus depriving the person of the reasoning power to recognize his own condition. Without recognition and treatment of symptoms (shivering, loss of limb coordination, exhaustion) by a companion, this condition could lead to stupor, collapse, and death.

Early detection is critical, since a person may become hypothermic in a matter of minutes and can die in less than 2 hours if unattended. Immediate treatment is:

1. Prevent further heat loss by moving the victim to the best shelter available.

2. Replace wet clothing with dry garments.

3. Insulate the victim from the ground and wind.

4. Keep the victim warm. Place the victim in a sleeping bag that has been prewarmed by another person. Provide warmth through skin-to-skin contact (by placing the stripped victim in a sleeping bag with another stripped person). Providing warm (not hot) rocks or canteens, or fire on each side of the victim also will help.

Adult leaders should know the symptoms of hypothermia and correct treatment procedures, and should continually observe campers on the trail, in or on the water, for early diagnosis of this dangerous condition.

PRINCIPLES AND METHODS
OF SCOUT CAMPING

The way a troop is organized year-round is the way the troop camps: under troop leaders but camping by patrols. The purpose of Scouting is actively behind Scout camping methods:

- Scouts camp in tents, not buildings, because camping in a building requires little of the Scout and teaches him little.

- Scouts cook by patrol because this is one of the ways to strengthen the patrol and its leadership. It teaches teamwork.

- Scouts carry their packs to the campsite instead of riding because physical fitness and self-reliance are two of our objectives. Scouts learn not only how to do things for themselves, but also how much they can do.

- Scouts set up their tents in patrol groups to maintain the identity and comradeship of the patrol.

Scout camping demands skill and know-how. Its emphasis is on adventure rather than convenience. It is designed to strengthen patrols and their leaders, not to subordinate them to the troop and its adult leadership. Decades of experience show that the more a troop adheres to the Scout method of camping, the more the Scouts like it.

Leadership for Troop Camps

The troop should camp under its own registered adult male leadership. The senior patrol leader of the troop should play his normal role in the troop camp. If he can't attend, an acting SPL may be designated.

Each patrol should be led by its elected or a designated acting patrol leader.

Policies for Scout Camping

MINIMUM CAMPING EXPERIENCE. At least 10 days and nights of camping per year is the minimum objective for a Scout troop. It is the responsibility of the troop committee and leaders to meet or exceed this objective.

CAMPING IN ANOTHER COUNCIL'S CAMP. A Scout troop may attend any Boy Scout camp anywhere in the country. Reservations are generally handled on a first-come, first-served basis. New troops should be encouraged to use their own council facilities, but all troops have the privilege of attending the camp of their choice. Arrangements to attend camp in another council must include a tour permit. These are available through your council service center.

CONFLICTS WITH RELIGIOUS OBSERVANCES. The Boy Scouts of America recommends that Scouting activities should not preclude Scouts from attending religious services and that there should be no loss of credits for the individual, patrol, or troop if the Scout elects to remain at home in order to attend church.

When Scouts are away from religious services, with approval of their parents and religious leaders, an approved religious service should be conducted by persons who have authority to do so, or

Duty to God is first in our lives

arrangements should be made for Scouts to attend religious services of their faith in nearby communities.

TROOP-OWNED CABINS OR CAMPS OFF THE COUNCIL SITE. The Boy Scouts of America actively discourages troops from developing permanent campsites or cabins. The reasons, based on experience, are as follows:

- The costs of such developments are nearly always far out of proportion to the amount of use given the facility by one troop.

- Ownership of a site tends to discourage the use of other sites, so the troop's outdoor adventure becomes limited.

- Camping in buildings does not contribute to the objectives of Scouting and provides little, if any, opportunity to learn and practice Scoutcraft skills.

- Protection of the property is difficult, if not impossible, and vandalism is almost a constant threat.

- Enthusiasm for buildings and permanent camps is highest before and during their development. It wanes as soon as they are completed, but the burden of repair, maintenance, and insurance grows with the years.

- Permanent troop camps often become hangouts where the kinds of outcomes and behaviors are contrary to those sought by Scout leaders.

Tour Permits

Your troop must obtain a local tour permit from your local council whenever it plans to camp (1) off council property but within 500 miles of home or (2) on the property of another Scouting council. Your council may or may not require a local tour permit to use its own facilities, but in any case will require at least a reservation.

Your troop must obtain, through your council, a national tour permit if it plans to travel and/or camp (1) 500 miles or more from home or (2) outside the continental United States. A minimum of 3 weeks is required to process your application for a national tour permit.

Tour permits are designed to safeguard you and your troop. They help assure parents that high standards of health, safety, and vehicle accident insurance are being met to ensure the well-being of their child. Finally, they keep the council informed of your plans and facilitate emergency contacts if necessary.

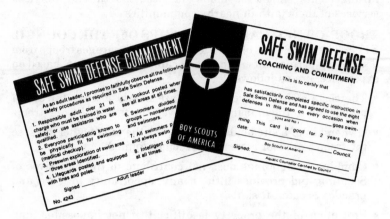

As an adult leader, I promise to faithfully observe all the following safety procedures as required in Safe Swim Defense.

1. Responsible adult over 21 in charge who must be trained in water safety, or use assistants who are qualified.
2. Everyone participating known to be physically fit for swimming (medical checkup).
3. Preswim exploration of swim area — three areas identified.
4. Lifeguards posted and equipped with lines and poles.
5. A lookout posted where [he can] see all areas at all times.
6. Swimmers divided [into] groups — nonswimme[rs and] swimmers.
7. All swimmers p[aired] and always swim [in pairs.]
8. Intelligent d[iscipline] at all times.

Signed _____
Adult leader _____
No. 4243

SAFE SWIM DEFENSE
COACHING AND COMMITMENT
This is to certify that

_____ has satisfactorily completed specific instruction in Safe Swim Defense and has agreed to use the eight defenses in this plan on every occasion when _____ (Unit and No.) goes swim-ming. This card is good for 2 years from date: _____.

Signed: _____
Boy Scouts of America _____ Council.

Aquatic Counselor Certified by Council _____

BOY SCOUTS OF AMERICA

Training in the Safe Swim Defense is
recognized by this certificate.

Safe Swim Defense

Council-operated Scout camps have compiled an enviable record of safety in and on the water. The record of troops camping on their own and conducting their own swimming program is less enviable and is sometimes marred by tragic water accidents that are nearly always preventable. You can virtually eliminate the possibility of such tragedies in your troop by following all eight of these simple defenses.

1. **Qualified Supervision.** Swimming must be supervised by an adult (at least age 21). This person must be qualified in water safety (BSA Lifeguard; Red Cross Advanced Lifesaving; or YMCA Senior Lifesaver) or must use assistants so qualified. Preferably have more than one adult qualified to supervise.

2. **Physical Fitness.** Require evidence of fitness for swimming activity with a complete health history from physcian, parent, or legal guardian. Adjust all supervision, discipline, and protection to anticipate any potential risks associated with individual health conditions. In the event of any significant health conditions, an examination by a physician (recommended BSA form, No. 4412) should be required.

3. **Safe Swimming Area.** The bottom is carefully examined for hazards. They are either removed or marked off-limits. The usable swimming area is then marked off for three classes: maximum 3½ feet for nonswimmers, from shallow water to just over the head for beginners, deep water (up to 12 feet) for swimmers. Use plastic jugs or balloons attached to rock anchors with twine. Then attach buoy lines (twine and floats) between markers.

4. **Lifeguards on Duty.** Two Scouts who can swim well are stationed as lifeguards. They are stationed ashore and equipped with a 100-foot lifeline. In the event of emergency one Scout swims with the line to the person in trouble and the other pulls both of them to shore.

5. **Lookout.** Station a lookout on the shore where everything can be seen and heard in all areas. This person may be the adult in charge of the swim and may give the buddy signals.

6. **Ability Groups.** Divide into three ability groups: nonswimmers, beginners, and swimmers. Keep each group in its own area. Nonswimmers have not passed a swimming test. Beginners pass this test: Jump feetfirst into water over the head in depth, level off, swim 7.5 meters (25 feet) on the surface. Stop, turn sharply, resume swimming as before and return to starting place. Swimmers pass this test: Jump feetfirst into the water over the head in depth, level off, and begin swimming. Swim 75 yards/meters in a strong manner using one or more of the following strokes: sidestroke, breaststroke, trudgen, or crawl; then swim 25 yards/meters using an easy resting backstroke. The 100 yards/meters must be swum continuously and include at least one sharp turn. After completing the swim, rest by floating. These qualification tests should be renewed annually, preferably at the beginning of each season.

7. **Buddy System.** Scouts check into the swim area in pairs, stay within 10 feet of each other, and check out in pairs. They are "lifeguards" for each other. A check is called every 10 minutes to be sure all pairs are together and to count them against the number checked in.

8. **Discipline.** Be sure everyone understands and agrees that swimming is allowed only with proper supervision and use of the complete Safe Swim Defense. Advise parents of this policy. When everyone knows the reason for rules and procedures, they are more likely to follow them. Be strict and fair, showing no favoritism.

Safety Afloat

Safety Afloat, a policy adopted in 1981 by the Boy Scouts of America, is related to using watercraft in the same way that the Safe Swim Defense program applies to swimming. By enforcing these nine measures you can prevent most watercraft accidents.

1. **Qualified Supervision.** A responsible adult must supervise all activity afloat and must be experienced and qualified in water safety (BSA Lifeguard, Red Cross Advanced Lifesaving, or YMCA Senior Lifesaver) and in the particular skills related to the watercraft being used, or use assistants so qualified. Ability to meet current requirements for Canoeing, Rowing, Small-Boat Sailing, or Motorboating merit badge qualifies a person in respect to safe handling of that watercraft. One adult supervisor is required for each 10 people, with a minimum of two adults for any one group. All adult supervisors must complete Safety Afloat and Safe Swim Defense training, and at least one must be certified in CPR basic life support.

2. **Physical Fitness.** All persons must present evidence of fitness assured by a complete health history from a physician, parent, or legal guardian. Adjust all supervision, discipline, and protection to anticipate any potential risks associated with individual health conditions. In the event of any significant health conditions, an examination by a physician (recommend BSA form No. 4412) should be required.

3. **Swimming Ability.** A participant who is not classified as a swimmer (see item 6, page 203) may ride as a passenger in a rowboat or motorboat with an adult "swimmer." In all other watercraft, a person must pass the "swimmer" test to participate.

4. **Personal Flotation Equipment.** U.S. Coast Guard approved personal flotation devices (PFDs) shall be properly worn by **all** engaged in activity on the open water (rowing, canoeing, sailing, motorboating). The only exception would be for persons classified in the current season as **swimmers** in closely supervised situations (such as instructional activity) when when the trained adult in charge has determined that the conditions are such that personal flotation equipment may be safely stowed loosely in the craft within easy reach of the occupants.

5. **Buddy System.** All activity afloat necessitates using the buddy system. Not only does every individual have a buddy, but every craft should have a buddy boat when on the water.

6. **Skill Proficiency.** All participants in unit afloat activities must be trained and experienced in watercraft handling skills, safety, and emergency procedures. (a) For unit activity on white water, all participants must complete special training by an Aquatics Instructor BSA or qualified equivalent. (b) Powerboat operators must be able to meet requirements for Motorboating merit badge or equivalent. (c) A minimum of 3 hours training and supervised practice is required for all other unpowered watercraft.

7. **Planning.** *Float Plan.* Obtain current maps and information about the waterway to be traveled. Know exactly where the unit will "put in" and "pull out" and what course will be followed. Travel time should be estimated generously. Review plan with others who have traveled the course recently.
   Local Rules. Determine which state and local regulations are applicable, and follow them. Get written permission to use or cross private property.
   Notification. File the float plan with parents of participants and a member of the troop committee. File float plan with council office when traveling on running water. Check in with all those notified when returning.
   Weather. Check the weather forecast just before setting out and keep an alert weather eye. Bring all craft ashore when rough weather threatens.
   Contingencies. Planning must identify possible emergencies and other circumstances that may force a change of plans. Appropriate alternative plans must be developed for each.

8. **Equipment.** All equipment must be appropriate for the craft, water conditions, and the participants, and must be in good repair. Spare equipment or repair materials must be carried. All equipment must certify state and federal regulations.

9. **Discipline.** All participants should know, understand, and respect the rules and procedures for a safe activity afloat. Rules for safety do not interfere with fun when fairly applied.

NOTE: For large boat (26 feet or longer) operations, standards, and procedures as outlined in the *Safe Boating Instructor's Guide,* No. 6662, and the *Advanced Seamanship Instructor's Guide,* No. 6660, may be substituted for Safety Afloat standards.

Wilderness Use Policy

In this policy statement the term "Wilderness Areas" includes all private or publicly owned backcountry lands. Many troops and posts enjoy the vast wilderness and backcountry areas across America each year. Studies indicate the need for an immediate reduction in the overall number using specific wilderness areas and in the numbers in each individual group. Large groups (more than 11) wear out campsites and tend to destroy solitude with excessive noise.

The Boy Scouts of America recommends the following practices to all troops and posts using wilderness or backcountry areas:

- Limit the size of groups generally to no more than 8 to 11 persons, including at least one adult leader (maximum: 10 persons per leader).

- Organize each group (patrol or crew) to function independently by planning their own trips on different dates, serving their own food, providing their own transportation to trailhead, securing permits, and camping in a separate and distinct group.

- When necessary to combine transportation and planning or buying, small groups should still camp and travel on the trail separately from other groups of the same unit.

- Use chemical backpacking stoves, particularly where fuel supply is limited or open fires are restricted.

- Contact authorities of area well in advance of trip to learn and comply with permit requirements and regulations.

- Stress proper wilderness behavior in pretrip training.

- Emphasize the need for preserving solitude and minimizing group impact through proper camping practices.

- Develop a unit environmental ethic. Practice it everywhere the unit goes.

- Match the ruggedness of high adventure experiences to the physical ability and maturity of those taking part.

- Write High Adventure, BSA, for cave-exploring policy.

- Use biodegradable (not metal or glass) or plastic food containers. Carry out unavoidable trash of your own and that left by others.

- Dig holes only for latrines—cover them completely before leaving.

Liquid-Fuel Policy

Each council has the option to permit or prohibit use of liquid fuels for Scouting functions. If the council approves the use of liquid fuels (including white gasoline, propane, butane, kerosine, and related petroleum products), such use must be limited to occasions when knowledgeable adult supervision is given. Knowledgeable means that the adult must have had previous training or experience in using the equipment with that particular fuel. Scouts must be carefully shown how to operate the equipment (including lighting, refueling, extinguishing, and packing) and advised on precautions that must be taken to avoid hazards, before they are permitted to operate the equipment with the adult present.

No Flames in Tents
Flammability Warning—
Camping Safety Rules

NO TENT MATERIAL IS FIREPROOF, AND ALL OF THEM CAN BURN WHEN EXPOSED TO HEAT OR FIRE. FOLLOW THESE RULES.

- Only flashlights and electric lanterns are permitted in tents. NO FLAMES IN TENTS is a rule which must be enforced.
- Liquid-fuel stoves, heaters, lanterns, lighted candles, matches, or other flame sources should *never* be used in or near tents.
- Do not pitch tents near open fire.
- Do not use flammable chemicals near tents: charcoal lighter, spray cans of paint, bug killer, and repellent.
- Be careful when using electricity and lighting in tents.
- Always extinguish cooking and campfires properly.
- Obey all fire laws, ordinances, and regulations.

It is recommended that "No Flames in Tents'" be stenciled on the flaps of your troop's tents.

PATROL AND TROOP CAMPING EQUIPMENT

Troops with an active program and good community support often own a great deal of equipment. Most of it, of course, is used for outdoor programs and need not be stored at the troop meeting place. Other troops with active outdoor programs may rely on rented equipment for special activities.

Some equipment, of course, is not easily rented, and the troop must undertake to supply such equipment itself. A good quality tent, for example, will last 5 to 10 years if properly cared for, or it can be ruined by a single misuse.

In many troops, most equipment is owned by the troop rather than by the patrols. It is purchased with troop funds. It may be practical, however, to assign certain camping equipment to patrols and hold them responsible for it. This is particularly good if the troop has no central storage facility.

To simplify matters, we will consider that all important equipment is bought by the troop. Whether or not any or all of it is assigned to patrols does not affect the points made.

Acquiring Equipment

In general it is best to buy good quality equipment. Although the price is low, bargains seldom turn out to be that. Cheap merchandise often turns out to be unsuitable for Scout use, or it may not be durable.

An example of this is found in buying tents. You might be able to buy Army wall tents at a fraction of their retail value. They are sturdy and will outlast most other tents, even higher priced ones. But they are made to be transported in trucks and not on Scouts' backs. A backpacking experience requires lighter weight tents. The other extreme is buying inexpensive "bargain" tentage and finding that it will not withstand even moderate use. You will find equipment of the national Supply Division of the Boy Scouts of America to be of good quality and designed for Scout use.

Some troops make some of their own equipment. In this way they have exactly what they need at costs far less than buying commercially available equipment. Tents, grills, tarps, and other items can be made by or for the troop.

Before you buy new equipment, you need to consider:

• Is it suitable for the use intended?

- Where will it be stored?
- Are there any hidden costs (such as stakes and poles for tents or a trailer to haul the canoes)?
- How long can it be expected to last?
- Should it be insured against fire, theft, etc.?
- Is it safe for Scouts' use?
- What training is required for those who will use it?

Maintaining Equipment

1. Label every piece of troop equipment prominently with the troop number. Paint it on canvas. Ink it on flags and books. Burn it on wood. Scratch it on metal. Some units color-code their equipment by painting or labeling all items with strips of the same color.

2. Keep a complete inventory of all troop equipment. Add to it whenever a new piece is acquired. Subtract from it at least twice a year by taking a complete inventory of all equipment and removing items that are no longer usable.

3. Store the equipment in a place that can be locked. Provide keys only to a few persons, such as quartermaster, Scoutmaster, and one troop committee member. Never allow anyone else to rummage through equipment.

4. Persuade your senior patrol leader to appoint as quartermaster a highly organized Scout who will take personal pride in keeping equipment in good order. Give that Scout total responsibility.

5. Have the quartermaster establish a check-in/check-out system for equipment. Be sure he serves as a support service for the patrols and the program.

6. Encourage your Scouts to take pride in their equipment and to take responsibility for keeping it in good condition. Have a last-minute inspection of all campsites before leaving to determine—among other things—whether any equipment has been left behind. Encourage Scouts to report loss or damage of equipment so it can be replaced or repaired promptly.

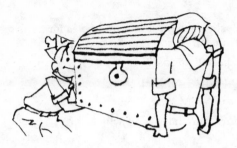

Stick to the basics, don't go with the frills.

BASIC TROOP EQUIPMENT

The equipment your troop needs is, of course, based on its program. At the same time, recognize that the equipment a troop owns helps to determine its program. Plan your purchases so as to expand types of outdoor activities your troop can do.

For Scoutcraft Instruction and Practice

- 6-foot ropes, ends whipped or burned (for nylon), ¼ inch or larger in diameter
- Whipping thread, heavy-duty
- Triangular bandages
- Compasses, magnetic
- Rulers
- Graph paper
- Chalkboard and chalk
- Topographic maps of your area
- Binder twine
- 15-foot ropes for lashing
- First aid kit
- Models of homemade packs, tin-can craft, tent, fly, etc.
- Slides or filmstrips of Scouting skills
- Pencils and paper supply

Flags

- Troop flag
- U.S. Flag
- Flag standards
- Flag belts (for carrying flags in parades)
- Rain covers for flags
- Flagpoles
- Flagpole emblems
- Pulleys and rope

Records and Literature

- Bulletin board
- Advancement wall chart
- Patrol records
- *Troop Record Book*, No. 6509
- *Troop Financial Record Book*, No. 6508
- *The Official Boy Scout Handbook*, No. 3227
- *The Official Scoutmaster Handbook*, No. 6501
- *Boy Scout Songbook*, No. 3224
- *The Official Patrol Leader Handbook*, No. 6512
- *Boy Scout Program Helps*
- *Fieldbook,* No. 3201
- Game books
- Troop logbook

Equipment For Camping

Camping equipment and program are closely related. The kind of camping you plan to do should influence the equipment you use. In turn, the equipment you buy or make and thus become committed to determines, in part, the program you carry out.

Tents. Whether for short-term or long-term camping or both, use two-boy tents that can be carried, set up, and taken down by Scouts. Tents should permit free circulation of air to reduce problems with condensation. Tents should be a minimum of 7 feet long by 5 feet wide. All official Scout items meet these specifications.

Since most troops do their long-term camping on council sites where tentage is either provided or rented, your concern in buying tents is probably to meet the needs of short-term camping. For a balanced program that does not restrict your troop to campsites by roads, choose tents that can be backpacked.

Every patrol should have a dining fly for cooking and serving food. For short-term camping, a 10- by 10-foot tarp usually will do.

Cooking Gear. Each patrol should have its own set, suitable for patrol cooking. Temporary cooking utensils can be made from cans.

Individual cook kits are needed only if the program involves a lot of one-man cooking.

Personal Clothing and Equipment. Your troop should make recommendations on what type of equipment to buy and what type not to. Clothing should be suitable for weather conditions. The Scout uniform is excellent for most camping.

Orientation of parents when new Scouts join should include advice about buying uniforms and equipment.

First Aid and Lifesaving Equipment. The troop should own, maintain, and carry a first aid kit for use in its outdoor program. Lifesaving equipment for water and ice sports should be made or purchased with the advice of your council officials.

Firefighting Equipment. At least minimal equipment should be bought, maintained, and on hand ready for use when the troop is in the field. Get the advice of your council and firefighting specialist as to the exact equipment to use. It will include rakes, shovels, and water and sand buckets.

Camping Equipment. This equipment is listed as the requirements for one patrol of eight. It should be adapted for different-size patrols and multiplied by the number of patrols in the troop to find the troop requirements. Equipment for leaders and Scouts not in patrols is in addition to patrol requirements.

- 1 tent for every two Scouts, many different Boy Scout models
- 1 camp shovel, No. 1269
- 1 bow saw, No. 2369 or No. 2365
- Tent poles and stakes as required
- 1 patrol flag and pole
- 1 cooking set (Trail Chef, No. 1049, or equivalent)*
- 2 plastic water basins, No. 1361*
- 2 plastic water containers, No. 1357*
- 1 plastic table cover
- 1 dining fly or tarp, No. 1424
- 1 chef's tool kit, No. 1486, or equivalent
- 1 hot-pot tongs, No. 1214
- 1 combination salt/pepper shaker, No. 1411
- 1 dishmop
- 1 dunking bag, No. 1950*
- Plastic bags for food storage
- 1 complete first aid kit, No. 8110

---

*Quantity determined by patrol size.

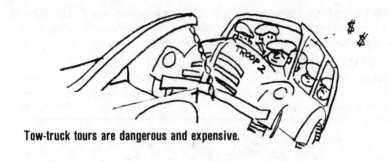

Tow-truck tours are dangerous and expensive.

Troop Vehicles

Troops may possess one or more vehicles, but ownership should rest with the chartered organization, i.e., "First Methodist Church Troop 110 Trailer." The acquisition and maintenance of a troop vehicle by the chartered organization is a major undertaking and is not recommended. Consider the following:

HIDDEN COSTS. A well-meaning person or company may offer a vehicle for nothing or next to nothing, but the annual costs of maintenance, fuel, storage, insurance, license, and registration can quickly mount to several hundred dollars or more. The troop committee must consider the potential use of such a vehicle realistically against the costs likely to be incurred.

STORAGE. A vehicle used solely to transport gear and driven only by qualified adults will not create liability questions that insurance can't handle. But any vehicle used to transport Scouts opens life-or-death questions and inevitably involves financial and moral liability in the event of injury or death. It is not easy for a troop with limited resources to maintain a passenger vehicle of any kind in top mechanical condition. Neither is it easy to justify at any time risking the lives and safety of Scouts, whether or not all legal precautions have been taken. It is better to charter buses and professional drivers on those relatively rare occasions when the troop travels by bus than to incur the responsibility entailed in bus ownership.

Transporting anyone in the bed of a truck is against Scouting policy, as well as the laws of some states. This includes camper shells and camper units that rest in the bed of a pickup. Vans and one-unit recreational vehicles are acceptable for transporting Scouts if a seat belt is provided for each passenger.

DIVERSION. Keeping a vehicle may become a fairly time-consuming matter and may divert the attention of interested adults from boy program to automotive mechanics.

PRIVATE CARS. Parents are usually willing to provide transportation in private cars. In this way they feel they are making a contribution to the program and often become interested in helping in other ways.

Behind your outdoor program are many people and resources to help you.

RESOURCES FOR OUTDOOR PROGRAMS

Many outdoor resources are available to assist Scoutmasters and troops. People, training, literature, and equipment are available to Scoutmasters who seek them out. Planning and conducting outdoor experiences for Scouts can involve lots of time and effort. The wise Scoutmaster finds ways to delegate authority to others so that his time is available for giving counsel and leadership for his Scouts as individuals and patrols, as well as for the entire troop.

People

Parents, troop committee members, the troop leadership corps, and assistant Scoutmasters can help fulfill many needs for the troop to conduct a high-quality outdoor program. District and council camping committee members may visit troop functions occasionally to see how things are going, to help the troop attend summer camp, and to offer assistance. Experienced Scoutmasters are among the best people resources for new Scoutmasters because they know the needs and the solutions to most of the questions that are asked. Roundtables provide a regular opportunity to seek help from other Scoutmasters. The council and district professional staff are also available to provide assistance. Many questions can be answered by the support staff in the local Scouting service center.

In addition to roundtables, council and district training sessions are offered for unit leaders from time to time. Wood Badge training is designed to help a Scoutmaster do a better job. If you, as Scoutmaster, need help or training, seek it out promptly rather than waiting for it to happen. Many people are delighted to help if asked.

Campmaster Corps

If your council has a campmaster corps, they may be one of your best outdoor program resources. Campmasters are Scouters who are skilled in various outdoor specialties. They serve three to five times a year by being available to assist troops on short-term camp-outs, usually conducted on council property. Campmasters supplement the Scoutmaster by offering instruction in outdoor activities where the Scoutmaster needs help to develop the outdoor skills of his Scouts. Different campmasters have different outdoor knowledge and skills so you will need to determine who can best fulfill your troop's needs.

Literature and Visuals

A wealth of outdoor-related literature and visuals is available to every Scoutmaster to help develop a high-quality outdoor program. Here is a brief synopsis of available materials.

The Official Boy Scout Handbook, No. 3227, contains the basics of outdoor knowledge and skills that every Scout should know.

The Fieldbook, No. 3201, covers advanced outdoor skills above and beyond those described in *The Official Boy Scout Handbook*.

Skill award booklets include basic outdoor skills related to specific skill award requirements.

Merit badge pamphlets—many merit badges are outdoor-related. Outdoor merit badge pamphlets thoroughly describe the knowledge and skills for specific outdoor specialties.

Look'n'do Series comes in two forms: (1) filmstrip or (2) slides with cassette tape. Fundamental outdoor skills are depicted to help new or inexperienced Scout troops quickly acquire ability in camping, hiking, cooking, first aid, and other areas. This series is one of the best outdoor education tools available to troops.

Campways Tours and Expeditions, No. 3734, describes all aspects of planning a Scout tour or a trek into remote backcountry areas, and lists literature on tours and expeditions. The Campways Service card on the back cover of the booklet may be used to obtain information on campgrounds available to Scouts.

Campways Service lists of campgrounds available to units (by states) may be obtained by writing to the Camping and Conservation Service, Boy Scouts of America, 1325 Walnut Hill Lane, Irving, TX 75038-3096.

The Official Patrol Leader Handbook, No. 6512, provides patrol leader with information about leadership skills for conducting successful outdoor experiences.

Boy Scout Program Helps is published annually in several issues of *Scouting* magazine. Many of the helps are outdoor related.

Boy Scout Leader Program Notebook is a pocket notebook distributed by *Boys' Life* that contains a monthly calendar and ideas for conducting troop meetings.

Troop Committee Guidebook, No. 6505, contains the essentials for a troop committee to effectively support outdoor programs planned by the troop leadership.

USGS topographic maps are as near as your mailbox. Write to the U.S. Geological Survey to get indexes for topographic maps for your area and information on how to order maps. For maps of states east of the Mississippi River write to Maps Information Office, U.S. Geological Survey, 1200 South Eads St., Arlington, Va. 22202. For maps of areas west of the Mississippi River write to U.S. Geological Survey, Box 25286, Federal Center, Denver, Colo. 80225.

Campways, BSA

This program:

1. Makes uniform agreements for Scout use of property controlled by the U.S. Forest Service, the National Park Service, the Army Corps of Engineers, the Fish and Wildlife Service, military installations, state parks, private landowners, and councils of the Boy Scouts of America.

2. Makes available travel information including adventures and opportunities near overnight group campsites.

3. Has information on leadership, food service, equipment, and transportation.

4. Provides a system of permits to help in planning and to control standards of operation, and

5. Provides a system by which troops may make reservations at prearranged overnight campsites anywhere in the U.S.A.— joining the camping facilities of council camps in a campways network.

When you represent Scouting, you are a special guest in the out-of-doors.

COMMUNITY RESOURCES

Your community, together with the area around it, contains more resources for your troop than you might suppose. Consider for a moment these possibilities for supporting your troop and making its program varied and interesting.

Places To Visit. Sometimes your troop can have an educational experience by seeing something in action. Does your community have:

An airport?	A historical site?
A fish hatchery?	A firehouse?
A factory or a mine?	A police station?
A museum?	A military base?
A nature center?	

Places for Outings. Your troop needs to go places and do things. Does your community have in it or near it:

An outdoor or indoor swimming pool?	An activity field?
	A supervised rifle range?
A lake or ocean front?	A riding academy?
A navigable (by rubber raft or canoe) stream or canal?	A trail system?
	A ski slope?
A public park?	A climbable mountain?

Equipment. Troops do not always have to own everything they need. Sometimes it is better to rent or borrow it. Can you in your community:

Rent skis, canoes, etc.?	Rent a car, truck or trailer?
Borrow or rent tents?	Charter a bus?
Get castoff materials from a local factory?	

Program Material. Do you have a public library? Can you copy documents there? Rent or borrow films, slides, filmstrips? Borrow records or tapes?

Is there a bookstore in town?

Is there a paid recreation director?

Is there an educational film library?

Is there a nature education center?

CAMPING AND CONSERVATION AWARDS

In addition to skill awards, badges of rank, and merit badges several other outdoor-oriented awards are available to Scouts who complete the requirements. These special awards are designated to encourage increased Scout participation in outdoor activities.

National Camping Award

To stimulate camping in troops, the Boy Scouts of America offers a certificate to troops meeting the following requirements:

1. *Patrol Activities.* Each patrol of the troop participated in at least three of the following activities during the last 12 months:

   • Attended camporee.

   • Held a day hike.

   • Did a conservation project.

   • Attended a Scout retreat.

   • Conducted a Scouting Anniversary Week outdoor project.

   • Conducted a father-and-son campout.

   • Attended an adventure trail or a klondike derby.

2. *Short-Term Camp.* All patrols in the troop were represented in four or more short-term campouts during the past 12 months.

3. *Long-Term Camp.* All patrols in the troop were represented in a long-term (6 or more consecutive days and nights) camp and at least 50 percent of the total boy membership of the troop attended.

Apply for the award through your council. A National Camping Award ribbon, No. 7758, is presented to troops on application. Use *Our Camping Log,* No. 3690, to keep your records and make application.

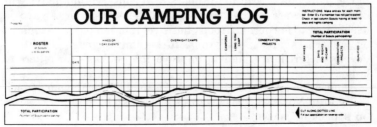

Historic Trails Award

The Boy Scouts of America has approved more than 200 historic trails throughout the nation. Each of these trails has some special historical significance. Some follow routes of Indians or early pioneers while others concentrate on historic landmarks.

Scouts who camp and hike for 2 or more days along one of these trails, who become acquainted with their historical significance, and who help restore and preserve historic features are eligible for the Historic Trails Award. Application is made through your council using form No. 4408. The Historic Trails Award is a distinctive patch that may be sewn on a pack or jacket.

When a trail meets the specifications of the Boy Scouts of America it is listed in a *Nationally Approved Historic Trails* booklet available at each council service center. This booklet contains addresses of contacts for each of the approved historic trails. Application to include a trail in this national listing is made through your council on a special form that specifies the criteria.

50-Miler Award

This award is given to Scouts who hike, canoe, or otherwise cover 50 or more miles without using motorized transportation. The trek must be at least 5 consecutive days in duration and each participant must perform 10 hours of a conservation activity or otherwise improve the environment. The 50-Miler Award is designated to encourage troops to travel into remote backcountry or wilderness areas and, thus, to become increasingly fit, to develop self-reliance, and to improve the outdoors for others to enjoy.

Application for the 50-Miler Award is made through your council using form No. 4408. This award is also a patch that may be sewn on a pack or jacket.

Hornaday Award

Hornaday Badge

Hornaday Award

The William T. Hornaday Award was initiated by the director of the New York Zoological Park and bears his name. Since its inception in 1914, this award has been highly prized. It is designated to recognize Scouts and units for exceptional and unusual Scouting service to conservation or environmental quality.

The Hornaday Award is granted in five different forms:

1. Unit certificate to a den, pack, patrol, troop, post, or a group of five or more Scouts or Explorers for unique conservation or environmental quality project.

2. Badge to a Scout or Explorer for outstanding service to conservation or environmental quality within a council.

3. Bronze Medal to a Scout or Explorer for exceptional service to conservation or environmental quality, within a council.

4. Silver Medal to a Scout or Explorer for unusual and distinguished service to conservation or environmental quality on a state or regional basis. Not more than six silver medals will be awarded each year. Applications are reviewed once a year for this award.

5. Gold Medallion to an adult Scouter or Explorer leader for unusual and distinguished service to conservation or environmental quality on a state, BSA region, or national basis. Emphasis will be, whenever possible, based on national impact.

The Hornaday Unit Certificate and the Hornaday Badge are awarded by your council. Application is made through your council.

The bronze and silver medals are awarded by the national office of the BSA upon the recommendation of the council and the Hornaday Awards Committee. This award is made only when a qualified Scout or Explorer is nominated by his or her council.

The silver medal is the highest possible attainment for a Scout or Explorer in conservation.

The gold medallion is awarded annually to one adult Scouter who is nominated by his council or by a recognized conservationist. The winner is determined by the national Hornaday Awards Committee which meets once a year for this purpose. The gold medallion is the highest conservation award for a Scouter.

The Hornaday application, No. 21-107, describes what must be accomplished to attain each award. It is available from your Scouting service center. Requirements for the bronze and silver medals generally involve several years of concentrated effort.

World
Conservation
Award

World Conservation Award

To qualify for the World Conservation Award a Scout must earn the following:

1. Environment and Conservation skill awards.

2. Environmental Science merit badge.

3. Either Soil and Water Conservation or Fish and Wildlife Management merit badge.

4. Citizenship in the World merit badge.

The purpose of this unique award is to make Scouts aware that all nations are closely related through natural resources and that we are interdependent with our world environment.

Application for the World Conservation Award is made using a special form available from your council service center. When a Scout has satisfied all requirements he is awarded a special patch, No. 140, depicting a panda bear.

Challenge

As Scoutmaster you have the ability to involve Scouts in outdoor programs that will help build their character, encourage participating citizenship, and develop their physical, mental, and emotional fitness. Camping is one of the primary tools that the Boy Scouts of America uses to achieve these goals.

Every Scout should have a long-term summer camp experience each year. Scouts often spend more time acquiring knowledge and skills in 1 week of summer camp than they do in troop meetings throughout the year. Summer camp is a highlight of a Scout's experience.

In addition to summer camp every troop should have 10 days and nights of camping during the year. Successful troops often plan an outing every month. This gives troop meetings a purpose in preparing for outdoor experiences.

Boys join the Boy Scouts of America with high expectations for camping and other outdoor activities. This becomes your challenge as Scoutmaster. Every troop needs an outdoor program that will meet, if not surpass, these high expectations of boys. Your Scouts are depending upon you for outdoor experiences that will make their lives meaningful.

You can blow the whistle on boredom.

Chapter 12

Advancement

There are six ranks along the trail to Eagle.

THE official statement of purpose of advancement in Boy Scouting is: "The Boy Scout advancement plan is designed to encourage Scouts to accomplish a progressive series of learning experiences in the areas of citizenship, character, and personal fitness objectives of the Boy Scout program. It provides for measuring and recognizing these experiences."

When a Scout reaches the age of 18, he is no longer eligible to take part in the advancement program. (See page 138 for exception.)

ADVANCEMENT AND
THE TROOP PROGRAM

Advancement is an integral part of the troop program—both indoors and out. The requirements for badges of rank and merit badges suggest hundreds of troop meeting, hike, and camp activities. As Scouts take part in these troop programs they learn skills and so are helped to advance. They don't quite automatically advance through participation, although advancement is a result of participation. Advancement is a personal and individual thing. Each boy advances according to his own interests and abilities. Each boy advances by personally demonstrating his own capability. He does not advance by being a passive participant in troop program.

Boys in a troop will be in many stages of advancement. Some will just have joined, while others might already have become First Class Scouts or Eagle Scouts. The troop may not always work on the requirements for a single skill or advancement recognition. Some boys already will have it, others won't be interested, and some will be deeply involved in working on some other phase. However, when those skills are used, the situation changes. Not all are working to earn a single recognition; all are joining together to achieve or to become good at something. Boys who have developed a skill can teach others or move to a more advanced level of the same skill.

For example, as a troop uses a skill such as cooking, some Scouts will be doing basic cooking for the Cooking skill award. Those who already have it will prepare to earn the Cooking merit badge. And, those who already have the merit badge can pass their knowledge on to the others.

Advancement Options

On completion of the joining (Boy Scout) requirements, the Scout has many options as to the directions his advancement may take.

Skill Awards. There are 12 skill awards, each built around a related group of skills or knowledge. They are designed to provide early recognition along the advancement trail and to motivate a Scout to develop skills and knowledge for everyday living, advancement in rank, full participation in Scouting, and a wide choice of things to do.

The individual tests for skill awards may be passed to troop-approved boy and adult leaders. A Scout may work on several skill awards at the same time, as he strives to qualify for an advancement in rank, keeping track of requirement completion in his *Official Boy Scout Handbook*.

When all tests for a single skill award are finished, the Scout will be presented a belt loop in recognition of his achievement. Care must be taken to be sure that Scouts understand skill awards are but stepping-stones to qualify for a badge of rank.

Merit Badges. There are more than 110 different merit badges, each related to a career, hobby, or Scouting skill. They are aimed at helping a boy discover his abilities and interests as he explores the merit badge subjects. They also help a boy become proficient in the areas of service to others and personal fitness. Merit badges demand more than skill awards. Often they have led Scouts into adult careers.

Adult merit badge counselors—recruited either by the district or the troop, and approved by the council—review and discuss the requirements for a merit badge with the Scout. On completion of the requirements an appropriate badge is presented to the Scout.

Badges of Rank. This is the advancement route leading to Eagle. There are four parts to each of the first three badges of rank (Tenderfoot, Second Class, and First Class):

1. Active participation in patrol and troop.
2. Scout spirit—living according to the ideals of Scouting.
3. Earning skill awards and merit badges (only merit badges for Star, Life, and Eagle).
4. Completion of a Scoutmaster conference.

In the case of Star, Life, and Eagle, there are two additional parts:

1. Service projects.
2. Troop leadership.

The badge of rank is presented to the successful Scout at a troop ceremony.

Guidance

Although the options in advancement are wide open to the Scout, you should guide him in his decisions. You will have a Scoutmaster conference with each Scout when he joins your troop. This is a good time to talk about the advancement program and the available options. Talk to him about his expectations, and what the troop expects of him.

In talking with him, find out what his interests are. This will help you guide him in selecting the path he will follow on the advancement trail.

Sometimes a fellow needs a friend to help him find his way.

ADVANCEMENT

Every badge of rank leads a Scout
higher up the Eagle trail.

THE FOUR STEPS
IN ADVANCEMENT

He learns. Some learning can be done on his own. He can read his *Official Boy Scout Handbook* and the merit badge pamphlets. But, most of his learning will come from others in his patrol and troop. The troop program will help. His patrol activities will be directed toward the skills he needs.

This means that one of the troop's continuing efforts will be to create learning experiences.

Every troop hike, camping trip, and other activity offers potential learning experiences. Scouts learn to pitch tents by pitching them, to use a compass by finding directions, and to cook a meal by having to eat it.

Scouts can visit forest preserves, fish hatcheries, museums, airports, and government agencies as members of a troop. These experiences will provide endless chances for boys to learn in a natural way.

Learning also can be done by the group method. Groups can be formed to learn citizenship skills, conservation, safety, and others.

Troops can invite outside experts to come and help them learn at meetings and other activities.

He Is Tested. The Scout is usually tested on one requirement at a time rather than taking a "final exam." He may pass tests over a period of several weeks on a single skill award or merit badge.

The language of the requirement determines the kind of testing. If it says *describe, tell,* or *explain*, words alone will suffice. No demonstration of the skill is required. If it says *show, demonstrate,* or *identify*, the Scout must do just that. *Telling* is not enough. He must do it.

These are the officers who may test Scouts.

For skill award requirements, all of the following may test Scouts:

Patrol leaders.

Webelos den chief.

Other qualified boy leaders.

Leadership corps members.

Instructors.

Scoutmaster and assistant Scoutmasters.

Troop committee members.

Specific people within the above groups should be named, and the subjects in which they are qualified should be stated. No blanket approval should be given to any group to examine in all requirements. There could be unqualified people in the group.

Merit badges may be tested only by qualified merit badge counselors approved by your council. Most districts publish the names and addresses of counselors available to Scouts in the district. To supplement the district counselor list, the troop may develop its own list of counselors. These should have council approval.

A smooth-running advancement program depends on a readily available up-to-date list of merit badge counselors and trained in-troop personnel to test skill awards.

He Is Reviewed. The board of review for Tenderfoot, Second Class, and First Class is conducted by the patrol leaders' council. A member of the troop committee will sit with this group as an adviser.

ADVANCEMENT

The boards of review for Star and Life are conducted by three or more members of the troop committee. The Boy Scouts of America has placed the Eagle Scout board of review in the hands of the troop committee or district or council committee responsible for advancement. The council will decide which method(s) may be used.

The review process is followed only for badges of rank. Skill awards and merit badges are not reviewed before they are presented, but the work done in earning them may be reviewed at the board of review.

The purpose of the review is to make sure that all requirements have been met. This means a check of both the technical skills and the Scout's attitude and practice of the ideals of Scouting. Care must be taken that the review does not become a reexamination. Spot checking is all that need be done.

Scouts are reviewed individually. At the end of the review, the Scout is dismissed while the review members discuss whether he is qualified. They call the Scout back to let him know whether he is qualified to receive the award. If he is not, the review team members tell him what he must do to gain approval. The review is the final approval needed for all badges of rank except Eagle. The Eagle application also must be approved by the your district, council, and the national office.

The Scoutmaster and assistant Scoutmasters do not sit on the review group for any of the badges of rank. However, the Scoutmaster usually discusses the qualifications of the candidates with review members before the review. He also introduces the Scout who is being reviewed to the members of the adult board of review and may be called on to clarify a point.

A Scout should be in as complete a uniform as he owns when reviewed.

A report of the review is filed with your council, where it becomes part of the advancement record of the troop.

He Gets the Badge. At the close of the next troop meeting following a review, Scouts approved for a badge of rank are given their badges in a brief ceremony before the whole troop. (An exception is Eagle, which must be approved by the local council and national office before presentation.)

Most troops also have courts of honor or other events such as open houses, parents' nights, etc., when they recognize every Scout who advanced since the last such event. They also use this opportunity to recognize Scouts who have been elected to office or have otherwise distinguished themselves. While the badges were presented earlier at a troop meeting, the certificates can be presented at this formal court of honor.

Explorer Advancement

An Explorer who has attained First Class in a Boy Scout troop may continue the advancement program and become an Eagle Scout by meeting the requirements as prescribed in *The Official Boy Scout Handbook*. Requirements for tenure may be met as a registered Explorer. Leadership requirements may be met in the post as president, vice-president, secretary, or treasurer. The Scoutmaster conferences will be conducted by his post Advisor. The board of review shall be by his post committee.

Webelos Scout Advancement

The Cub Scout program has an advancement plan similar to the Scout advancement plan. To earn the Arrow of Light Award, the highest Cub Scout award, some of the requirements involve visiting a troop meeting, taking a hike or camp, and participating in a Scout-oriented outdoor activity. Just as Scouts become frustrated when they can't find merit badge counselors, Webelos Scouts become frustrated when there is not a troop to help them meet their requirements for advancement

Other portions of Webelos Scout advancement involve activity badges, which involve skills similar to skill awards and merit badges. When a Webelos Scout joins your troop, find out which activity badges he has earned and what the requirements are. This can help you guide the new Scout as he starts the Boy Scout advancement plan.

Aquanaut   Artist   Athlete   Citizen   Craftsman

Engineer   Forester   Geologist   Naturalist   Outdoorsman

Scholar   Scientist   Showman   Sportsman   Traveler

JOINING REQUIREMENTS

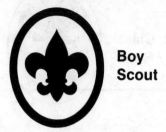

Boy Scout

1. Complete fifth grade and be at least 10½ years old.

OR

Be 11 years old or older, but not 18 years old.

2. Understand and intend to live by the Scout Oath or Promise, Scout Law, Scout motto, Scout slogan, and Outdoor Code.
3. Know the Scout sign, Scout salute, and handclasp and when to use them.
4. Understand the significance of the Scout badge.
5. Take part in a Scoutmaster conference.

ADVANCEMENT REQUIREMENTS
(with comments in italics)

Tenderfoot Rank

1. Be active in your troop and patrol for at least 2 months.

   "Active" means more than just attendance. It means taking part actively in troop and patrol meetings, camps, and service projects.

2. Scout spirit: Repeat from memory the Scout Oath or Promise and Law. Explain the meaning of each point of the Law in your own words. Demonstrate that you have practiced these ideas in everyday life.

   "Repeat from memory" refers to the Scout Oath or Promise and the Law. Under the title to each point of the Law in The Official Boy Scout Handbook *is a statement of interpretation in bold type. The Scout does not need to memorize these statements.*

3. Earn Citizenship and one other skill award.
4. Take part in a Scoutmaster conference.

Second Class Rank

1. Be active in your troop and patrol for at least 2 months as a Tenderfoot Scout.

   The time period starts the day of his successful board of review for his previous award. This rule is followed for each rank.

2. Show Scout spirit.

   "Scout spirit" primarily means living according to the ideals of the Scout Oath or Promise and the Scout Law. It is the intent of this requirement, which is included in each rank, that a Scout should do his best and also show improvement as he moves from one rank to the next.

3. Earn Hiking, First Aid, and one other skill award (so that you have five in all).

4. Take part in a Scoutmaster conference.

First Class Rank

1. Be active in your troop and patrol for at least 2 months as a Second Class Scout.

2. Show Scout spirit.

3. Earn Camping, Cooking, and one other skill award (so that you have eight in all).

4. Earn First Aid merit badge.

5. Swimming. Tell what precautions must be taken for a safe swim. Jump feetfirst into water over your head in depth. Swim 50 m (or 50 yd.). During the swim, stop, make a sharp turn, level off, and resume swimming.

   This requirement may be waived by the troop committee for medical or safety reasons.

6. Take part in a Scoutmaster conference.

Star Rank

1. Be active in your troop and patrol for at least 4 months as a First Class Scout.

2. Show Scout spirit.

3. Earn five more merit badges (so that you have six in all), including *any* three more from the required list for Eagle.

   There are 14 merit badges on the required list for Eagle. First Aid was earned for First Class rank. Any of the remaining 13 may be used to meet this requirement for Star and Life ranks. For the Eagle rank, 11 are specified.

4. While a First Class Scout, take part in service projects totaling at least 6 hours of work. These projects must be approved by your Scoutmaster.

   Service projects shall be meaningful service not normally expected of a boy as a part of his school or religious activities. The work may be done by the Scout alone, with other Scouts, his patrol, or the troop. The service should not be part of a project which the Scout is already doing outside of Scouting. The idea is to get a Scout to do things not normally expected of him as a troop member or as a member of his family. He should be reaching out for new ways to help others. Star and Life service projects may be approved for Scouts assisting on Eagle service projects.

5. While a First Class Scout, serve actively for 4 months in one or more of the following positions (or carry out a Scoutmaster-assigned leadership project to help the troop): patrol leader, senior patrol leader, assistant senior patrol leader; den chief; scribe, librarian, historian, quartermaster, bugler, chaplain aide, member of the leadership corps, instructor; junior assistant Scoutmaster.

   If the Scout meets this requirement by carrying out a Scoutmaster-assigned project to help the troop, such a project shall be at least equal in difficulty to comparable service in one of the leadership positions.

6. Take part in a Scoutmaster conference.

**Life
Rank**

1. Be active in your troop and patrol for at least 6 months as a Star Scout.

2. Show Scout spirit.

3. Earn five more merit badges (so that you have 11 in ell), including any tlvee move from the required list for Eagle.

4. While a Star Scout, take part in service projects totaling at least 6 hours of work. These projects must be approved by your Scoutmaster.

5. While a Star Scout, serve actively for 6 months in one or more of the leadership positions listed in requirement 5 for Star Scout (or carry out a Scoutmaster-assigned leadership project to help the troop).

6. Take part in a Scoutmaster conference.

**Eagle
Rank**

1. Be active in your troop and patrol for at least 6 months as a Life Scout.

2. Show Scout spirit.

3. Earn a total of 21 merit badges (10 more than you already have), including the following: (a) First Aid, (b) Citizenship in the Community, (c) Citizenship in the Nation, (d) Citizenship in the World, (e) Communications, (f) Safety, (g) Emergency Preparedness OR Lifesaving, (h) Environmental Science, (i) Personal Management, (j) Personal Fitness OR Swimming OR Sports, and (k) Camping.

   Only one of the merit badges may be used in items g and j. If the Scout has earned more than one in item g or j, he chooses one to meet the requirement and lists the remaining toward the total of 21.

   NOTE: If you have a permanent physical or mental disability you may become an Eagle Scout by qualifying for as many required merit badges as you can and qualifying for alternate merit badges for the rest. If you seek to become an Eagle under this procedure, you must submit a special application to your council service center. Your application must be approved by your council committee for advancement BEFORE YOU CAN WORK ON ALTERNA-TIVE MERIT BADGES. (See page 139.)

4. While a Life Scout, serve actively for a period of 6 months in one or more of the following positions: patrol leader, senior patrol leader, assistant senior patrol leader; den chief; scribe, librarian, quartermaster, member of the leadership corps, junior assistant Scoutmaster; chaplain aide; instructor.

    The interpretation is the same as for Star and Life requirement 5, except note that the Scout cannot qualify by "carrying out a Scoutmaster-assigned project," and some leadership positions do not qualify.

5. While a Life Scout, plan, develop, and give leadership to others in a service project helpful to your religious institution, school, or community. The project idea must be approved by your Scoutmaster and troop committee and reviewed by the council or district before you start.

    Key words are "plan, develop, and give leadership to others." A greater degree of leadership is shown when the "others" that are given leadership are from outside the Scout's own troop. For Star and Life service, the Scout could be a follower. For Eagle, he must be a leader. The project need not be original, but the Scout must plan the details, organize the work and manpower, and direct the successful carrying out of the project. The total time involvement must be considerably more than is required for Star and Life service. Time is not spelled out because in this case the planning time might be more than the working time. The project must be meaningful and be of value when successfully completed. Two Scouts working for Eagle cannot both receive credit for the same project by working together. Projects which benefit any part of the Boy Scouts of America's program are not acceptable.

6. Take part in a Scoutmaster conference.

 **Eagle Palms**

After becoming an Eagle Scout, you may earn palms by completing the following requirements:

1. Be active in your troop and patrol for at least 3 months after becoming an Eagle Scout or after award of last palm.

2. Show Scout spirit.

3. Make a satisfactory effort to develop and demonstrate leadership ability.

4. Earn five additional merit badges beyond those required for Eagle or last palm.

    These merit badges may have been earned anytime since joining.

5. Take part in a Scoutmaster conference.

You may wear only the proper combination of palms for the number of merit badges you earn beyond Eagle. The Bronze Palm represents 5 merit badges; Gold 10; and Silver 15. For example, if you earn 10 merit badges and two palms, you would wear only the Gold Palm. If you earn 20 merit badges and four palms, you would wear a Silver and a Bronze Palm.

Camping
Skill Award

1. Present yourself to your leader, properly dressed, before going on an overnight camping trip.
   Show the camping gear you will use, including shelter and food. Explain how you will use the gear.
   Show the right way to pack and carry it.
2. Go on two overnight camping trips with your troop, patrol, or other Scouts, using the gear.
   On each overnight camp, do the following:
   a. Carry the gear on your back for at least 2 km (1¼ mi.) to your camp. After camping, carry it 2 km (1¼ mi.) back.
   b. Pick a good place for a tent.
      Pitch a tent correctly in the place you picked and sleep in it overnight. Store the tent correctly after use.
   c. Make a bed on the ground. Sleep on it overnight.
   d. Follow good health, sanitation, and safety practices. Leave a clean camp.
   e. After each trip, tell your leader what you achieved and learned. Tell how good camping practices proved useful.
3. a. Whip the ends of a rope.
   b. Tie the following knots: square knot, sheet bend, two half hitches, clove hitch, taut-line hitch, bowline. Show their correct use.
4. a. Lash poles together with the following lashings: square, shear, and diagonal lashings. Show their correct use.
   b. Use lashing for making a simple useful camp gadget.

NOTE: If you use a wheelchair, crutches, or if it is difficult for you to get around, you may substitute "transport the gear" for "carry the gear on your back" in requirement 2a. You must travel under your own power.

Citizenship
Skill Award

1. a. Describe the flag of the United States. Give a short history of it.
   b. Explain why you should respect your country's flag.
      Tell which special days you should fly it in your state.
   c. Using a flag and with another Scout helping you, show how to hoist and lower the flag, how to hang it horizontally and vertically on a wall, and how to fold it.

d. Tell when to salute the flag and show how to do it.

2. a. Repeat from memory the Pledge of Allegiance. Explain its meaning in your own words.
   Lead your patrol and troop in the proper ceremony of reciting the pledge.
   b. Tell about the meaning of our National Anthem and how it was written.

3. a. Explain the rights and duties of a citizen of the United States.
   b. Tell about two things you have done that will help law-enforcement agencies.
   c. Explain what a citizen should do to save our resources.

4. Do one of the following:
   a. Visit a community leader. Learn about the duties of the job or office. Tell your patrol or troop what you have learned.
   b. Learn something about a famous U.S. person of your own choosing. Tell your reasons for picking that person and give a short report of what that person did to gain this recognition.
   c. Make a list of 10 things, places, or sayings that have some relationship to the history of the United States. Explain their meaning.
   d. Know the history and tradition of your state, commonwealth, or territorial flag.

Communications Skill Award

1. Do the following:
   a. Make a phone call correctly and answer properly.
   b. Show how to make an emergency phone call. Put these emergency phone numbers near your home phone.
   c. Do two of these:
      (1) Introduce a guest.
      (2) Make an announcement.
      (3) Tell of some special past event.

2. Teach a Scout skill to two or more Scouts.

3. Get a message to others without speaking or writing using two of these:
   a. Silent Scout signals.
   b. Manual alphabet.
   c. Sign language for the deaf.
   d. Indian sign language.
   e. Sports signals.
   f. Morse code.
   g. Semaphore code.
   h. Scout trail signs.

4. Tell how to get to a place selected by your leader. (It must be 1 km [0.6 mi.] away and not in a straight line.) Use speaking, writing, and sketches.

5. Take part in or plan an emergency mobilization for your patrol or troop.

6. Know five emergency distress signals.

Community Living Skill Award

1. Explain what is meant by the terms: public utility, public service, government, community problems, community organization, volunteer or private agency, government agency, ethnic group, tradition, resources, crime resistance.

2. Do three:
   a. Make a list of five organizations working in your community. Visit one. Tell what it does.
   b. List five activities that take place in your community during a month. Explain the reason for each. Take part in one. Tell what you did.
   c. Make a list of five community problems. Explain how each affects you, your family, and the community.
   d. Tell some of the history, traditions, contributions, and ways of living of two ethnic groups in your community.
   e. Visit your police department. Find out what you can do to help reduce the likelihood of crime in your home and neighborhood. Tell about your visit.
   f. Take part in a service project that will help a volunteer or private agency in your community. Tell what you did.

3. Describe two public services. Visit a place that provides one of these services. Tell about your visit.

4. Show that you know how to get around using a map or transportation schedule.

NOTE: "Community" is the place where you live.

Conservation Skill Award

1. Show by what you do that you follow the Outdoor Code when you are in the outdoors.

2. a. Explain the main causes and effects of water pollution. Tell how we can have clean water.
   b. Explain the main causes and effects of air pollution. Tell how we can have clean air.

3. a. Make a list of present major sources of energy and the major alternate sources.
   b. Make a list of 10 ways in which you and your family can save energy.

4. a. Take a walk around where you live for 2 hours and make two lists related to conservation:
      List things that please you.
      List things you feel should be improved.
   b. Plan and carry out your own conservation project. Get it approved by your patrol leader before you start.

5. Take part in one of these projects with your patrol or another Scout:
   a. Clean up a roadside, picnic ground, vacant lot, stream, lake shore, or ocean beach.
   b. Work on erosion control of stream bank, gully, or trail.
   c. Plant trees, do forest improvement or insect control.
   d. Improve backyard or other wildlife habitat.
   e. Help with energy conservation.

Cooking Skill Award

1. Show you know how to buy food by doing the following:
   a. Plan a balanced menu for three meals—breakfast, lunch, and supper.
   b. Make a food list based on your plan for a patrol of eight Scouts.
   c. Visit a grocery store and price your food list.
   d. Figure out what the cost for each Scout would be.

2. Sharpen a knife and an ax properly and give rules for their safe use.

3. Use a knife, ax, and saw correctly to prepare tinder, kindling, and firewood.

4. a. Locate and prepare a suitable fire site.
   b. Build and light a cooking fire using not more than two matches.

5. a. In the outdoors, cook, without utensils, a simple meal. Use raw meat (or fish or poultry) and at least one raw vegetable, and bread (twist or ashbread).
   b. In the outdoors, prepare, from raw, dried, or dehydrated food, for yourself and two others:
      (1) A complete breakfast of fruit, hot cooked cereal, hot beverage, and meat and eggs (or pancakes), and
      (2) A complete dinner or supper of meat (or fish or poultry), at least one vegetable, dessert, and bread (biscuit or bannock).

6. After each cooking, properly dispose of garbage, clean utensils, and leave a clean cooking area.

NOTE: When laws do not let you do some of these tests, they may be changed by your Scoutmaster to meet the laws.

Environment Skill Award

1. a. Tell what is meant by environment.
   b. Describe how plant life, animal life, and environment relate to each other.
   c. Explain the oxygen cycle.
   d. Explain the water cycle

2. Tell how sun, air, water, soil, minerals, plants, and animals produce food used by man.

3. a. Make a 3-hour exploration of a forest, field, park, wetland, lake shore, ocean shore, or desert. Make a list of plants and animal life you recognize.
   b. In the outdoors, spot and name 10 wild animals by sight or sign (mammals, birds, fish, reptiles, mollusks).
   c. In the outdoors, spot and name 10 wild plants.
   d. Know how to identify poison ivy, poison oak, and poison sumac.

4. Do one:
   a. Study a plot of ground, 1 m² (10 sq. ft.). Report on the plants and animals you find.
   b. Make a closed terrarium that includes animals. OR make an aquarium that includes both plants and animals.
   c. Keep a daily weather record for at least 2 weeks. Tell how weather affects the environment.

5. Display at least six newspaper or magazine clippings on environment problems.

Family Living Skill Award

1. Tell what is meant by: family, duty to family, family council.

2. a. Make a chart listing the jobs you and other famliy members have at home.

b. Talk with your family about other jobs you may take on for the next 2 months.

3. Show that you can look after yourself, your family, and home. Do four of these:

   a. Inspect your home and grounds. List any dangers or lack of security seen. Tell how you corrected one.
   b. Explain why garbage and trash must be disposed of properly.
   c. Look after younger children for 3 hours. Use good health and safety practices.
   d. List some things for which your family spends money. Tell how you can help your family in money matters.
   e. Tell about what your family does for fun. Make a list of fun things your family might do at little cost. Do one of these with a member of your family.
   f. Carry out a family energy-saving plan.

4. Explain how you can get help quickly for these problems: medical; police; fire; utility; housing; serious family problem. Post a list of these directions in your home.

First Aid Skill Award

1. a. Explain what first aid is. Tell how to act in case of an accident.
   b. Tell the dangers of moving a badly injured person.
   c. Tell the best way to get medical help quickly. Show that you keep the names, addresses, and phone numbers for medical help where you can find them quickly.

2. a. Show how to treat shock.
   b. Show what to do for "hurry" cases of serious bleeding, stopped breathing, internal poisoning, heart attack.

3. Show first aid for the following cases: cuts and scratches; burns and scalds; blisters on feet; bites or stings of insects, chiggers, ticks; bites of snakes and mammals; skin poisoning; sprained ankle; object in eye; and nosebleed.

4. Explain first aid for puncture wound from splinter, nail, or fishhook.

5. Use a bandage to hold a dressing in place on the head, hand, knee, and foot.

6. Make an arm sling.

7. Tell the five most common signs of heart attack. Tell what action you should take.

Hiking
Skill Award

1. Tell how to take a safe hike:
   a. Cross-country, day and night.
   b. Along a highway, day and night.

2. a. Tell how to keep from getting lost.
   b. Tell what to do if you are lost.

3. a. On a map, point out 10 different symbols, including contour lines. Tell what they represent.
   b. Orient a map.
   c. Point out on a map where you are.

4. a. Show how a compass works.
   b. Give its eight principal points.

5. a. Show how to use a compass and map together.
   b. Using a compass and map together, follow a route you marked on the map far enough to show you know how.

6. Take a hike in the field.*
   a. Before leaving, have your plan approved by your leader, including purpose, route, and clothing.
   b. Take an 8 km (5-mi.) hike in the field with your troop, patrol, or two or more other Scouts. Wear the right clothing. Take the right equipment. Follow good hike rules.

7. Take a hike in your town.*
   a. Before leaving, have your plan approved by your leader, including purpose, route, and clothing.
   b. Take an 8 km (5-mi.) hike in a place of interest outside your neighborhood with your troop, patrol, an adult, or two or more other Scouts. Wear the right clothing. Take the right equipment. Follow good hike rules.
   c. After you get back, tell what you did and learned.

NOTE: If you use a wheelchair, crutches, or if it is difficult for you to get around, you may substitute "trip" for "hike" in requirements 1 and 7, and "trip to a specific objective" for "hike in the field" in requirement 6. You must travel under your own power.

*The hikes for requirements 6 and 7 must be taken on separate days.

Physical
Fitness
Skill Award

1. a. Show that within the past year you have had a health examination by a doctor licensed to practice medicine.
   If the doctor told you some things to do, tell what you are doing about one of them.
   b. Show that you have had a dental examination within the past year.

2. a. Record your best in the following tests: _____ push-ups; _____ pull-ups; _____ sit-ups; standing long jump _____ m _____ cm;
   run walk _____ mins. _____ secs.
   b. Set goals to do better.
   c. Keep a record of how you are doing for 30 days.

3. a. List the four groups of basic foods needed in the daily diet of a boy your age.
   b. Tell how this diet helps your body.

4. a. Satisfy your adult leader that you have good daily health habits.
   b. Tell how the use of tobacco, alcohol, and drugs can hurt your health.

Swimming
Skill Award

1. a. Tell what must be done for a safe swim with your patrol, troop, family, or other group.
   b. Tell the reasons for the buddy system.

2. Jump feetfirst into water over your head. Swim 100 m (or 100 yd.), with at least one change of direction. For the first 75 m (or 75 yd.) use any stroke. For the last 25 m (or 25 yd.), use the elementary backstroke. Right after the swim, stay in the water and float for a minute with as little motion as possible.

3. Water rescues:
   a. Show reaching.
   b. Show throwing.
   c. Describe going with support.

4. Show rescue breathing.

Required badges for Eagle have silver borders:
all others have green borders.

THE MERIT BADGE PROGRAM

The purpose of the merit badge program is to provide the following:

1. Opportunities for Scouts to plan and carry out projects toward their own growth and development.

2. Chances for Scouts to learn about a wide variety of interesting subjects.

3. Orientation in these fields to serve as a springboard to further interest.

4. Help to the Scout in discovering his talents and abilities.

5. Useful skills in many subjects leading to capable, confident, participating citizenship.

6. Involvement in activities of great interest.

The merit badge plan is open to all Scouts, including those who just joined. A Scout may earn any merit badge at any time.

Procedure

When a Scout is interested in working on a particular merit badge, you provide him with a signed merit badge application and the name of a counselor. You sign the application to show the counselor that you approve of the Scout working on this badge.

The Scout contacts the counselor and makes an appointment. He has as many visits with the counselor as necessary to learn the skills and pass the tests. When the counselor is satisfied that the Scout has met the requirements, the application is signed and the Scout brings it to you. You have it recorded in the troop records and list it on the Advancement Report, which you send to the local council service center. At the same time, you order the badge, which is *presented at the next troop meeting.*

It is important that all advancement standards be maintained. Awards become meaningless if Scouts do not have to meet specific standards. Your leadership can control standards within the troop. If in questioning the Scout about earning the merit badge you find that certain merit badge counselors are failing to require Scouts to meet the standards, you can withhold awarding it. You must notify the troop committee member responsible for merit badge counselors or the district committee that recruits, trains, and supervises merit badge counselors.

Chapter 13

Training Junior Leaders

The badge doesn't make the leader, training does.

ONE of your most important jobs as Scoutmaster will be to see that your troop's junior leaders are successful in their jobs. The fact that a Scout is selected as senior patrol leader, patrol leader, scribe, or any other position means he will need some training. That's something that you and your assistants should consider as a top priority.

When a boy leader knows what is expected of him, he is more likely to succeed. If he learns some simple techniques of leadership, his fellow Scouts should respond to him. The result is a better patrol or troop and a group of happier Scouts.

Recognition. The trained leader emblem, No. 280, may be worn by a junior leader who has completed the operations workshop for the position he currently holds.

INTRODUCTION TO LEADERSHIP

As soon as a Scout gets a new leadership job in your troop, you should try to sit down with him and talk about it. He will likely feel honored at being chosen but may not understand that responsibility goes with the job. The following outline will help you get a new junior leader started on his way to success. It is designed for patrol leaders, but may be adapted for other offices.

LEARNING OBJECTIVES: At the end of this session, each patrol leader should be able to:

- State the duties of a patrol leader.
- Describe in his own words the promises Scouting makes to each Scout.
- State how to help build patrol spirit.
- Describe the eight points of the Baden-Powell patrol.
- Identify the element of attitude in solving problems.
- State some of the things that must be done in order to get along with others.
- Explain how the patrol leaders' council works.
- Plan and conduct a successful patrol meeting.

MATERIALS NEEDED:

- Your own copy of *The Official Scoutmaster Handbook.*
- Copies of *The Official Patrol Leader Handbook* for each person present.
- Paper and pencils for note taking.
- Copies of *The Official Boy Scout Handbook* for each person present.

Method	Personal coaching for not more than two or three boys. The suggested location is the home of the Scoutmaster or one of the boys.
Welcome to Scouting's Toughest Job	Tell the new patrol leader(s) that you are happy to have him as a new patrol leader. Give him a copy of *The Official Patrol Leader Handbook.* Tell him it is his to keep. The purpose of this visit is to review some of the things in the book that will help him do his job. Tell him that you want him to succeed as a patrol leader, and that what you cover will help him understand what to do and how to do it.
Duties to the Patrol	Now, turn to the inside cover of the *Patrol Leader Handbook.* Read aloud The Patrol Leader's Code. It is a good idea to have this typed on a 3x5 card

beforehand so you may give each patrol leader a copy to keep and study. If not, suggest that he write it on the notepaper you have furnished. Tell him that you will explain each point before the introduction is finished.

The Promises of Scouting

Ask him to open his *Patrol Leader Handbook* to page 4. Read aloud the message from the Chief Scout Executive. Now review in your own words the information on pages 6-7. On page 8 read the paragraph that begins, "Open your *(Boy Scout) Handbook....*" When you have read this, give out a loan copy of *The Official Boy Scout Handbook* and ask him to turn to page 9 in that book. Ask the Scout to read this page aloud.

If more than one patrol leader is present you may wish to alternate paragraphs. When they have finished the reading ask them to tell you what it means to them. Discuss this as necessary. Now go back to the *Patrol Leader Handbook* and review the rest of the material on pages 8 and 9.

Building Patrol Spirit

Review pages 10-11. Give particular emphasis to the section on Together and Planning. Discuss patrol flags (page 12) and slides, yells, songs, etc. (page 13).

The Baden-Powell Patrol

Ask the patrol leaders to turn to page 15. Review the information on the Baden-Powell patrol. Continue on pages 16-21 to discuss each of the eight points covered. Answer questions as they arise. Encourage discussion.

Problem Solving

Discuss the information on attitude, pages 22 and 23. Stress the fact that the patrol will mirror the attitude of its leader. Ask the patrol leader to tell you what he thinks the last paragraph on page 23 means. This has sometimes been referred to as the "Power of positive thinking!"

Getting Along With Others

Remind the patrol leader that one of the 12 points of the Scout Law is: A Scout is friendly! Talk about the ideas on page 24. Stress the magic words "please" and "thanks" (page 25). Continue to discuss each major topic thorough page 34. Remember, however: Don't preach. Give the Scout plenty of time to ask questions or take notes. This is important material. Each boy must absorb it at his own pace. But he must understand it to be a successful patrol leader.

The Patrol Leaders' Council

Have him turn to page 35 in the *Patrol Leader Handbook*. Ask what the illustration at the top of the page means. Discuss the relationship between the patrol and the troop. Talk about the patrol leaders' council (page 36 through the top of page 42).

Successful Patrol Meetings

Turn to page 58. Discuss the where, when, what, and how of successful patrol meetings. Look at the patrol meeting clock on page 61. Ask why this is important. Talk about the three "C's" and "P's." Now turn to pages 62-71 and show how these six elements—ceremony, checking, coaching, projects, plans, and play—are used in each successful patrol meeting.

Close your introductory session after you have discussed the importance of closing ceremonies. Tell the new patrol leader how pleased you are to have him as a junior leader in the troop. Welcome him again as an important member of the patrol leaders' council. Give him the date, time, and location of the next meeting. Tell him you look forward to seeing him there.

If the meeting has been in the patrol leader's home, say a few words to the parents before leaving. If it has been in your home, have some light refreshments and a brief fellowship period.

There are many additional training opportunities for you and your junior leaders. Let's take a look at two of them.

Junior Leader Orientation Workshop

The Junior Leader Orientation Workshop, No. 6520, is a 1-day event usually a responsibility of the district training committee. It may involve the total district or a group of neighboring troops. It is conducted by key boy leaders of participating troops. Each Scoutmaster and his troop's junior leaders are invited to attend as a group so that leaders and boys get the same information.

The workshop will explore some of the functions of leadership which the junior leaders will learn and put into practice. Those with similar troop jobs will meet in small groups to discuss the duties of their office and how to carry them out. Finally, time is scheduled for the Scoutmaster and his boy leaders to meet and plan their troop junior leader training program.

Troop Operations Workshop

The junior leader orientation workshop will give your boy leaders a good overview of their jobs. Now it's time to get into the details of your own troop and how to make it succeed. The troop operations workshop is designed to guide you through the training of your own patrol leaders and other selected junior leaders.

As Scoutmaster, you will want to give your personal leadership to this training. Your assistant Scoutmasters, members of the troop committee, and outside consultants can help. This gives the Scouts a chance to work with several adults and makes the training more lively and interesting. Be careful, however, not to overpower the junior leaders with too many adults.

Planning the Training

Select a location. The secret of a good junior leader training program is to make it a new experience for the Scouts. It is a get-together of the Scoutmaster and his leadership team, so it should be limited to the patrol leaders' council and other selected troop officers. The location should be away from the troop's normal area of activity. Check with parents, committee members, and folks from the chartered organization for a vacation cabin, hunting lodge, or other hideaway. Consider church camps, youth camps, or similar locations with indoor facilities. The training can be conducted as part of a special junior leader camping trip but the extra effort required for outdoor cooking and tent living can detract from the real purpose of the program. Housekeeping should be easy.

Select a Date. The outline that follows is laid out for a Friday evening and all day Saturday, with an optional Sunday program. This is not necessarily a recommendation to choose these days. Take care to see that the junior leaders are not drawn away from their religious obligations. The training outline is made up of discrete blocks of time. These sessions can be arranged to fit a variety of weekend situations.

Advance Preparation. The senior patrol leader will have a vital role to play in the workshop. Review the details with him. Be sure he knows exactly what is expected and has carefully thought through the program.

If your troop took part in the junior leader orientation workshop, much of the advance planning has been done. As leader of the patrol leaders' council, the senior patrol leader can be responsible for checking attendance and assigning the planning of meals. Appoint service and program patrols and generally organize the weekend. Each assistant Scoutmaster and other adult should have an assignment backing up the youth.

Check and double-check to be sure all of the supplies are at hand and ready for use. Your council service center can help in supplying some of the material needed.

Conducting the Training

The Objectives. Every good training program needs objectives. They help ensure that sure you will arrive where you want to go. At the end of the troop operations workshop weekend, each participant should be able to:

- List the responsibilities of his position.

- Explain the responsibility leaders have to each other, boy to boy and adult to boy.

- Explain the elements of a good troop program.

- Determine the training needs of his patrol and the troop.

- Describe how the *Look'n'do* series can be used to assist in skill award training.

- Use the available planning tools to develop a troop or patrol program.

- Explain the patrol method and how it works in a troop.

- Use the skills of leadership to assure that every Scout has a good experience as a member of the patrol and troop.

Materials Needed. The following materials are called for in the troop junior leader training outline. Make every effort to have these supplies at hand for the most effective training.

- *The Official Scoutmaster Handbook,* No. 6501, one per adult leader.

- *The Official Boy Scout Handbook,* No. 3227, each person brings his own.

- *The Official Patrol Leader Handbook,* No. 6512, one per patrol leader.

  Boy Scout Program Helps, No. 7260.

- *Boy Scout Leader Program Notebook,* No. 26-002, one per person. (If Program Notebooks are not available for all junior leaders, a small pocket notebook can substitute.)

- *Boy Scout Posters,* No. 18-915 (posted around the training room).

- *The Troop's First 6 Months,* No. 6549 (if a new troop).

- *See'n'do* Guidebook.

- *Council Planning Calendar,* No. 26-007 (If not available, substitute the Scout diary calendar or a monthly planning calendar from a local business firm).

- *Troop Planning Worksheet,* No. 26-005 or No. 7254.

- *Troop Meeting Plan,* No. 4425, 12 per patrol.

- *Boys' Life* magazine.

- *Scouting* magazine.

- Local council calendar of activities.

- Local council camp promotion and planning material.

- *Look'n'do* audiovisuals and scripts (as examples):

  Camping; No. AV-599 filmstrip, No. AV-643 slides.

  Hiking; No. AV-573 filmstrip, No. AV-631 slides.

  Cooking; No. AV-581 filmstrip, No. AV-634 slides.

  First Aid; No. AV-598 filmstrip, No. AV-636 slides.

- Slide or filmstrip projector, screen, extension cord.

- Easel pad, felt pens, masking tape for posters.

- Three-ring binder, note paper, and pencils; each person brings his own.

Presenting the Subject. The workshop should be as lively and active as you can make it. Plan about 40 minutes for each session unless otherwise noted. Some games, songs, and other activities are suggested in the outline. These help let off steam. Remember that boys learn more from seeing and doing than from listening. Keep things lighthearted and positive for the best response.

TROOP OPERATIONS WORKSHOP OUTLINE

FRIDAY EVENING
The troop junior leaders and adults gather at an agreed-upon location to travel to the overnight site.

Upon arrival, set up the meeting room, assign living quarters, and store food and equipment.

SESSION 1—THE LEADERSHIP TEAM JOB
(Scoutmaster presides)

(Note: If the group has participated in the junior leader training workshop, this will be a brief review. If not, a more detailed coverage will be needed but limit it to about 20 minutes.)

Opening Ceremony
Ask the senior patrol leader to conduct an opening ceremony selected from the *Patrol Leader Handbook,* being sure to point out the source.

What's My Job?
Remind the leaders of what was discussed at the junior leader orientation workshop and to recall the introduction they received when they were appointed to office. Ask each junior leader to describe his job in his own words.

After the first patrol leader has responded, ask the other Scouts with the same job to add anything he may have overlooked. Repeat this for each multiple position.

Confirm Their Opinion

When each junior leader has responded, briefly review the leaders' duties outlined on pages 51-53 in the *Patrol Leader Handbook*.

The Leadership Team

Point out that this group of youth and adult leaders is often called a "leadership team." It functions much like a football team. The senior patrol leader is like the quarterback, calling the plays after a huddle with the patrol leaders' council. The Scoutmaster is a coach on the sidelines, ready to help when needed. Each team member has a position to play and a job to do when the ball is snapped. Each player knows what the other players are to do and can count on them to be in the right place at the right time. In football, this makes a winning team. In Scouting, it makes a winning troop.

(Now is a good time for another action song.)

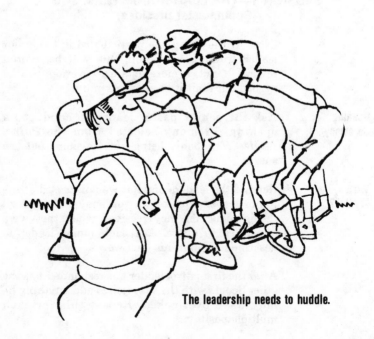

The leadership needs to huddle.

SESSION 2—BRAINSTORM TIME
(Senior patrol leader presides)

What's Going To Happen

The senior patrol leader explains that we're going to find out how may ideas we can get out of this group. Wild ideas are OK, but try not to get silly. Here's the assignment:

> "If you were a member of the greatest Scout troop in the whole world, what do you think should be in the troop's program?"

The Rules

Point out that this is called "brainstorming" and there are some simple rules:

1. We want as many ideas as possible.
2. Shout out your idea in two or three words; don't try to explain it.
3. All ideas are good, but try not to be silly.
4. No fair criticizing an idea.
5. You can build on someone else's idea.
6. Everybody takes part. If you think of it, say it!

You will probably need two people to note the ideas on easel pad sheets. Ask a couple of adults to do this so all the junior leaders can share in the brainstorm.

Brainstorm

Start getting ideas down. Urge everybody—youth and adults—to contribute.

The brainstorm leader's job is to keep the ideas coming. Most boys will list the simple and obvious ideas first—go swimming, take a hike, go camping, etc. Ask questions to open up new ideas. What kind of hike? Where could we go?

Keep an eye on the balance of suggestions. Trigger new subjects with questions like, "How about some skill award things?" Or "Any ideas on a troop Good Turn?"

Summary	When it appears that the group has a good list, call the brainstorm to a halt. Post the easel pad sheets on the wall for all to see.
	Explain that in the morning the group will go over these ideas and pick some that it thinks the troop would really want to do. Meanwhile, everyone should look over the list and feel free to add items.

CLOSING PERIOD (Scoutmaster presides)

Quiet the Group	Ask the best song leader to lead a quiet song. This will quiet the group down from the brainstorm excitement.
Review	Thank the senior patrol leader for his efforts and the junior leaders for their good ideas.
Scoutmaster's Minute	Refer to the Boy Scout posters that have been hung in the room. Point out that everyone is familiar with the Scout Oath and Law, and the motto and slogan. The Boy Scout aims and the Boy Scout methods may be new ideas, however.
	Review the aims and methods briefly, explaining that junior leaders are not only Scouts—they are *leaders* of Scouts. They can do a better job of helping the boys they lead if they keep these aims and methods in mind.
Closing Ceremony	Ask the senior patrol leader to lead the group in a closing ceremony selected from the *Patrol Leader Handbook*.
Fellowship	Now is the time for an evening snack. Make it something special.

Reveille, breakfast, and cleanup.

SESSION 3—YOUR TROOP PROGRAM
(Scoutmaster and senior patrol leader)

**Review
the Past**

Briefly review last year's troop activities. Which ones seemed to work well? Which ones didn't work? Explain that there are six questions that a group can use to evaluate a program. Write them on the easel pad or use a prepared poster:

1. Did we do it?

2. Did we do it right?

3. Did we do it on schedule?

4. Did every member take part?

5. Did they enjoy it?

6. Do they want more?

Apply these questions to last year's program.

Look Ahead

Explain that now we're going to look ahead to next year. We did some things in the past that are worth repeating and got some good ideas from the brainstorm session.

Post the Troop Planning Worksheet on the wall and distribute notebooks, calendars, pencils, and other supplies.

Point out that some suggested themes are shown on the worksheet and are detailed in *Boy Scout Program Helps.* They are there if needed but if we have some better ideas, that's great.

Pick and Choose

Now go through the ideas from the brainstorm session and group those that seem to go together. Ask the troop scribe to list these on the easel pad and suggest each patrol leader keep his own notes.

Next, go through past programs that might be worth repeating and list them.

Finally, check the suggested monthly themes and see if they fit the ideas that have been listed. Some may, some may not. Can new themes be suggested that will fit?

Check the Resources

Review the district and council calendar of events for dates of the camporee, Scouting show, summer camp, Scouting Anniversary Week, roundup, and other activities.

Next check on holidays, religious dates, school activities, chartered organization events, and the Scoutmaster's personal calendar.

Build a Program

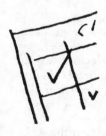

Now is the time to put it all together. Agree on programs and activities that the troop members would like to do. Move the approved items from the various lists to the appropriate square on the Troop Planning Worksheet. Each junior leader should also enter the items in his notebook. Cross out the items on the lists that were not chosen, but keep the lists posted; you may want to go back to them.

State that now they have a basic troop program, and that they're going to *make it happen* this afternoon, but now it's time for break.

**ACTION BREAK—
OUTDOOR GAME**

(The assistant senior patrol leader or the program patrol leader should lead the group in an outdoor action game. Select one that is new to the troop from the *Patrol Leader Handbook*. If possible, choose a game related to a skill award requirement. It will prepare the group for the next session. Set up the projector and screen during the game so you're ready for session 4).

Take advantage of what's there.

SESSION 4—TRAINING TO GROW
(Scoutmaster and senior patrol leader)

**Where
Are You?**

Ask each junior leader to open *The Official Boy Scout Handbook* to page 530. Here is his personal advancement checklist. How many have been using it? It's a great way to keep track of progress toward the next rank. Ask each person who hasn't done so to check off quickly the requirements he *has met* toward his next rank.

Ask how many need a skill award. Ask them to find the skill awards requirements beginning on page 538 and check off in the left margin the things they could do *right now*.

Point out that the requirements that are not checked are what the Scout needs to learn how to do. That means training is needed.

Patrol Advancement

Now ask everyone to check chapter 7 beginning on page 126 of *The Official Patrol Leader Handbook*. Here are hundreds of things that junior leaders can do to help patrol and troop members grow through advancement.

Point out the two steps to earning skill awards— learning the skill and testing and checking (pages 127-8). Remind patrol leaders that they can check off skill award requirements *provided they have met the requirements themselves.*

Training for Learning

Explain that some Scouts can read *The Official Boy Scout Handbook* and learn what they need to earn a skill award. Most Scouts, however, need help and that calls for some training. Also note that most skill awards require the Scout actually *to do* something, not just know about it. That calls for an action program.

Where Do We Train?

Ask the junior leaders to suggest where this training should take place. List the responses: troop meetings, patrol meetings, on hikes, in camp, personal coaching, etc. Make the point that some type of training is a part of almost everything we do in the troop or patrol.

Pass out copies of *Troop Meeting Plan*. Training is involved in skills development, patrol meetings, and interpatrol activity, and can be a part of the preopening and the game.

Ask the group to thumb through chapter 4 of *The Official Patrol Leader Handbook* to find training opportunities. They're in checking, coaching, and projects, and can be a part of plans and play.

Train Without Pain

Many people think "being trained" isn't exciting. So Scouting hides the training in the fun and adventure of a good program. Ask the group to look over the program that they've outlined to see where specific training is offered and where hidden training is possible.

Look'n'Do

Explain that most people learn best by observing (looking at) an activity, then doing it. An audiovisual series called *Look'n'Do* can be a help in training Scouts for the skill award requirements. Explain that the slides or filmstrip should be stopped from time to time so the Scouts can try out what they've seen on the screen.

Effective Teaching

Ask for a volunteer from the group who has no idea of how to run the projector you'll be using. (You may have to brief a Scout in advance to be sure he acts like he doesn't know how.)

Explain that we're going to give a little demonstration of effective teaching. Write "Effective Teaching" on the easel pad. State that the objective is to teach the Scout to run the projector properly. Write "objective" on the easel pad and stress that you need to know what the person should be able to *do* as a result of the training.

Ask the Scout to thread the machine or set up the slide tray and start the show. When he hesitates or fumbles, point out that you've now made a discovery—that he doesn't know what to do, what he needs to know, or what he wants to know. Write the word "discovery" on the easel pad.

Now demonstrate to the Scout exactly how the machine is threaded or set up, how to turn it on, frame the picture, and advance slides or strip. State that you are teaching and he is learning. Write "teaching—learning" on the easel pad.

Now let the Scout try his hand at running the projector. Explain that this gives him a chance to apply what was taught to see if it has been learned. Write "application" on the easel pad.

How did the Scout do? Pretty well? Make a few little mistakes? Explain that asking and answering these questions is evaluation. Write the word on the easel pad.

If the Scout made a few errors, show him how to do it again and point out that because people seldom learn everything the first time, you recycle—show them again. Write "recycle" on the easel pad.

Six Elements Explain that these six elements make up almost any effective teaching situation. Ask the group to keep them in mind as they see some samples of the Look'n'Do series.

Objective	Application
Discovery	Evaluation
Teaching-Learning	Recycle

Look'n'Do Audiovisual Using the newly trained projectionist and a preselected Scout as narrator, show samples of two or three of the Look'n'Do visuals.

These are useful tools to use in a troop meeting to prepare Scouts for the camping, hiking, cooking, and first aid skill awards. Suggest that these might be kept in mind to be included in the troop program.

Adjourn Now it's time to get ready for lunch.

LUNCH BREAK (Prepare lunch, clean up, have a rest period.)

SATURDAY AFTERNOON ACTIVITY (Something out-of-doors would be good. Try a nature hike combined with a scavenger hunt or an activity out of part 2 of *The Official Patrol Leader Handbook*.

Get a handle on your program.

SESSION 5—MAKING IT HAPPEN
(Scoutmaster, senior patrol leader, consultants)

Warm Up

Lead off this session with a good action song and one or two handclaps out of *The Official Patrol Leader Handbook.*

Programs Need Plans

Ask the Scouts to imagine how they would carry a bucket full of water if it didn't have a handle. (If you have a real bucket handy, let a Scout try it.) It's awkward, takes both hands, and you're likely to spill some of the water. With a handle, it's easy.

Explain that good plans are the "handle" on a program. Without good plans, a program is awkward and hard to manage, and, like the water in the bucket, you could lose some of it.

Planning Steps

Getting on top of a high wall is hard without a ladder. Getting on top of a *program* is much easier with a ladder of planning steps. As you explain each step briefly, write it on the easel pad or use a prepared poster:

1. *Define the job.* Write down exactly what you want to happen. Make it as detailed as you can. You may want to split the big job into smaller jobs and work on a mini-plan for each.

2. *Locate the resources.* List what you have to work with—things *and* people. Make a list of what you need and where you might get it.

3. *List the alternatives.* Think about this carefully. If I do this, what will happen?

4. *Decide what to do.* Look at the job, the resources, and the possible consequences and decide on a course of action.

5. *Outline the plan.* Now write down the steps that must be taken to reach the goal. Put them in order. Decide who will be asked to carry out each step. Ask them for help and be sure they know exactly what's to be done.

6. *Carry out the plan.* Start taking the steps you've listed. Check on the progress of the people you've asked to help.

Evaluate. Keep these six points in mind as the plan unfolds. Be prepared to change the plan if it looks as if problems are developing.

Enjoy

A well-carried-out plan will result in a successful program.

Post the six steps on the wall for all to see. They'll need them for the balance of this session.

Pick a Project

Form the group into patrol leadership teams. The patrol leader and his assistant will work together. Spread the other junior leaders evenly among the teams. Ask an adult to work with each group as an adviser.

Refer to the Troop Planning Worksheet. Ask each team to pick a project coming up in the next 2 months and develop a plan to carry it out using the six steps to planning.

Explain that the patrol leader is the chairman of the team and he should turn to his adult adviser only if he gets stuck. The Scoutmaster and senior patrol leader are available if there are any questions.

Planning Project

When each team has chosen its project, suggest that they work wherever they will be most comfortable. Set a time when the group will reassemble for reports on progress.

As the teams work on their plans, the Scoutmaster and senior patrol leader should circulate among them to monitor progress and help as needed.

Reports

When the group reassembles, ask each patrol to report on its plans. Suggestions from other groups are welcome, but be sure these are positive. If the plans are not complete, challenge each team to have its plan complete by the next meeting of the patrol leaders' council.

Summary

Thank the patrol leaders for the leadership they have given to the planning project. Remind them that this is "for real." If they are not completely satisfied with the plan, they should review it during the balance of the afternoon to be sure it's as good as they can make it.

What's Next

Explain that the group will be dismissed for the rest of the afternoon for free-time activity, but that the Scoutmaster would like to spend a few minutes with each junior leader, so they are asked to stay close by.

Announce the time for supper and dismiss the group.

SCOUTMASTER CONFERENCE— GETTING TO KNOW YOU

The Scoutmaster should spend time visiting with each junior leader during the balance of the afternoon. Make this informal—sitting on a log or strolling through the woods. Aim to breach the "wall" which sometimes blocks communication between boy leaders and their Scoutmaster. Try to draw the boy out; find out what he needs and how he thinks. Use your best counseling technique. Even if needed, save corrective counseling for another time.

DINNER— SOMETHING SPECIAL

Make this a real event. Try a barbecue, steak fry, chili feed, or one of the adults' famous Dutch oven specials.

Cleanup.

Note: If the group will not be staying over until Sunday, now is the time for a brief summary and departure.

Special Note: If remaining, be sure that plans are firm for Sunday religious services. One possibility is to attend services at nearby churches (in uniform). If this is not practical, the group should plan its own worship service under the direction of the chaplain's aide. If some members of the group observe Saturday as a religious day, arrangements should be made accordingly.

SATURDAY EVENING

SESSION 6—PLANNING FOR FUN

The Mission

Gather the group and explain that a fun campfire is scheduled for later in the evening, and tomorrow morning would be a great time for a theme hike. Divide the group into two teams. One is headed by

TRAINING JUNIOR LEADERS

the senior patrol leader, the other by the assistant senior patrol leader.

Here's the mission: The senior patrol leader's team is to plan and conduct the evening campfire. There are some good ideas in *The Official Patrol Leader Handbook*. Ask the team to try some ideas new to the troop members to see how they work.

The assistant senior patrol leader's team will plan a theme hike for tomorrow morning. *The Official Patrol Leader Handbook* should be their principal resource.

Planning Time Be sure each group knows how long their activity should last and how long they will have for planning.

Adjourn to the planning sessions. Reassemble when it's time for the campfire.

JUNIOR LEADER CAMPFIRE (Senior patrol leader in charge.)

Harmonize around the campfire.

CRACKER BARREL (Fellowship after campfire.)

SUNDAY MORNING (Reveille, breakfast, cleanup.)

WORSHIP SERVICES (Attend services of local churches. Make arrangements ahead of time. Be sure to involve the chaplain aide, if the group must conduct its own religious services.)

Attend church services.

JUNIOR LEADER THEME HIKE (Assistant senior patrol leader in charge.)

A hike is a walk with a purpose.

Serve those you lead.

SESSION 7—SUMMARY AND CHALLENGE (Scoutmaster)

What We Did   Assemble the group upon returning from the theme hike. Briefly review what was accomplished during the weekend:

- Each leader knows his job and has proven he can work with others. We're a team.

- Junior leaders have lots of good ideas. They are creative people.

- Training is needed to help our troop and patrol members grow through advancement. We know how to do this.

- We developed a program and laid plans to make it work.

- We had fun, got to know each other better, and explored our own strengths and the strengths of others.

**Thanks
To All**   Thank the entire group for their active participation. Pay particular tribute to the adult leaders who assisted in many ways.

What's Next   Point out that the challenge is to put what was learned to work. The Scouts of the patrols and troop need the leadership team—all of the leaders must be dedicated to doing their best to serve those they lead.

LUNCH   (Make this quick and easy.)

CLEANUP   (Be certain that the facility is in better shape than when the group arrived.)

DEPARTURE

Chapter 14

Troop Administration

"By Jove! Your troop has met all of the 10 Tests of Successful Scouting. Yours is one of this year's Honor Units."

RUNNING a Boy Scout troop is a little like running a business. There are some practical matters—a place to meet, money for program, recordkeeping, and recruiting for the future. All of these concerns can be managed by others with your general supervision. You need to be involved in each one just long enough to find someone else to become responsible for that part of troop administration. If you do that, you can devote most of your effort to the program and the Scouts.

YOUR TROOP MEETING ROOM

Usually troops are provided a meeting place by their chartered organization. Where this cannot be done, it becomes the task of the troop committee to locate and arrange for suitable facilities.

Following is a checklist of minimum conditions for a suitable troop meeting room:

- Large enough
- Attractive but not lavish
- Properly lighted and heated
- Ventilated
- In a safe building
- Preferably on the ground floor
- At least two exits with doors opening outward
- Toilet and drinking water facilities

The Meeting Place Inspection form, No. 6140, provides a more detailed checklist of health and safety factors.

When the troop goes outside its chartered organization for space, there should be a written agreement about when and how the space is to be used, and what rent, if any, will be charged.

Even when the troop uses facilities owned by its chartered organization, the troop has an obligation to spell out the proposed use. On the basis of the troop's annual plan, the meeting room should be reserved by written request specifying the dates and hours when the meeting room will be used by the troop. If there is heavy use of the building, any change of use should be reported to the organization so that others may use the room.

The troop should keep the meeting room and its equipment in good order. Regardless of the condition in which the troop finds the room, it should always leave it in better condition. Any damage should be reported promptly and paid for. The floor should be cleaned after use, chairs stacked, and any requirements of the building's owners or supervisors scrupulously observed.

Some troops are lucky enough to have more or less exclusive use of a room. They can decorate and equip it as a Scout meeting room. Most troops, however, do not have such an arrangement. This calls for ingenuity in developing portable screens, bulletin boards, etc., that can be dismantled and stored easily.

An ideal troop meeting room would have one large room for the whole troop, one or more small group rooms adjacent to it, and storage space convenient both to the outside and to the main room. Few troops are lucky enough to have the ideal, however, and have to make do with less than the best.

One of the best ways to defeat the problem of an inadequate troop meeting room is to schedule many of the troop's activities elsewhere. In fact, the chief handicap of a really great meeting room is that it tends to keep the troop there when it really belongs outside.

Scouting policy does not support the construction of buildings particularly to house Scout troops. The cost is seldom justified by the amount of use. The management of the property is burdensome and costly. Buildings erected for Scout use almost always turn out to be unsuitable: too small, poorly lighted and heated, and very often unsafe.

It is a rare community or neighborhood that has no public building suitable and available for Scout troop meetings. There are thousands more schools, churches, firehouses, and rooms than there are Scout troops.

MONEY FOR THE PROGRAM

Like any organization, a Scout troop needs to have a budget and a treasury. The money to operate the troop comes from the Scouts themselves. As much as possible, Scouts should earn their own way for dues, uniform, personal equipment, and expendable supplies. It is part of the character-developing process. Scouts work on unit money-earning projects to meet troop needs.

Preparing a Troop Budget

The basic records for creating a troop budget are found in the *Troop Financial Record Book*, No. 6508, and the *Troop Record Book*, No. 6509. For an established troop, it is important to have these record books up to date and available for use in preparing the troop budget. A new troop may find the sample troop budget helpful in preparing its first budget.

The *Troop Financial Record Book* will provide additional help to a new troop in developing its first budget. This book also describes in detail a simple and workable system for developing a troop budget.

There are four steps to the process and you get things started. This is the way the *Troop Financial Record Book* states it:

1. A rough draft of the budget is prepared by the Scoutmaster, troop treasurer, and troop scribe. This is a pencil draft, subject to change.

2. The patrol leaders' council reviews the rough draft of the budget carefully and puts it into final form.

3. The troop committee gives final approval to the budget and assumes the responsibility for the next step.

4. The parents and Scouts are informed about the budget so that all will understand the individual Scout's responsibility in making it work.

The *Unit Budget Plan,* No. 28-426, is available from the Registration Service, BSA, or through your local council service center.

Collecting Dues and Keeping Records

Scouts must be expected to keep their dues payments up to date. They should be kept informed of their dues status, and both they and their parents should be advised of nonpayment. A Scout troop

A SAMPLE TROOP BUDGET
(Membership 30)

EXPENSES

Reregistration (30 x $3.00)	$90.00
BOYS' LIFE (30 x $6.60)	198.00
Reserve (30 x $1.00)	30.00
Basic Expenses	447.00
	$765.00

INCOME

Unexpended balance from last year	$60.00
Dues (30 x 50 weeks x 30¢)*	150.00
Money-earning projects	255.00
	$765.00

*Many troops have dues of 50¢ per week.

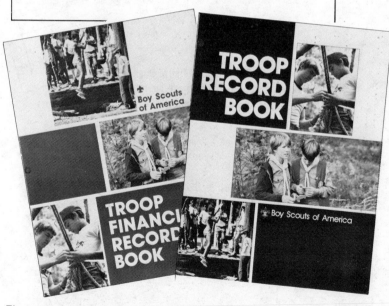

The treasurer, a troop committee member, uses the Troop Financial Record Book; and the scribe, a Boy Scout, uses the Troop Record Book.

TROOP ADMINISTRATION

can only encourage good money practices by helping Scouts to learn to meet their obligations.

Some troops may collect dues on a monthly basis and still adhere to this system and its benefits. Annual collection of dues is not approved by the Boy Scouts of America for these reasons: (1) Annual dues are large enough to prohibit some boys from joining, and (2) Such collection usually means the parents pay the dues and the boy loses the sense of responsibility and the training that comes from paying dues weekly.

The record system described below has worked satisfactorily for a great many years in thousands of troops.

1. Before the first meeting each month, the troop scribe checks the *Troop Record Book* and prepares each Patrol Monthly Dues Envelope, No. 3816, with members' names and dues accounts. He confers with Scoutmaster and distributes to patrol scribes weekly. The names of inactive Scouts are not listed.

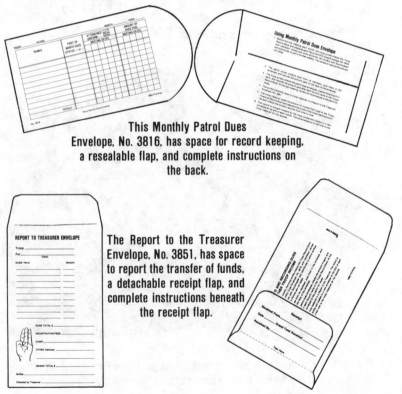

This Monthly Patrol Dues
Envelope, No. 3816, has space for record keeping,
a resealable flap, and complete instructions on
the back.

The Report to the Treasurer
Envelope, No. 3851, has space
to report the transfer of funds,
a detachable receipt flap, and
complete instructions beneath
the receipt flap.

2. The patrol scribe collects dues from its members, puts them in the envelope, and records the amount paid on the face of the envelope.

3. The troop scribe collects the patrol dues envelopes, checks the amount in each, and records the amount paid after each Scout's name in the *Troop Record Book*. At the next meeting, he returns the envelope to the patrol for reuse.

4. The scribe transmits dues to troop treasurer in a Report to the Treasurer Envelope, No. 3851.

5. The troop treasurer posts the amount of income from dues to the *Troop Financial Record Book* and deposits the funds in the troop's bank account. He also checks the scribe's records from time to time.

6. The record is brought forward by the troop scribe and posted to a new envelope at the end of each month. The old envelope is turned over to the troop treasurer for his records.

Boys' Life

Because of the importance of good reading in character development, the Boy Scouts of America has published *Boys' Life* almost since its beginning as a movement. The magazine is available to members at half the regular subscription rate. You should consider it as much a part of troop program as camping or advancement. New Scouts should be signed up for the magazine when they join, and subscriptions renewed from troop dues when the troop reregisters.

Registration Fees

When a Scout joins a troop, he should pay the full registration fee, regardless of the time of year. You should then forward, with his application, the actual amount owed for a partial year's registration. The balance should be credited to the troop treasury to begin building a reserve against which the boy's reregistration may be paid from the dues which the boy has paid.

When the troop reregisters, the troop should pay the Scouts' registration fees entirely, since this is one of the services the Scouts "buy" through their dues payments. Scouters should be responsible for their own fees since they have not contributed to the troop treasury by dues payment.

Paying Bills

As you may see from your own experience or from the sample budget, a troop with even a modest program may take in and spend some hundreds of dollars a year.

Every troop should have a checking account in a local bank. Most troops require two signatures for drawing checks.

The troop treasurer should pay all troop bills by check and should watch carefully to see that the troop's budget is not being exceeded.

As Scoutmaster you should be provided with a petty cash fund. You can then buy small items out of that fund and turn in receipts to replenish the fund as needed.

Money-Earning Projects

When last year's unexpended balance plus this year's anticipated dues income do not total as much as planned expenses, the troop must engage in one or more money-earning projects.

Every money-earning project should pass these tests in order to conform with Scouting's policies and not negate some of the purposes of the program.

1. Has your chartered organization, troop committee, and Scouting council approved your project, including the dates and method of the proposed money-earning project?

2. Are your plan and the dates selected so that there will be no competition with money-raising programs and policies of your chartered organization, Scouting council, or the United Way?

3. Is your plan free from any stigma of gambling, in harmony with local ordinances, and consistent with the ideals and purposes of the Boy Scouts of America?

*4. If a commercial product is to be sold by boys, will it be sold on its own merits and without reference to the needs of Scouting either directly (during the sales presentation) or indirectly?

*5. If tickets are sold by your troop for any function *other than* a Scouting event (such as a troop supper or Scouting circus), will they be sold by your boys as individuals without depending on the goodwill of Scouting to make the sale possible?

---

*The Scout uniform must not be worn when selling a commercial product, service, or entertainment.

Scouts are not permitted to solicit money for any purpose.

6. Will the buyers get their money's worth from any product they purchase, function they attend, or services they receive?

7. If a money-earning project is planned by your troop for a particular area, do you respect the rights of other Scout troops in the same neighborhood?

8. Is it reasonably certain that people who need work or business will not lose it as a result of your troop's plan?

9. Will your plan protect the name and goodwill of the BSA and prevent it from being capitalized on by promoters of shows, benefits, or sales campaigns?

10. If any contracts are to be signed by your troop, will they be signed by an individual without reference to the Boy Scouts of America and in no way bind the local council or the Boy Scouts of America to any agreement or financial responsibility?

Some Sample Money-Earning Projects

Exhibit: merit badge show, hobby show
Sale of Scout-made items: kitchen gadgets, birdhouses and feeders, barbecue aids
Waste collection: papers and magazines, cans, bottles, computer cards
Rummage sale
Subscription bridge party
Bake sale
Garage sale or auction
Lawn or automobile care
Care of pets, gardens, etc., while owners are away
Suppers: pancakes, spaghetti, turkey, covered dish

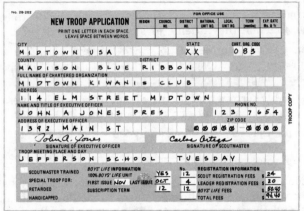

New Troop Application, No. 28-202, is a carbon interleaved form with three copies and a page of instructions.

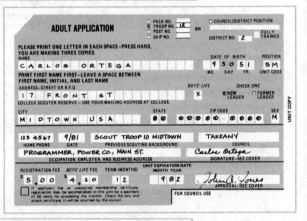

Adult Registration Application, No. 8273, is also a carbon interleaved form with an original and two copies.

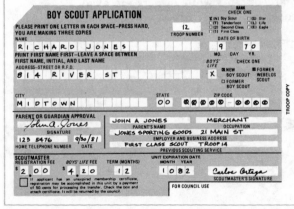

Boy Scout Application, No. 8271, is a similar form and provides a temporary membership certificate.

REGISTERING A NEW TROOP

The chartered organization being registered for the first time submits three types of forms. Directions for each form are furnished with it.

Troop charter application: Complete all required information; submit two copies and keep one.

Adult applications: Each adult being registered with the troop completes an application. The troop submits two copies of each application and keeps one.

Boy applications: Each Scout completes an application. The troop submits two copies and keeps one.

REREGISTERING YOUR TROOP

Near the end of your charter year, your council will provide an application for charter renewal. This is a computer printout of information previously furnished to the national office. Thus, your task of reregistering the troop is much less than that of registering it in the first place. You need only update the printed information.

Before your charter expires, your council probably will conduct a charter review meeting at which the progress of the past year and the plans for the coming year will be reviewed. This is a fine opportunity for you, your fellow leaders, and your troop committee to meet with representatives of the local council to review just where you are and where you are going. Once this meeting has been held, your charter renewal application can be completed, submitted, and processed.

Instructions on how to bring your Troop Charter Renewal printout up to date are printed on the reverse side of the troop copy.

Most troops hold uniform reviews (inspections) from time to time during the year. Every troop should conduct one at the time of charter renewal. This review is conducted by the Scoutmaster and his staff. They check badge placement and ensure that all Scouts are following the troop selected uniform options.

Registering New Scouts and Leaders During the Year

Any new Scout or adult who joins between troop registrations is registered by submitting the appropriate boy or adult application.

As in other cases, submit two copies and keep one. The prorated fees must be paid with the application. It is important that this be done as soon as the boy joins, since he is not officially a Scout until he is registered. Don't hold applications and fees until you have several. Transmit each one when it is received.

Transfers

When a Scout is moving to a new area, give him a copy of a Transfer Application, No. 28-401, showing his record to date. That will enable him to continue with full credit.

Likewise, when a boy who has been a Scout elsewhere asks to join,

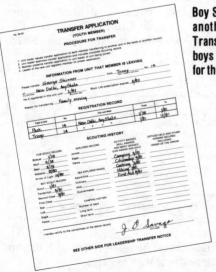

Boy Scout membership is transferable to another Boy Scout troop. Use this Transfer Application, No. 28-401, for boys who are leaving your troop, and ask for this form from the boys transferring to your troop.

ask him for his transfer record to bring your troop records up to date. Transfers list advancement, offices held, and registration dates.

PATROL AND TROOP RECORDS

It is not necessary for a troop to build a set of records from blank sheets of paper. Most of its records can be kept on standard forms and in standard record books developed by the Boy Scouts of America and improved with decades of experience. Patrol and troop records are of three major types—statistical, informal, and display. Each is discussed here in turn.

Statistical Records

1. *The Troop Record Book*, No. 6509, contains individual information on each Scout—registration status, leadership positions held, advancement, attendance, dues, and camping participation. It is kept by the troop scribe.

2. *The Troop Financial Record Book,* No. 6508, contains the troop's budget plus month-by-month details of actual income and expenditures. It is kept by the troop treasurer.

3. Copies of charter applications and Scout and adult applications should be kept together in one place to support troop records. They are best filed in a three-ring binder and kept by the Scoutmaster. Copies of advancement reports to the local council should also be kept in this way.

4. The Individual Scout Record (sheet), No. 6518, has space for a complete history of a Scout.

Informal Records

Patrols and troops often keep logbooks of their activities. These include accounts of troop or patrol activities, newspaper clippings, photographs, or other memorabilia kept as a living record of what Scouts have done together.

Display Records

Among the records that troops sometimes display at troop meetings are the following:
Advancement status (an attractive wall chart is available).
Attendance and dues status.
Interpatrol contest status.

NEW SCOUTS

Your troop needs to actively recruit new members or it will pass slowly out of existence as the older boys move out of Scouting.

For that very reason Scouting's congressional charter challenges each Boy Scout troop to make room for every boy who is qualified to join. Recruiting new Scouts should be carried out on a year-round basis. However, there are some times of the year when recruiting is most effective.

SPRING ROUNDUP. The ideal recruiting method is for one boy to invite another boy to join. This should be encouraged, or it won't happen. Your troop might set aside a couple of weeks each year for a special recruiting effort. Check on newly available boys in May or June so they can be included in the troop's summer camp adventure.

FALL ROUNDUP. Also, make another special recruiting effort in September as the troop starts another program year. Urge Scouts to invite their friends to come to troop activities during this time. Plan a troop program that will be of special interest to new boys. Make these boys feel welcome at meetings. Greet them warmly and urge them to get into troop games and other activities.

A new Scout is a very important person, make him feel welcome.

Register new Scouts as soon as they join.

SIGNING THEM UP! When a new boy shows that he is interested in joining, give him an application for membership. Ask him to fill it out, have his parents sign it, and bring it back to the next meeting along with his registration fee. When he has passed his Boy Scout requirements, you can register him through the council.

ROUNDUP HELPERS. Your Scouting service center has these recruiting aids:

- Be a Boy Scout, No. 6521, a postal card for you and your senior patrol leader to send a personal invitation to join your troop.

- How To Join the Boy Scouts, No. 6524, a flyer that explains the Boy Scout joining requirements and lists the tests for the Tenderfoot rank.

- *Join the Scouts for Fun and Adventure,* No. 6526, an 8-page, full-color booklet with reprints from the exciting pages of *Boys' Life* magazine.

- *What Parents Should Know About Our Scout Troop,* No. 6511, a folder with a title that says it all.

A Boy Scout in your troop can become a Webelos den chief.

Webelos-to-Scout Transition

One excellent source of new boys is graduating Webelos Scouts. Cub Scouting is for boys 8 through 10 years old and Webelos Scouts are the 10 year olds. Their program prepares them to be excellent new Boy Scouts.

Webelos Scouts don't automatically become Boy Scouts, but if proper relations are built, a Cub Scout pack can be a "feeder source" of new boys year after year. This is called *Webelos-to-Scout transition* and should bring in six to eight new boys each year. Here are some key steps:

1. *Find a Cub Scout pack.* If your chartered organization doesn't have one, your commissioner or district executive can help find one for you.

2. *Get to know its leaders*—in particular, the Cubmaster and Webelos leader(s).

3. *Select people from your troop to work closely with the pack.* The best way is to have a den chief* (boy leader) from your troop for

---

*Your den chiefs can use the *Den Chief Handbook*, No. 3211.

each Webelos den and a Webelos resource person (ASM or committee member) to help the pack.

4. *Learn a little about the Webelos program yourself.* Browse through the *Webelos Scout Book.* You'll see how Webelos Scouts can be prepared for your troop.

5. *Schedule joint Webelos den-troop activities.* Maybe a troop hike in the fall, a court of honor in the winter and a troop overnight with Webelos Scouts and their dads in the spring. Always invite Webelos Scouts to an Eagle court of honor.

6. *Meet the Webelos parents.* Visit a pack meeting. Webelos dads can become assistant Scoutmasters and/or troop committee members when their sons join.

7. *Ask the boys to join your troop*—at least a month before they have to decide.

8. *Welcome the boys when they graduate* and take part in the ceremony.

9. *Make sure the Webelos Scouts feel welcome in your troop.* Be sure they are all happy in their patrols and aren't hazed or "initiated."

If the Webelos den is very closely knit, you might let them stay as a patrol in the troop with their den chief as patrol ledaer.

Also, if Webelos Scouts complete skill award requirements in the den, the den chief can sign their *Official Boy Scout Handbooks* for the requirement after they officially join the troop.

When done right, Webelos-to-Scout transition requires only four or five meetings per year and pays off with a continuing source of new boys.

Chapter 15

Games and Activities

In Scouting, we can make a game out of hard work.

WHEN Baden-Powell discovered late in the 19th century that certain military training was best done with games, he was a pioneer. Fifty years later, he was still a pioneer. Today, distinguished institutions, such as Harvard Business School, have lent respectability to the gaming method of learning. Trainees in all sorts of fields pay hundreds of dollars per day for training using methods commonly used by Scouts before World War I—for which *they* paid 25 cents a year!

The game is not just a fun thing to sandwich between periods of hard work and dull lectures. It is central to the Scouting method. The whole program is a game. The more a Scouting meeting resembles a lecture hall, the less likely it is to teach.

Almost everything Scouts do can be done or learned or practiced—or all three—as a game. This includes not only the obvious skills such as knot tying and swimming that readily lend themselves to games and contests, but even everyday chores like KP and tent pitching.

Consider this use of the gaming method to handle an unpleasant job. A troop found the council camp greatly in need of a cleanup during one weekend visit. They resolved to do something about it on their next visit. The council readily agreed that if the troop could get trash to the parking lot, the council would get a truck and cart it out of camp.

The Scoutmaster announced that he was going into the junk business on Saturday morning of the next camp-out. He would pay, he said, top prices for junk of all kinds.

Scouts took baskets, bags, and wheelbarrows with them to camp. Between nine and noon they rounded up—by patrol—literally tons of trash and brought it to the Scoutmaster in the parking lot. True to his word, he paid top prices—in stage money.

That evening the troop auctioned off $15 worth of food, candy, and equipment to be paid for in stage money earned by trash selling that day. A firemaking set sold for $7,000 in stage money. A watermelon went for $12,000. A candy bar sold for $900. Everybody went to bed happy, camp was cleaner than it had been in years, and not one adult had to ask one boy to stoop over and pick up some trash. The pile in the parking lot filled the truck three times.

The genius of the game method is that it gets more done in less time, leaving everybody happier than before. Since almost every boy likes almost every game, the game method is almost certain to be a hit whenever it is applied.

So if you have been thinking of games as a comic relief to put in the middle of the deadly serious business of Scouting, think some more. The business of Scouting *is* a game. Games are the basic method of the whole program.

PRINCIPLES FOR USING GAMES

Games Must Fit Your Troop. The size and members of your troop are not just like all others. Some games will work better than others. Try them out and see. Never quit trying new games and game methods.

Everybody Should Be Active. Scout games are not spectator sports for a few to play and many to watch. Those who are left out will soon find their own entertainment, and you probably will not approve of what they find.

The Patrols Are the Teams. There is no team like a patrol. It is already formed and it needs to work together. Don't break up patrols to play a game. Keep them intact and strengthen them through games. In relays the small patrol will have some members compete twice to equalize.

Let Boy Leaders Lead. It is good leadership experience to lead games. Pass the ball around to as many boy leaders as you can.

Try Many Games. Don't throw out a game because it "doesn't sound good." Some of the games most popular with Scouts fit that category.

HOW TO LEAD A GAME

1. Name the game (if it has a name). This will give it a handle by which to identify it next time it is played.

2. Line the troop up in formation to play.

3. Explain the rules. Make them short, but clear.

4. Demonstrate the game. Have a quick runthrough so everyone can see how it is done.

5. Ask for questions.

6. Run the game. Be sure you stick by the rules announced.

7. Don't play a troop meeting game that can't be explained in 2 minutes. It's too complicated for this use.

SCOUTCRAFT GAMES

These games involve skills such as first aid, cooking, compass work, observation, and axmanship. Some are only suitable for outdoors; some may be played both indoors and outdoors.

Games are not always contests in which speed counts. A contest involving putting patrol cook kits together may involve both speed and quality of work. A wood chopping contest—for safety reasons— is won by the patrol chopping a log in the fewest strokes, not the fastest time.

One of the most successful games is the county-fair or adventure-trail type. This game—which can be played indoors or outdoors—is a combination of several skills. Each patrol is given a scorecard and directions. Each begins at a different station and rotates among different stations in the meeting room, outside the building, or in camp. At each station there is a problem to solve, a skill to demonstrate, or a task to perform. There is a judge at each station who observes the patrol at work and awards points according to directions given him in advance. The patrol with the greatest total points wins the whole game.

Games are so useful in learning and practicing skills that they belong in almost every troop meeting. Here is a selection of games to introduce you to the idea.

Newspaper Study

Equipment. One newspaper per patrol.

Patrols in patrol corners, each with the same day's issue of a newspaper. On signal, patrols start a search for news items which definitely illustrate the Scout Law. Items are cut out and sorted according to the points of the Law. Patrol with most clippings in given time wins.

Which Direction?

Equipment. Map, compass, and eight direction cards for each patrol. Each card has names of two locations on the map.

Maps and compasses are placed at a distance in front of each patrol. First Scout in each patrol runs up and is handed a card by a judge. Using the compass, the Scout must orient the map and determine the direction from the first location on the card to the second location. He writes direction on the card and hands it back to the judge. If within 5° of the correct direction, he may run back and touch off the next Scout in his patrol, who runs up and gets a new card with two new locations to plot. If the Scout was more than 5° off, he must redo the problem until he is within the allowable error. First patrol through is the winner.

Kim's Game

Equipment. Miscellaneous small articles, paper, and pencils.

Patrols gather before a tray covered with a cloth. The cloth is lifted for 1 minute, and the Scouts are permitted to study the 20 to 30 small articles which are revealed: button, pocketknife, clip, nut, coin, pencil, Scout badge, string, etc. Patrols retire, go into a huddle, and make lists of the items. One point for each article remembered, 2 points subtracted for articles mentioned which were not on the tray.

Bowline-Sheet Bend Draw

Equipment. One 2 meter rope per contestant.

Each patrol forms into pairs in facing lines. On "Go" each member ties a bowline around his own waist. The first of a pair to finish then ties the ends of his partner's rope to his own with a sheet bend. When finished, both lean back against the ropes with their hands in the air. The winner is the first patrol in which all boys are leaning back and all knots are holding.

Knot "Champ-Nit"

Equipment. As needed.

Each patrol is in a corner, with the patrol leader in charge. Under his direction, members race to tie a square knot (for instance), and drop it to the floor. The winner steps out and the rest of the patrol repeats the contest. Continue until only the "champ-nit" of the patrol is left. The troop assembles, and patrol champ-nits compete to find the troop champ-nit. This method may be used for numerous Scout activities. The merit of it is that the Scout most in need of practice gets the most of it.

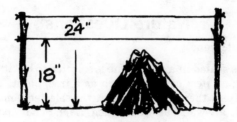

String Burning

Equipment. Stakes, string, wood, ax, knife, two matches for each team.

Two Scouts form each team. Each team stretches two strings tightly between two vertical sticks—one string 45.72 cm (18 in.) above the ground, the other 60.56 (24 in.). The team gathers wood, prepares it, and makes a fire lay under the strings. The top of the fire lay must be below the lower string. Only natural tinder and wood may be used. On signal, the fires are lighted. No team may use more than two matches. After lighting, the fires must not be touched, nor may extra wood be added. The winner is the team whose fire burns through the top string first.

Name It

Equipment. As needed, also paper and pencils.

The troop's nature expert collects specimens of things with which every Scout should be familiar, such as a puffball, milkweed pod, cattail, pine cone, wasp nest, leaves, insects, etc. About 15 of them are attached to cardboard, numbered consecutively, and placed

before the troop. Each boy makes a list of the items he recognizes. These are turned over to the judge, who gives 1 point to each correct answer. The total points divided by the number of boys in the patrol gives each patrol's standing.

Nature Questions

Equipment. None.

Scouts are seated in a circle. One is selected to be "it." He selects, in his mind, an item of nature such as a tree, plant, animal, bird, fish, or any part thereof. He whispers the selected item to the game leader so his answers can be checked. Each Scout, in turn around the circle, asks one question that can be answered with a "yes" or "no", in an attempt to narrow down the possibilities, and then makes one guess as to what the item is. The Scout who correctly identifies the object during his turn becomes "it" for the next round.

What's the Sign?

Equipment. For each patrol, a pencil and a large sheet of paper with the names of 20 conventional map signs.

Patrols line up in relay formation, facing lists tacked to the opposite wall. On signal, Scout No. 1 runs up to the list and draws a map sign next to its name. He runs back and touches off the next player, who runs up, and so on, until all signs are drawn in. Score 2 points for each correct sign, plus 10 points for the patrol finishing first. See *The Official Boy Scout Handbook.*

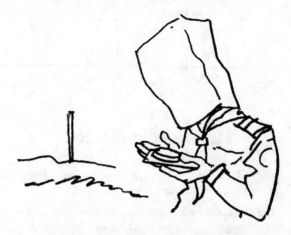

Blindfold Compass Course

Equipment. Brought by contestant: compass. Furnished by judges: large paper sack, marked stake. Outdoor area.

One boy represents the patrol. He takes an azimuth reading to a numbered stake 30.48 m (100 ft.) away. A large paper sack is then placed over his head, which just enables him to see the ground and the compass held close to his chest. He is turned around on the spot three times, then takes a compass reading and proceeds toward the stake. When he figures that he is at the goal, he halts and calls the judge. Closest contestant wins.

How Do I Get Back?

Equipment. Silva compass or ruler and protractor and paper and pencil for each patrol.

Leader says: "I started this hike going in the direction of 60° for 1 kilometer. Then I changed direction to 190° and went 1 more kilometer. What direction should I follow to get back to where I started?" The patrol that plots the course and comes up with the answer (310°) first is the winner. Use your imagination, compass, and map scale to create other situations using the map in *The Official Boy Scout Handbook,* page 195.

Map-Reading Race

Equipment. Brought by team: compass. Supplied by judges: sketch map with two or more objectives, stakes with identification cards. Outdoor area.

Form four-man teams, or use patrols as teams. Each team is given a sketch map showing magnetic north, scale, and two or more objectives, not too far from the starting point. The team orients the map, plots the azimuth to the first objective, goes to it, finds what it is (low stake with a colored card for each competing team attached to it), and takes a card as evidence of having found the spot. They then plot the azimuth to the second objective, and find a similar card there. When all objectives have been reached, the team returns to the starting point with the cards. The first team back with a card from each objective wins.

Knot Step Contest

Equipment. A 2 meter rope for each Scout.

Line up Scouts at one end of the room. Call out the name of a knot. Each Scout ties the knot. Judges quickly check the knots. Each Scout who tied his knot correctly can take one step forward. The leader calls out another knot and the same procedure is followed. The first Scout to reach the opposite wall is the winner.

Knot-Tying Relay

Equipment. Staff; 8 ropes 2 m (6 ft.) long.

Patrol teams of eight boys each (in case of a small patrol, one or more Scouts each must tie two knots) line up in relay formation, about 2 paces from a staff which is held horizontally 1 meter off the ground. Eight ropes are laid out below the staff. On signal, Scout No. 1 runs up, ties the proper knot, runs back, and tags off No. 2, who runs up, ties his knot, and so on, in the following order: (1) square knot; (2) sheet bend; (3) fisherman's knot (for these, join ends of rope with tight knot, staff running through loop); (4) clove hitch; (5) two half hitches; (6) timber hitch; (7) taut-line hitch; (8) bowline. First patrol through wins.*

*For each incorrect knot, add 1 minute.

RECREATION AND FITNESS GAMES

These games rely on basic skills such as running, pulling, jumping, balancing, etc. They are usually quite active and call for the use of several types of fitness: endurance, muscular coordination, eye-hand coordination, etc.

The game of dodge ball is a good example of such games. The person who is "it" must be able to catch the ball, pick a target, and throw accurately. The other players rely on agility and speed to avoid being hit.

One feature of Scout recreation and fitness games is that most tend to equalize boys of different size, weight, and strength. In the game of swat tag, for example, a soft object such as a stuffed sock is placed in the hands of one Scout, who proceeds to beat the next Scout with it until the latter makes his way around the circle and back to his position. Very often a large boy loses his apparent advantage in chasing the small boy next to him; the small boy's superior speed and agility enable his quick escape from the slower and stronger boy.

Recreation and fitness games can be formalized into contests in which skills are called for and points accumulated. Standard fitness tests, including such events as the 600-meter run-walk, the 50-meter dash, etc., can be the basis for interpatrol contests.

Common sports such as softball, hockey, touch football, basketball, and soccer can be played in their original or modified forms, although the other elements of the Scouting program should not be left out in order to accommodate such sports. Nor should Scout troops become athletic teams in a league with other troops or teams.

Informal sports in which all Scouts can take part can be a natural part of a troop's program. Judgment should be applied to time, place, and length. We are not teaching sports, but using them to accomplish our aim.

Here is a selection of some of the most popular recreation and fitness games.

The starred (★) games are good preopening activities because boys can be added as they arrive at the meeting.

Jump the Shot ★

Equipment. Long rope with soft weight (sandbag) in end.

Form the troop in a circle, with one boy in the center. He swings the rope around the circle below the knees of the others, who must jump over it. Anyone hit by the rope or bag is given 1 penalty point. When the game is halted, the Scout with the fewest points wins.

Poison ★

Equipment. None.

Mark a circle on the ground, 2 paces in diameter. The troop forms a circle outside it, with Scouts of the various patrols alternating. All Scouts join hands and move rapidly around the circle, while each Scout tries to force the two next to him to step into the inside circle. Any Scout stepping into the circle is "poisoned" and receives 1 penalty point. At the end of the game, the patrol of the Scout with the fewest points wins.

Dodge Ball ★

Equipment. Large ball such as basketball or volleyball.

The Scouts form a circle, with one as "it" in the center. The ball is tossed to a Scout in the circle. The object of the game is to hit "it" below the waist with the ball. When hit, he changes places with the Scout who hit him, and the game continues. When played indoors, it might be good to restrict all throwing to two-handed passes to cut the force of the throw.

Do This-Do That ★

Equipment. None.

Before beginning, determine the length of time for the game. The leader, in front of the troop, performs certain movements, preceding each with "Do this!" or "Do that!" All movements following the order "Do this!" must be executed immediately by all players, while movements following "Do that!" must be ignored. Players making mistakes step back one step. The Scout nearest the starting line at the end of the game is the winner.

Swat 'Em ★

Equipment. A rolled newspaper.

The troop forms a circle. Each Scout stands with his hands held cup-shape behind him. "It" circles mysteriously about the ring, carrying a rolled newspaper. He leaves it in the hands of one of the players in the circle, who from that moment on has the privilege of swatting the boy at his right on the back, below the neck, as long as that boy is on the journey around the circle and back to his own

place in the circle again. When this chase is completed the new holder of the swatter is "It" and the first "It" takes his place in the circle.

Steal the Bacon ★

Equipment. One neckerchief.

Two teams form lines facing each other, 30 feet apart. They number off, starting on opposite ends, so that there are two Scouts for each number, one in each line. The leader places the "bacon" (a neckerchief) on the ground in the center. The leader calls a number and the two Scouts with that number dash out, each trying to seize the "bacon" and get home before the other tags him. Score one point for getting home safely or for tagging the Scout who has the "bacon."

Crows and Cranes

Equipment. None.

Divide the troop into two teams lined up facing each other, one side called the "Cranes," the other the "Crows." When the leader calls out "Cranes!" or "Crows!" all on the team named must turn and run to the wall in back of them, trying to reach it before members of the other team tag them. If a boy is tagged before reaching the wall, he is captured and becomes a member of the other team. This can be kept up until one team has captured all those on the other side. The leader can add fun by dragging out the words and by giving occasional false alarms—for example: "Cr-r-r-rows" or "Cr-r-r-ranes" or "Cr-r-r-rash."

British Bulldog

Equipment. None.

One or two older Scouts take position as "bulldogs" in the center of the room—or area—facing the troop. At "Go," the rest of the troop charges from one end of the room and tries to reach the other end without being caught. To catch a player, the "bulldogs" must lift him off the floor long enough to yell "1-2-3 British bulldog." When a player is caught, he too becomes a "bulldog" for the next charge. No more than three bulldogs may tackle a player. If a struggling player is not lifted completely off the floor while he slowly counts to 10, he is declared free for another charge. The game continues until one free player is left—he is the winner.

Song Stumper

Equipment. None.

The troop forms a circle, grouped by patrols. Each patrol has a song leader in front of it. The game leader is in the center of the circle. When he points at one of the patrols, the patrol members must begin a song immediately and continue singing it until the leader points to another patrol, which must begin a different song. If a patrol begins a song which has already been sung, or doesn't start singing immediately, it is eliminated. The leader should keep this moving fast, pointing to a new patrol when the patrol has sung only a few phrases of a song. The last patrol in the contest is the winner.

Dual Contests

Equipment. None, or as noted in each event.

These are two-boy contests.

Indian Hand Wrestling. Each contestant places the outside of his right foot against the outside of the other's. Both brace themselves by placing their left feet a long step to the rear. They grasp right hands and attempt to throw each other off balance. The one who first makes the other move his feet or lose his balance is the winner.

One-Legged Hand Wrestling. Each contestant holds his left leg behind him in his left hand, and grasps the other's right hand. Then each tries to throw the other.

Stick Pull. The contestants are seated, facing each other, with the soles of their feet touching. They grasp a strong stick between them, using both hands. On signal, they pull, each trying to raise the other.

Stick Twist. The contestants stand facing each other with their arms raised, grasping a stick between them with both hands. On signal, they force the stick down between them, each trying to twist it from the other's hands.

Indian Leg Wrestling. The contestants lie down with their backs flat on the ground, side by side, but with their legs in opposite directions. On signal each lifts his inside leg to vertical position, then on the next signal tries to lock that leg with the opponent's and twist him over.

Kneel Knock. Contestants kneel facing each other, hands grasped behind their backs. They try to knock each other off balance, using only the shoulders.

Palm Boxing. Contestants stand facing one another on a single length of rope on the floor. Without moving their feet, they box palm hitting palm, attempting to knock one another off balance. The contestant who is forced to move either foot from the rope to restore balance is the loser.

Belt Tug. Contestants are on their hands and knees, facing one another. Two belts are looped together, and one loop is placed over the head of each contestant. The object of the contest is to try to pull the loop off the opponent's head without rising from the kneeling position or touching the belt with the hands.

Hand Slap. Two contestants stand facing each other. Their hands are extended, one player's palms up and the other player's palms down on top of the first player's hands. The object is for the player whose palms are up to slap the back of the other player's hand or hands before he can move them out of the way. If he succeeds, he scores a point, they return their hands to the original position, and he tries to score another point. If he misses, positions are reversed; the other Scout turns his palms up and becomes the aggressor.

Duck Fight. Contestants squat and grasp their ankles with their hands. On signal, each tries to knock the other off balance or cause him to release the hold on his ankle. If a Scout falls to the ground or releases his ankle hold, it is a point for his opponent.

Rooster Fight. The contestants stand facing each other. Each brings his right leg up behind his left and grasps it at the ankle with his right hand. Then, balanced on one leg, he tries to knock the other off balance or cause him to release his ankle hold.

Spies in the Woods

Equipment. Pieces of paper on cardboard backing. Pencil for each player. Outdoor area.

Place cardboard-backed pieces of blank paper 2 feet above the ground on various trees and shrubs in the game area. Two or three of the leaders (depending on size of the area) are spies. They roam about the area. Each player tries to locate the papers and write his name on each of them without being seen. If a spy sees a player within 15 feet of a paper, he puts that player's name in his "black book." For scoring, names in the spies' books are subtracted from the number of signatures on the papers. The patrol with most successful players wins.

Capture the Flag

Equipment. Two signal flags. Large outdoor area.

Each team has its own territory in which its Scouts are free to move as they please, but into which opponents enter at their peril. The territories are separated by a boundary line such as a brook or a trail, etc. Any Scout crossing this line may be captured by the enemy.

The teams assemble close together at a starting point near the center of the line, each team in its own territory. On a signal the teams proceed to set up their flags at any point within 100 paces of the starting point. The flags must be visible, although it is permissible to place them inconspicuously.

After 3 minutes another signal is given for the start of the game. The object is to enter the enemy's territory, capture the flag, and carry it across the line into home territory without being caught. Scouts may be posted to guard the flag, but must not get nearer than 10 paces to it, unless an enemy Scout goes within that distance. They may then follow him.

Any Scout found in the enemy's territory may be captured by rules set in advance, such as grasping and holding him long enough for the captor to say "Caught!" three times. When a Scout is captured he must go with captor to the "guard house"—a tree or rock 10 paces from the boundary line.

A prisoner may be released by a friend touching him, provided the prisoner at that time is touching the guard house with a hand or a foot, whereupon both return to their own territory. If the rescuer is caught by the guards before he touches the prisoner, he, too, must go the guard house. A rescuer may rescue only one prisoner at a time.

If the flag is successfully captured, it must be carried across the line into home territory. If the raider is caught before he reaches home, the flag is set up again at the point where it was rescued and the game goes on as before. If neither side captures the enemy's flag within the time agreed upon (say, half an hour) the game is won by the team having the most prisoners.

NOTE: Additional ideas for games can be found in the back of *Patrol and Troop Activities,* No. 6543.

If you can sing and lead songs, great! If not, find someone who can.

SINGING

There are many occasions for group singing in Scouting. An opening or closing ceremony may involve singing. A campfire usually opens and often closes in song. Hiking, working together, or sometimes just sitting around waiting for the bus to come may cause a song to spring up with no one in particular leading it.

Singing is a natural aid to morale. It does not *create* morale, and you cannot count on song as a substitute for good program. But it can liven things up or tone them down, according to the mood desired. It can add fellowship and fun to almost any Scouting occasion.

How can you get singing started? Here are some ways:

1. Get copies of the *Boy Scout Songbook.* It has a great variety of songs for every occasion.

2. Get some Scouts interested who can accompany singing on an instrument such as a banjo, guitar, harmonica, or ukelele.

3. Start with familiar songs. Sing just one at a meeting. If it goes over, try another song next meeting. If it doesn't, wait a few weeks and try another song.

4. Introduce songs by having an individual or small group sing them—with accompaniment if possible—and then have the troop join in.

5. As interest in singing develops, expand the repertoire—learn a lot of songs. A good singing troop knows dozens of songs.

STORYTELLING

By the dying campfire, or by a simple indoor campfire composed of three candles set in an aluminum pie pan, a well-told story can create almost any desired mood. The storyteller can invoke laughter, terror, inspiration, and patriotism at will.

Half the work of storytelling is done by the campfire itself. It sets a mood, and you just follow it. To do the same thing in the light of day or with all lights on might be impossible.

Where do good stories come from? Your local library is full of them: fiction and fact, heroic stories, mystery stories, military tales, legends, ghost stories, science fiction, and even accounts of real-life persons.

Since most of us talk better than we read aloud, a telling sounds better than a reading. So read the story yourself, get familiar with it, and then retell it to the Scouts.

Tell the boys in advance that the story is whatever it is—sad, inspiring, exciting, etc.—and that you must have their undivided attention. There must be no talking, no unnecessary motions, and no interruptions. Warn them that any discourtesy will cause you to stop right where you are and not finish. Make these the standard rules when stories are told and insist on them.

Give them details so they can imagine the characters and action in great detail: "He was a giant of a man, taller than most, and much, much heavier. He must have weighed 250 pounds. His huge hands could grip a basketball at the top. His grey hair was straight and thin, and there were wrinkles in his face—the wrinkles of pain and sorrow. He shuffled when he walked."

Telling stories is easier than you suppose. With practice you can get better. However, a story is a rare treat and should not be expected at every campfire. But, with much persuasion, you or someone else should be ready with a good story to be told at the right time. Stories make a surprising impression on youth—far greater than our usual estimate of their sophistication would allow.

THE SCOUTMASTER'S MINUTE

The Scoutmaster's minute is often a story. It is distinguished by its brevity and singleness of purpose. It may be an account from a newspaper, a short poem, a personal experience, or something out of Scouting's history.

Such stories are often helped by building them around a familiar object. A phonograph record can be used to introduce a story about Thomas Edison and his incurable curiosity about things. A fishhook can be used to show how it is easy to get into something (like a habit) and how hard it is to get back out. A magnet can be used to deflect a compass needle, illustrating the effect of temptation on life's objectives.

Citizenship subjects are good material for Scoutmaster's minutes.

Some suggested Scoutmaster's minute presentations follow. They may be used as is, but, more constructively, they will give you ideas for other presentations.

Don't Get Hooked

(Stick a fishhook in a piece of cloth and show how difficult it is to back it out the way it went in.)

Scouts, it sure was a cinch to put this fishhook into the cloth, but you can see how hard it is to back it out.

It's just like a bad habit—awfully easy to start, but awfully hard to stop.

Some guys your age have started to smoke. It was easy to start—as easy as it was for me to put the fishhook into the cloth. Across our land millions and millions of smokers have tried to stop smoking and failed. They just couldn't get the hook out.

If it's so hard to stop and if so many smokers want to quit, then why start—why get the hook in—in the first place?

Some people think it's manly to smoke. Take a look around you. Look at who is smoking.

A Little Extra Effort

(You will need two poles and rope to secure them with a square lashing. Tie a square lashing.)

As you watch me tie these poles together, think about how this lashing might be compared to success in life. The wrapping turns hold the two poles closely together. But notice, they are not real tight, and with a little movement of the poles, the ropes loosen to allow slipping.

Now I add the frapping turns. I might have been satisfied without these turns, but notice what happens when I make the extra effort to add them. The frapping turns took up all slack in the first turns and tightened the entire lashing so the poles are now securely bound in place. Repeated movement won't loosen the ties that bind them together.

These frapping turns that finished the job took a little extra effort, but what a difference they made in the job! In life, you will constantly be given chances to put forth a little extra effort. When you have the chance, don't let these opportunities pass. Remember the frapping turns.

If you put extra effort into the things you undertake, you will find success in life, real lasting friendships, and the inner knowledge that, come what may, you have done your best.

A Key to Scouting

(Hold up a car key.)

I have here in my hand a key—a small item as you can see. Yet it will open the door to my car, and when properly placed and turned it will start the engine. With this little key I can visit faraway places, see wonderful sights, and do many things that were impossible only a generation ago. Is it any wonder that I always carry this key with me?

(Hold up a copy of The Official Boy Scout Handbook.*)*

Your *Boy Scout Handbook* is a lot like my car key. It is a small item, yet it will open the door to Scouting and will speed you on your way to adventure. Sure, you probably could get by without using your handbook. I could get by without my car key, too, but I'd have to walk and it would be slow. I certainly wouldn't get to see all the places I can reach by car.

Let's not leave our key behind as we enjoy Scouting. Use your handbook regularly. Take it with you to meetings and on hikes and camping trips. Let your handbook open the door for you.

Big Enough

Scouts, for hiking you have to use a map scale to measure distance between points.

Tonight I'm thinking of another kind of measuring. I get the feeling that we don't realize how often we measure ourselves, day after day.

When you look at a heavy package and say, "That's too heavy for me to lift," what are you measuring? The size of the package—perhaps. But even more you're measuring yourself. You are not big enough to handle this package—or perhaps you just think you aren't!

It may be our homework. We say, "It's too much," when we really mean, "I'm not enthusiastic enough about that much work."

You see, in cases like that we're talking about ourselves, really, rather than the amount of our homework.

Our big idea—all over America—is "Be of service." Some may say, "Oh, it's too much bother," but others will prove that they're big enough to measure up to this idea.

When we look at a job we take our own measure.

Our Flag and Our Oath

(Have three candles in a holder before you—one red, one white, and one blue.)

Have you noticed the strong bond between our flag and our Scout Oath? Let me show you. *(Light the white center candle.)* One of the colors in our flag is white. It is the symbol of purity, of perfection. It is like the first point of our Scout Oath, our duty to God.

(Light the red candle.) The color red in our flag denotes sacrifice and courage, the qualities of the founders of our country. Red is the symbol of the second part of the Scout Oath, too. Our duty to other people requires courage to help anyone in trouble and the self-sacrifice of putting others first.

(Light the blue candle.) Blue is the color of faith. It represents the faith of our founding fathers and reminds us of the third part of the Scout Oath. Our duty to ourselves requires us to be true blue, to be strong in character and principle, to live a life with faith in the importance of being good.

Scouts, rise! Let's have lights out, please. Now, Scout sign. Let us dedicate ourselves with our Scout Oath.

Magnetic Influence

(Demonstrate how a magnet destroys the validity of a compass by causing the needle to veer from North).

Scouts, you have learned to rely on your compass. You know that the needle points North and will guide you in the wilderness, but you have also seen what happens when a magnet is brought near the compass. The magnet is an ouside influence on the character of the compass.

Each Scout has an aim in life. He wants to grow up to be physically strong, mentally awake, and morally straight. The points of the Scout Law make up the magnetic field that directs the compass needle we follow.

Just like the magnet, there are influences trying to change our aim. There are temptations difficult to overcome—temptations to get by without working, to lie, to cheat, to follow the coaxings of friends, and the jeers or threats of enemies.

If you are going to grow up physically strong, mentally awake, and morally straight, you must not succumb to the attraction of the evil magnets in your life, but must be steadfast in your purpose of living up to the ideals of Scouting.

How To Catch a Monkey

Anybody here want to know how to catch a monkey? Well, I can tell you how they do it in India. They take a gourd, cut a small hole in it, and put some rice inside. Then they tie the gourd down securely and wait for the monkey.

Monkeys are greedy and selfish. I guess you could say anybody who is greedy and selfish is a monkey. Anyway, monkeys are so greedy and selfish that they fall for the gourd trick every time.

The monkey sticks his paw into the gourd to get the rice. He gets a handful—but then he can't get his hand out of the gourd. His fist won't go through the small hole. And he's so greedy and selfish that he won't let go of the handful of rice. He just waits there with his greedy fist wrapped around the rice until the men come and take him.

Well, you've got the moral to this story: Don't be greedy and selfish or you may make a "monkey" of yourself.

Night Is for Sleeping

You can always spot the greenhorn—the first-year camper—as soon as "Taps" sounds on the first night in camp. He's the guy that just can't quiet down when the time comes for sleeping.

The experienced camper, comfortable and warm in his bed, knows that night is for sleeping—knows that he'll have more fun and be in better shape for all activities the next day if he gets a good night's sleep.

The greenhorn is the fellow who makes an uncomfortable bed with either poor insulation or inadequate covers and wakes up in the wee small hours, cold and uncomfortable and unable to get back to sleep. The greenhorn can't stand to be cold and uncomfortable alone, so he wakes up a few other soundly sleeping fellow Scouts to share his discomfort. This, naturally, makes him an unpopular guy, not only with the fellows that he intentionally woke up but with all the other campers who are roused by the noise created by the greenhorn out chopping wood to keep warm.

Don't be a camp greenhorn. Night is for sleeping. Be quiet after "Taps" until you get to sleep, and if you wake up early in the morning, don't give away your inexperience by getting up. Stay in bed until "Reveille."

A Scout Is Cheerful

Two brothers once decided to leave their hometown and move to the city. Outside the city the first brother met an old man.

"How are the people here?" asked the first brother.

"Well, how were the people in your hometown?" asked the old man in return.

"Aw, they were always grumpy and dissatisfied," answered the first brother. "There wasn't a single one among them worth bothering about."

"And," the old man said, "you'll find that the people here are exactly the same!"

Later the other brother came along.

"How are the people in this city?" he asked.

"How were the people in your hometown?" the old man asked as before.

"Fine!" said the other brother. "Always cheerful, always kind and understanding!"

"You will find that the people here are exactly the same!" said the old man again, for he was a wise old man who knew that the attitude of the people you meet depends upon your own state of mind. If you are cheerful and frank and good-humored, you'll find others the same.

Stick to It

(Hold up an envelope that has been delivered by the United States Postal Service.)

Fellows, the postage stamp you see on this envelope was given the job of making sure that this important piece of mail was delivered to me. The stamp is pretty small but, in spite of its size, it did the job.

In your patrols, each of you has the responsibility of "delivering the mail" in order that your patrol becomes a success. Like the postage stamp, it isn't your size that determines how well you do the job but, rather, how well you stick to it.

We can't all be good at all things. Some are better at physical skills, some at mental tasks.

Remember the stamp. It did the job in spite of its size by sticking to the job. Make up your mind that you can do the same thing. Just determine to do your best—and stick to it until the job is done.

Respect for the Flag

(Have one red, one white, and one blue piece of cloth and a U.S. flag.)

What is our flag? You might say it's a piece of cloth. Would that be right? Well, it's true that these pieces of cloth could make a U.S. flag, but then we would have more than just a piece of cloth, wouldn't we? What is our flag, then? It's a symbol of our country, of the principles for which we stand. It's a guarantee of protection and security for us. And isn't it a thrill to see the flag flying at the top of a tall staff?

The blue in our flag is a symbol of faith and loyalty—the faith and loyalty of our country's founders. The red in our flag denotes sacrifice, the sacrifices made to establish our nation. The white of her stars and alternate stripes stands for purity of heart and mind. Yes, the colors stand for bravery, loyalty, and purity.

Is there anything in these pieces of cloth by themselves that demands our respect? No. They could be made into an apron just as easily as a flag. We could mop the floor with them or wipe our shoes with them. But the flag these pieces of cloth could make represents our great nation and everything the United States stands for. That's why, Scouts, we give our flag the respect and loyalty that we owe the United States of America.

Everyone Can Win

In a competitive rally we have winners and losers in the various events, yet it is possible for everyone to win something.

A losing patrol can win in spirit and morale, if the fellows work as a team and gain a better understanding of one another. It can win respect in the eyes of all Scouts, if patrol members show good sportsmanship.

A patrol that loses in competition can still win, if in the process of losing the Scouts in the patrol gain in the knowledge of Scouting skills so they will be more proficient in future meets of this type.

Sure, it's nice to win, but with the right attitude, losers frequently benefit more in the long run than do the winners.

Nobody enters a competitive rally planning to lose, but if this should be your lot, make the best of it—take advantage of the things learned in losing and determine to build your patrol teamwork and skill so that the next time someone else will be the loser.

Light Your Law

(Light an ordinary match, hold it up until it has burned for a few seconds, and then blow it out, break it, and throw it away.)

Scouts, you're all familiar with a common match, and know that with it you can start a fire—a fire that will keep you warm, cook your food, and add cheer after dark. After using the match to light your fire, you break it to be sure it is out, and discard it.

The Scout Law is somewhat like this match. We use it to light the good things inside us, but unlike the match we threw away, we should keep the Scout Law to use over and over—in our Scout activities, in our daily living at home, in school, in our work and play, and in the future as we grow into manhood. We don't discard the Scout Law after the troop meeting or even in later years when we are no longer Scouts. The things it represents are as true and meaningful to adults as they are to Scouts.

If you follow the Scout Law every day, the points of the Law will become so much a part of your life that when you grow up and enter the world of adults, you will be able to stand erect and look everyone squarely in the face and say, "I am a man."

Let's all stand, give the Scout sign, and repeat the Scout Law.

Be "In Uniform"

Fellows, what would you think of a policeman in full uniform except for trousers which were of a bright plaid material? How about a hospital intern wearing a sport coat over his white uniform while on duty? Or, what would you think of a train conductor wearing a fireman's cap or, even more absurd, an airline pilot wearing the silks of a jockey as he boarded his plane?

They'd all be "out of uniform," wouldn't they? With some of the outfits mentioned, you wouldn't be sure what they really were.

Scouts, we have a uniform, too. We have a full uniform—not just a neckerchief or just a shirt, but like the people I mentioned, we have a full uniform. When we don't wear the full uniform, we are just as "out of uniform" as the policeman with the plaid pants.

The Flag Code says that when we are "in uniform" we salute the flag with the Scout salute, but when "out of uniform" we salute by holding our right hand over our heart. How do you think a Scout should salute the flag if he's wearing blue jeans or chinos or some other nonofficial dress along with part of the uniform? He's not "in uniform," is he?

A Scout Is Thrifty

Fellows—here I have just a handful of sand, and in my other hand I have a piece of topsoil, just sod. Do you see much difference in them?

Yes, you're right. There's the difference between poverty and wealth here—the difference between starvation and prosperity for all people. This sand represents a civilization that once flourished and is now dead because of misuse of resources. People took from the soil and put nothing back.

But this sod is different for it contains the miracle power of growth. This sod is topsoil enriched through many years.

Our very existence depends on the narrow margin of about 6 inches of topsoil that covers much of our planet. Without it, we cannot survive.

If all the topsoil of the world eroded, what would people live on? Food can't be raised on sand or rock.

What things can we do, as Scouts and as citizens, to help people better understand the importance of this *(gesturing with sod)* and not just let our land drift to this *(sand)*—with the topsoil allowed to waste away?

Working Together

(Equipment—20 wooden matches held together by a rubber band. See that all matches are even in the bundle so the package will stand on end. Stand the matches on the floor in front of the Scouts.)

Scouts, you'll notice the matches in front of you stand easily when they are all bound together with the rubber band. But, look at what happens when I try to stand them after removing the band.

(Take the rubber band off and attempt to stand them up. Of course, they'll fall in all directions.)

Our troop is like this bunch of matches. As long as we work together as a team, bound together by the ties of Scouting, we will stand as a strong troop. But, if we remove those ideals of Scouting, and each man thinks only of himself, we'll be like that bunch of matches when the rubber band was taken off.

As we all live up to the ideals of the Scout Oath, Law, motto, and slogan, we will be wrapping ourselves with the band that will strengthen our troop and make sure that it stands for the things that make Scouting great.

What Money Can't Buy

(Hold up some money.)

All of you recognize this and know that it will buy certain things. It can purchase a candy bar, a stamp, or a little time on a parking meter. Add more money and you can do bigger things.

However, there are many things that money, no matter how much you have, cannot buy. Some of these include the love of your family, freedom, friendships, and the great out-of-doors.

You can't place a value on Scouting, either. We couldn't pay salaries enough to get all the help we have. Nor could we place a value on the memorable experiences, the camping trips, the hikes, the fun of campfires.

People can't pay us for the Good Turns we do, and isn't that a good thing? Such payment would take away the good feeling that we have when we do something for others.

Remember, this money can buy many things, but not the things that really count in human happiness and dignity.

Badge, Book, and Candle

(Place a Scout badge, The Official Boy Scout Handbook, *and a lighted candle on a table.)*

Scouts, since 1910 these three things have been significant in the Boy Scouts of America.

The badge is the symbol of Scouting throughout the United States. Similar badges are used by Scouts all over the world. It is the sign of a universal brotherhood of men and boys of the free world.

There are many books that are important to good Scouts; the handbooks to help us with Scoutcraft skills; the merit badge pamphlets with information about special skills; and, most important of all, the Bible to guide our daily lives.

A candle is a symbol of the light of Scouting that penetrates the darkness of hate, prejudice, war, strife, and distrust. It is a light that must be kept burning in the heart of every Scout, now, and as he grows into manhood.

The Good Turn

(Hold up an ordinary mechanical pencil with the lead turned in so it will not write. Use this pencil as if writing on a sheet of paper and then hold up the paper to show that there is no writing on it.)

Scouts, this pencil won't write. It doesn't leave a mark on this sheet of paper. But if we give it a good turn *(at this point turn the pencil so the lead comes out)*, it now becomes useful and will leave a mark on a sheet of paper.

The good turn we gave the pencil made it useful. The Good Turns we do in our daily living are the things that make us useful. The Good Turn enables us to be useful in our home, school, community, and nation. The Good Turn raises us above the ordinary. It makes our lives worthwhile.

Thank You, Dad

Now, fellows, don't answer this question out loud, but how long has it been since you said, "Thank you, Dad." I'm afraid that too often we take our fathers for granted.

I suppose it might be awkward to try to say—in words—"Thanks, Dad, I appreciate everything you do for me—and with me." And, of course, if we merely said those words and stopped there, they'd be a pretty empty kind of thanks, wouldn't they?

I wonder just how a fellow can go about saying thank you to his father and mother.

The best way that we can show our appreciation is by making our parents proud of us, happy over the kind of fellows we are and are trying to be.

No matter what else we do as a gesture to show appreciation on Father's Day, certainly we want to do our very best to be the kind of fellows that our dads can be proud of all through the year.

Picking on Him

On a hike or in camp we reveal our true selves most. Did you ever know a fellow who thought people were always picking on him?

I recall a boy who pitched his tent carelessly and it blew down on him in the middle of the night. He tried hard to blame it on someone else, but finally he had to admit to himself, "Well, I guess it was my own fault."

Another time he burned a steak. "It was the fire's fault," he insisted, until the other fellows laughed at him and showed him how the same bed of coals could help turn out a well-cooked steak.

Things usually happen to us because we set the stage for them. Actually, people are too busy to spend their time picking on us.

When something goes wrong, the first place to look for the cause is within ourselves.

Your Development

(Show a roll or package of camera film.)

If you look at this exposed film before development, you cannot tell what kind of picture it will make. Film looks exactly the same after snapping the shutter as it did before.

But after development, the image appears on the film and you can see what the picture will be when it is printed.

As I look at you Scouts, I wonder how your exposure has been. You all look the same on the surface, yet I know there are differences within each of you. Like the film, you have been exposed to good and bad things that will make an impression when you develop.

Unlike the film, you have brains. You know what is inside yourself and can do something to make certain your development is good.

Follow the ideals of Scouting—the slogan, motto, Scout Oath or Promise, and Scout Law.

If you live according to these high standards, you can be sure your development will be good as you grow older, and you'll be able to enter manhood fully prepared to be a good citizen of our great nation.

Your Basic Survival Tool

If someone told you that you would be dropped from a plane in the heart of the Canadian wilderness and could pick one tool, implement, or instrument to take with you, what would you choose? Would it be a rifle, pistol, or similar weapon? How about a tent or sleeping bag? Or would a box of matches be most useful?

An experienced woodsman was asked this question, and without hesitation he said, "My ax." He said that with his ax he could defend himself, build shelter, cut materials to make snares and fishing equipment to secure food. The steel in his ax would strike a spark from rocks in the area and provide him with fire. He said that in this day of marvelous inventions, only the simple ax could do all of these things and guarantee his survival.

If the ax is this important to the experienced woodsman, shouldn't we be a little more respectful of it? Shouldn't we learn how to use it correctly, to care for it, and always to keep it sharp and ready for emergency use?

The woodsman, when he said, "My ax," really meant, "My sharp ax, unrusted, with a tight head, ready for hard use." An ax that doesn't meet these standards is pretty useless. Let's be sure our axes are always ready for use.

Camp Is a City

As we look at local government, perhaps we can gain a better understanding of its duties and responsibilities, if we compare it with our own troop experience in camp.

A camp is a city in many ways. First of all, the camp has certain rules and regulations (laws) developed for the good of all campers. Then, of course, someone must enforce these laws, and it is the responsibility of troop leaders (police and courts) to see that camp regulations are followed. Wherever groups of people live there is a need for fire protection, and the camp is no exception. We organize a troop fire guard (firemen) while we are in camp to protect our property from the danger of fire.

Sanitation, including proper disposal of refuse and garbage, must be taken care of both in the city and in camp. In our patrol rotation of duties we have kitchen and campsite "cleaner-uppers" (sanitation department).

There are other similarities between camp and a city, but the ones I've mentioned are enough to point out the value of participating citizenship. You all know what happens in camp when we have indifferent citizens. Everyone suffers because of the failure of a few. The same thing is true in government.

Your Mark—Which Will It Be?

(Hold up a plaster cast of a track.)

Scouts, here you see permanent evidence that an animal (or bird) has passed along the way. Before we made the cast, the track was pretty temporary—a few hours of wind and rain and all signs of the animal's passing would be erased. By making the cast, we preserved the track for future generations of Scouts to view.

Our lives can make a temporary or permanent mark on this world according to the way we live. Most of us probably never will be great leaders of nations or famous in the arts or sciences, but we can still leave a permanent mark on this earth by the things we do for others.

The daily Good Turn is one way to start making your mark, because as you give of yourself to others in unselfish service, you are making changes in their lives and in yours. Those who change the lives of others make a permanent mark in the world, because the good they do lives on long after they have passed along the way.

Has each of you done his Good Turn today? Have you decided to consciously seek out opportunities for service to others and not just wait until you happen to see a need?

Decide now to leave your permanent track as you pass through the years.

Heat, Fuel, and Oxygen

(Hold a lighted candle while talking. Room lights may be turned off, if desired.)

Fellows, here you see a plain, ordinary candle—a candle such as we use in our investiture ceremony for new Scouts.

This candle needs three things to keep it burning. These three things are heat, fuel, and oxygen. The heat was provided by the match I used to start it burning. The fuel is the melted wax which is absorbed by the wick. The oxygen comes from the air around us.

If we remove any one of these three things, the candle will go out. If there is no heat, the wax will not melt. If the wax is not melted, the wick cannot absorb the fuel, and if the air were cut off, the candle would soon go out.

In the same way, Scouts, you and I need three things to do our tasks in life. These three things are related to your body, your mind, and your spirit.

In dedicating yourselves to the Scout Oath, you pledge that you will do your best to make these three things meaningful in your life. You pledge to keep yourselves physically strong, mentally awake, and morally straight.

We need these three things to do our job, just as the candle needs heat, fuel, and oxygen to keep burning.

A Scout Is Trustworthy

An architect who had just finished college was trying to get his business established and was having a hard time doing it. He still owed money for some of his college expenses and saw his debts piling up. Each day he became more and more worried, until he was looking around desperately for a solution.

Then a wealthy man, who had been a good friend of his father, came to him one day. "I want you to build me a house," he said. "Build it of the finest materials. Spare no expense. Build it just as if it were for yourself and you had all the money in the world. Here is an advance on your fee. I will be gone for some months, so take full charge."

It was like a dream to the young architect. The advance enabled him to wipe out all his debts, and he knew that he could be married soon. For when the house was finished, he could expect other good commissions. Then his reputation would be established solidly. So he set to work with great joy.

As the building progressed, the architect was struck with an idea. The owner would not be back for months. No one was keeping check on the building. He could build the house just as he pleased. So he began to use second-rate materials where they wouldn't show. As he went on in this way, he figured he would make an extra ten thousand dollars for himself, because, of course, he would charge the owner for the best materials throughout.

Well, the house finally was finished and the owner came back. The man was pleased. "It's beautiful," he said. "But, unfortunately, I will never live in it. While I was traveling, I made some investments in Europe that will keep me there, perhaps permanently. And I want you to have this house as a wedding present from me. It's so beautiful! It's a picture of your own character, true and loyal all the way through!

Imagine how the young architect felt! Yes, the house was a picture of his own character, and would be there to remind him of his cheating as long as he lived.

Chapter 16

Ceremonies

Ceremonies stress the importance of Scouting's ideals.

EREMONIES, in the early years of Scouting, were associated primarily with courts of honor and rank advancement. We have since come to realize the benefits of taking every possible opportunity to recognize participants in Scouting. These ceremonies can be made more impressive by planning and a little showmanship. Refer to *Scout Ceremonies*, No. 6542, for more help.

If a Scout has earned recognition, whether for a rank or for a troop-meeting uniform inspection, he deserves to receive it promptly and publicly. The major way we hold the interest of boys in Scouting (and that's the only way we can influence their development) is by recognizing their achievements. Prompt, dignified, impressive public recognition ceremonies influence attendance, advancement, and tenure!

Most experienced Scouts and Scouters have seen enough ceremonies to have their own ideas on how it should be done. Any one of them could put on a good one-man show, but one-man shows are rarely impressive and deny opportunity for involvement of others, both youth and adults, in the program. The easiest way to avoid one-man shows is to document your ceremony well ahead of time. First, examine the elements and sequence of events desired or required. Then, think them through—several times. When you have what you believe is an acceptable program, make a legible, complete list of events and participants. Next review the plan with appropriate Scouts and Scouters, keeping an open mind for suggestions. Solicit suggestions from key leaders involved— particularly the Scouts.

Ceremony Ingredients. What should go into the making of a good Scout ceremony? The ingredients will vary with the end product desired but the following might be considered.
Ceremonies should:

- Contain some element of rededication to the Scout Oath, Scout Law—a reminder of the ideals of our movement.

- Be based on building Scout spirit, or improving Scout participation.

- Include some element of patriotism, or appreciation of the American way of life.

- Include enthusiasm and sincerity.

- Be impressive, dignified, and brief.

- Tolerate neither horseplay nor embarrassment.

- Avoid elements or suggestion of initiation.

- Be planned by boys or a committee that includes boys, to ensure maximum boy appeal and perhaps greater effectiveness.

- Start *on time* and end as close to announced (or expected) time as possible.

- Feature boys, but where possible and appropriate, acknowledge the chartered organization and key adults who are active with the troop.

- Avoid discomfort, such as poor visibility, inability to hear speakers, long periods of standing at attention, and poor ventilation.

- Honor one Scout at a time, ensuring that he feels it is his special recognition.

- Ensure that the recipient is *facing the audience,* not the presenter.

- Be conducted as though a young man's future depends on it.

The only way to eliminate mishaps at the real event is to let the "goof" happen at practice sessions. Only by seeing the color guard "in formation" can you ensure that they are about the same height, don't have two left feet, know where the flags actually go, and are not scheduled to be in two parts of the ceremony at the same time.

Investiture Ceremony. *Troop is lined up along two sides of the room, the troop officers at the front of the room, parents seated. Patrol leader brings the candidate into the room which is lighted by a single candle.*

Scoutmaster: Who goes there?

Patrol Leader: I bring a candidate who has completed the Boy Scout requirements and wishes to join our troop and my patrol.

Senior Patrol Leader: Bring him forward. *When the candidate approaches, the senior patrol leader takes the lighted candle and says:* This candle represents the spirit of Scouting. It lights our way as Scouts in the same way it lights this room tonight. It reminds us to help other people at all times, to live up to the Scout Oath and Law, to Be Prepared, and to do a Good Turn daily. Are you ready to take the Oath?

Candidate: I am.

Scoutmaster: Scout sign. Repeat the Scout Oath with me: "On my honor..." *As you and the candidate repeat the Oath, light three candles from the spirit of Scouting, (1) duty to God and country, (2) duty to others, (3) duty to self, and say:* When we do our duty the world is a brighter place for everyone. Each person here tonight has witnessed your taking the Scout Oath or Promise. All of them will help you keep it. *Now, pin the Boy Scout badge on the candidate's shirt while the patrol leader pins the patrol medallion on his right sleeve. Exchange salutes. Patrol leader escorts the new Scout to his place in the patrol formation amid the cheers and applause of the troop and its visitors.*

OPENING CEREMONIES

The opening ceremony bridges the gap between all activities, conversations, and diversions and the beginning of the troop meeting. An opening should be used to begin all troop meetings and courts of honor. The opening will set the pace for all that follows. Openings, like all ceremonies, are important and deserve attention and planning.

A standard ceremony may be developed and used as a troop tradition, or meetings may be varied with several ceremonies.

An opening ceremony sets the tone for the meeting.

Your opening ceremony may be handled by the senior patrol leader or by an assigned patrol. Here are a few examples:

U.S. Flag Ceremony 1. Troop in horseshoe formation with flag at open end. Starting at one end, Scouts in turn take one step forward, salute the flag, and step back in place.

U.S. Flag Ceremony 2. Troop in single line. U.S. flag is spotlighted with a strong flashlight. One Scout reads the first verse from *The Star-Spangled Banner*. (This ceremony can be used at four meetings in a row using a different verse each time.)

Troop Flag Ceremony. Patrol leaders grasp troop flagpole with left hand and give Scout sign with right. Members of patrols form lines like spokes of a wheel with the flag at the hub by grasping one another's upraised right arm with their left hand and giving the Scout sign with the right. When all are in formation they repeat the Scout Oath and give the troop yell.

INSTALLATION AND REDEDICATION CEREMONIES

These ceremonies cover a wide range of applications. Such ceremonies add a touch of formality. When a Scout assumes a job in the troop as patrol leader or even as assistant patrol leader, make that step official by presenting his new badge of office with the seriousness it deserves. Make it an official happening in your troop. Try to put yourself in the place of the Scout or Scouter being honored, then do and say those things that would please you.

Make each one of these ceremonies special. It is important to tailor the ceremony; and like all ceremonies, good common sense and detailed planning are the keys to success.

The court of honor recognizes advancement.

COURTS OF HONOR

Courts of honor can be as varied in character as the troops which conduct them. They range from highly structured to extremely informal, and from totally adult-led to completely boy-run, although most are somewhere in between.

The important thing to remember is that their only purpose is to recognize boys. If you must recognize adults (such as introducing new adult leaders/committee members or making a presentation to retiring ones), it should be done at the beginning of the evening, prior to the opening of the court by your commissioner or other Scouting official. Once the court is formally opened, adults have no place in the proceedings except to honor boys for their achievements.

Ideally, the conducting of the court of honor is the responsibility of the troop committee. You, as Scoutmaster, should be included in the program, but you are not the presiding justice of the court of honor. Someone else should do that job.

FLAG CEREMONIES

The use of the U.S. flag, state, church, and troop flag is encouraged. These banners are important symbols in our lives. Use them in courts of honor and other ceremonies. However, care should be taken to ensure the use is meaningful. Don't let the use of the flag become mere "habit."

The flag portion of *The Official Boy Scout Handbook*, pages 414-27, are helpful in showing proper respect to the flag. More information is available on this subject in the pamphlet *Your Flag*, No. 3188, published by the Boy Scouts of America.

CAMPFIRE CEREMONIES

The campfire is a natural place for ceremonies. A troop may develop traditional opening, lighting, and closing campfire ceremonies or try something new each time. A troop campfire is an excellent place for most ceremonies from investitures to courts of honor. With a little imagination most ceremonies can be adapted for use at a campfire.

WEBELOS-TO-SCOUT TRANSITION CEREMONIES

The importance of conducting a good Webelos-to-Scout ceremony cannot be overstated. This is the single most effective method to retain a boy and his parents in Scouting. Far too many Webelos Scouts never join a Boy Scout troop simply because no troop made it easy for them to do so. To the Webelos Scout the troop does not appear to be a friendly place—the Scouts are all bigger than he is. A good transition ceremony can help make the newcomer welcome.

1. Make the boy feel important. He has accomplished something and should be recognized for it. A part of this recognition is the fact that he has earned the right to take the next step up the ladder of Scouting into the troop. Emphasize that it is the expected thing for a Webelos Scout to do.

2. Make him feel wanted in the patrol and in the troop.

3. Welcome his family into the troop.

GENERAL TIPS FOR GOOD CEREMONIES

A few props and techniques can really spice up any ceremony. These can range from simple to elaborate, depending on the need and the money you have available for the event.

Lighting. Lighting is important to most ceremonies. This ranges from performing a ceremony behind the campfire so the fire illuminates the participants to spotlighting recipients in a court of honor.

- Room lighting needs to be checked. Where are the switches? When will they be turned off and on and who will do it? Practice to plan the effect.

- Stage lighting can be simulated by using yard reflector lights or desk lamps. A regular table lamp can be used simply by shielding the audience from its glare with a piece of cardboard.

- Spotlighting should be used anytime a boy is recognized before a court of honor or any large audience. Spotlights can be from strong flashlights or a 35mm slide projector. In the case of the projector, you can reduce the size of the spot by masking the lens.

Decorations. A few decorations can transform a room into a special place for appropriate ceremonies.

- Crepe paper streamers or strips are inexpensive and easy to use.

- Make displays of Boy Scout neckerchief slides.

- Use posters and Boy Scout pictures.

- Create an unusual atmosphere with colored lights.

- Feature Scout skills in displays.

Audiovisuals. A large number of commercial and Boy Scout movies and slide programs are available and appropriate for formal ceremonies. Good sound equipment (tape or record) and carefully selected music will enhance a court of honor or other special ceremony. For example, showing movies or slides of an Eagle candidate's service project from beginning to end adds to the audience appreciation of the Eagle Award.

Special Troop Props. Specially designed or developed props can become a part of the troop's tradition giving the occasion a special flair each time it is used.

- Advancement boards arranged by rank or patrol may be made with names on individual cards punched for hanging when the Scout is recognized at the court of honor.

- Eagle plaque with the troop numeral and the new Eagle's name added to those of the others at the court of honor.

- Rustic candelabra of logs with holes drilled for candles may be used for many ceremonies featuring the points of the Oath and Law.

- Artificial campfire made with electric light bulb shining through a red or orange plastic cover. Set inside a log fire lay, this imitation fire provides a campfire glow around the room. Be careful of fire hazard—use flashlights, if in doubt.

- Light boxes can be made from paper bags partially filled with sand and illuminated by lighted candles placed in the sand. These light boxes may be used outdoors with proper precaution to prevent fire.
- Badge holder is a useful decoration to organize the badges and certificates that are to be awarded. It could be a felt-covered tray or a corkboard. Divide all items by the Scouts' names and be sure the presenter knows how to get the badges off.
- Flags lend themselves to the pageantry of a ceremony and may be given a special prominence by focusing a spotlight on them.
- Troop scrapbooks or the troop "Log of Achievement" may provide space for Scouts awarded higher rank to write a brief statement of their thoughts on becoming a Star, Life, or Eagle Scout.

CLOSING CEREMONIES

The closing ceremony brings the meeting or activity to a formal end. The following four ceremonies are examples:

Taps. Scouts sing taps. Each boy slowly raises his two hands in front of him during the words "from the lake, from the hill, from the sky," and lowers them during the rest of the song.

Scout Vesper Song. Form a circle. Scouts cross arms in front and grasp hands of Scout on either side making a continuous circle of crossed and joined hands. Sing the "Scout Vesper Song" from the *Boy Scout Songbook.*

Flag Ceremony. If a flag ceremony was used in the opening it is appropriate to retire the flag as a closing ceremony. Scouts could whistle the bugle call "To the Colors" as the flag is retired.

Scout Law Ceremony. Scouts are in a circle. They give the Scout sign. Each Scout grasps the upraised wrist of his neighbor with his left hand. The troop recites the Scout Law.

Chapter 17

Uniforms and Insignia

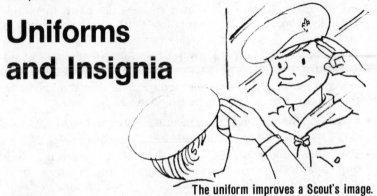

The uniform improves a Scout's image.

THE Scout uniform will help you achieve the objectives of Scouting. The uniform by itself can't make a good Scout or a good troop, but its use will improve both the Scout and the troop because it is a visible symbol of Scouting.

THE OFFICIAL UNIFORMS

Troop options in uniforming are available. These are explained in the illustrations. Details on wearing official insignia appear later in the chapter.

Encouraging Uniforming

In a troop with a strong tradition of 100 percent uniforming, a leader may need to make no special efforts to sustain uniforming. Each new Scout gets a uniform, wears it regularly and proudly, and little emphasis need be placed on it.

In a new troop or one where uniforming is less than 100 percent, however, it is a different story.

Leader Example. All uniforming begins and is maintained by the example of leaders. You, your assistants, and all boy leaders should be in full, correct uniform at all Scouting functions. There is little hope that boys will maintain pride in proper uniforming if their leaders do not. Incidentally, the costs of Scouter uniforms are deductible on your Federal income tax.

Uniform Exchange. Many troops buy old uniforms in good condition from Scouts who have outgrown them or left the troop.

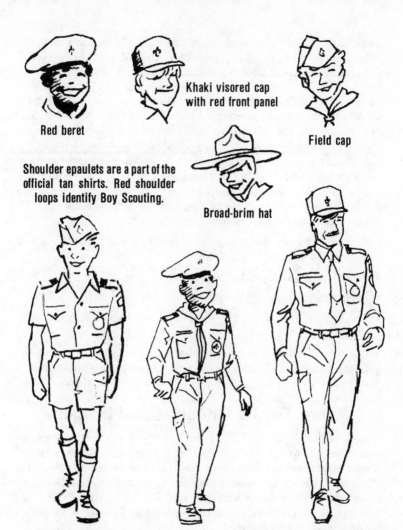

Red beret

Khaki visored cap with red front panel

Field cap

Shoulder epaulets are a part of the official tan shirts. Red shoulder loops identify Boy Scouting.

Broad-brim hat

If the troop votes not to wear neckerchiefs, shirts may be worn with the collars open. Boy Scout bolo ties may be worn, if desired.

Khaki uniforms, sold before the design change, will continue to be official uniforms of the Boy Scouts of America.

Your troop may choose its official uniform from the options shown. When the choice is made, all Scouts wear the selected uniform. The adult leaders and junior assistant Scoutmasters will wear the same official uniform, but it need not be the same as that chosen for wear by the Scouts in your troop.

These are resold to boys needing uniforms. They are known as "experienced" uniforms. It is important that no boy be deprived of Scouting because of lack of a uniform.

Inspections. An excellent way to encourage proper uniforming is by regular uniform inspections. Formal inspections should be held at least quarterly. It's not a bad idea to have quick, informal inspections once a month. In these informal inspections, the senior patrol leader or each patrol leader inspects the Scouts for general appearance and full uniform. This should take only 3 to 5 minutes.

For formal, quarterly inspections, use Uniform Inspection Sheets, which are available at your council service center.

Items to inspect may include some or all of the following:

- Personal grooming—face and hands clean, hair combed, fingernails trimmed and clean.
- Complete uniform—clean and neat.
- Pocket flaps buttoned.
- Insignia correct and properly placed, no excessive patches or badges.
- Observance of chosen troop options.
- Shoes.

Where To Get Uniforms and Insiginia

New uniforms, official equipment, and certain insignia can be purchased only from official Scouting distributors. These are retail stores that have been given a special franchise by the Boy Scouts of America to distribute these materials. Buyers must show that they are currently registered with the Boy Scouts of America to buy uniform parts and insignia. Other official equipment is available without evidence of registration.

Restricted badges and insignia are available only through the office of your council. This control assures that such restricted materials don't fall into unauthorized hands.

When To Wear the Uniform

Scouting Activities. The uniform is appropriate for nearly all Scouting activities. It is especially appropriate where travel is involved and Scouts will be in front of the general public. There may be activities within some Scouting functions that are not suitable for uniform wear, such as doing camp KP or cleaning out a creek bed.

Scouting Anniversary Week. Scouts should be encouraged to wear their uniforms during this week in February.

Special Scout Participation. Where Scouts act as color guards, march in parades, and escort distinguished visitors at public functions, the uniform is in order.

When NOT To Wear the Uniform

The uniform is not appropriate for Scouts or Scouters under three kinds of conditions:

1. When a commercial product or service is being sold, *even for Scout money-earning purposes.*
2. When the activity would tend to dishonor or discredit the uniform.
3. When the wearing of the uniform would tend to imply endorsement by Scouting of a product, service, or political candidate or philosophy. Scouts and Scouters are encouraged to take active part in political matters as individuals, but to do so in uniform would imply endorsement by the Scouting movement.

How the Uniform Can Help a Boy

It is not the purpose of the Scout uniform to hide the differences between boys or make them feel that they are all the same. Scouts come from many backgrounds. They have their own religious beliefs and family traditions. Scouting wants boys to take pride in these differences.

There is a way in which Scouts are alike. When he sees another person in a Scout uniform, he knows he is like that person because both have committed themselves to the Scout Oath or Promise and Scout Law. The Scout Oath or Promise and Law bind Scouts together. The Scout uniform is worn to identify openly with these beliefs.

The uniform stands for high ideals.

By wearing the uniform Scouts give each other support. Boys need that and they can give it to each other. It's good to discover that others share our beliefs. It means all Scouts are brothers.

By wearing the uniform Scouts declare their faith and commitment to important beliefs that bind them to *all* people. It's a way of making visible their belief in God, their loyalty to our country, their commitment to "help other people at all times."

Young people recognize the importance of taking a stand regarding their beliefs. They say: "If you believe it, be it." At some point in a Scout's experience he openly declared an acceptance of the Scout Oath. But the values of the Scout Oath and Law make a difference in a boy only when he acts upon them.

As Scouts wear the uniform, they are standing for some principles—in the open, where everyone can see. Scouts are standing with each other, not alone, declaring their intent to be "other people" oriented.

How the Uniform Can Help the Troop

1. When smartly worn, the uniform can help to build good troop spirit.
2. By investing in a uniform, a Scout and his parents are really making a commitment to take Scouting seriously.
3. The uniform makes the troop visible as a force for good in the community.
4. When properly worn on the correct occasions, it can attract new members.
5. Scouts in uniform create a strong, positive youth image in the neighborhood, thus helping to counteract the negative feelings some adults have about youth.

INSIGNIA

Most of the insignia of Scouting are worn on the uniform and become part of it. It is important for Scoutmasters to be well acquainted with insignia and their proper display.

Insignia are intended to show current status. Thus, a Second Class Scout does not wear a Tenderfoot badge, and a former patrol leader does not wear that badge.

Badges which have been worn and are no longer appropriate can be sewn on a trophy blanket or hide, or may be worn on the red patch vest. The vest is not to be worn with the uniform, however. The trophy blanket can be used as the top cover of a camp bed, and worn over the shoulders at campfires. In this way Scouts and Scouters can "show off" the things they have done.

In Boy Scouting the advancement program is intended for boys only. As a Scoutmaster or other leader, you should neither seek awards designed for boys nor wear them on your uniform. Advancement badges are not for adult wear. However, if you earned the Eagle rank, Quartermaster Award, Silver Award, Arrow of Light Award, religious emblem, and/or lifesaving award as a Cub Scout, Boy Scout, Varsity Scout, or Explorer, you may wear the embroidered square knots for these awards on your uniform. See pages 346-47.

Good taste suggests that you do not necessarily wear all the insignia you may be entitled to wear.

Alterations of Insignia Prohibited

No alteration of, or additions to, the official badges and insignia or in the rules and regulations governing their use or their location upon the uniform may be authorized by any Scouting official, local council, local executive board, or committee except the national Executive Board.

Special Local Badges and Insignia

Local councils are authorized to adopt special badges and insignia as awards for particular purposes in harmony with national policies and to permit their use upon the official uniform in accordance with the Rules and Regulations of the Boy Scouts of America, but such awards must be approved as to purpose and design by the national office in advance.

Badge Swapping

Scouts attending jamborees swap articles of a local or regional character among themselves. Swapping badges or rank, office, distinguished service, performance, achievement, distinction, and training is in violation of the Rules and Regulations of the Boy Scouts of America, which forbids the holding of these badges by any but members who have complied with the requirements.

Badges of Other Organizations

The general rule is that badges awarded by organizations other than the Boy Scouts of America may not be worn on an official uniform. There are exceptions. Among them are special badges approved by local councils in conjunction with the national Insignia and Uniform Committee, such as historic trails medals. Other exceptions are awards from other Scout associations and religious emblems.

Two Badges With the Same Meaning

Where two or more badges have the same meaning, only one may be displayed on the uniform at the same time. An exception to the rule is permission to wear the ribbon Eagle Award on formal occasions on the same uniform on which also appears the Eagle knot or Eagle embroidered emblem.

Badges of Identification

Community Strip. Lettered with the name of the community in which the troop is located. Limited to 17 letters and spaces. Worn on left sleeve with center touching the shoulder seam.

State Strip. Worn centered below and touching the community strip. It is not worn with the council strip.

Council Patch. Where approved by the local council, this patch may be worn in place of the community and state strip.

Troop Numeral. Worn centered on left sleeve with top just below the community, state, or council strip.

Veteran Troop Insignia. Worn by members of troops that have achieved 25 or 50 years of continuous registration. Worn touching the top of the troop numeral. The numeral should be lowered enough to permit insertion of the veteran bar between the community, state, or council strip and the numeral.

Universal Scout Badge. Worn as a lapel pin on a business suit or on any other contemporary clothing by adults registered with the Boy Scouts of America.

Universal Scout Jacket Badge. Worn by Scouts and Scouters on the left pocket or breast of the jacket or jac-shirt.

Patrol Medallion. Worn with top centered 2 inches below the shoulder seam of the right sleeve by members of the patrol shown on the medallion.

Leadership Corps Emblem. Worn with top centered 2 inches below the right shoulder seam of Scouts who are members of the leadership corps.

Nameplate. May be worn by Boy Scouts and Scouters on the right pocket flap of the uniform shirt. If Order of the Arrow pocket emblem is worn, the nameplate is worn above the Boy Scouts of America strip over the pocket.

JEFFREY BROWN

Interpreter strip. Worn by Scouts and Scouters who can speak another language. See *Boy Scout Handbook,* page 482.

ESPAÑOL

Shoulder Loops. Worn by Scouts and Scouters on the official tan long- or short-sleeve shirts. Color of the shoulder loops identifies the branch of Scouting: red, Boy Scouting; orange, Varsity Scouting; green, Exploring; blue, Cub Scouting; silver, council and district; gold, regional and national.

Badges of Office

These badges are worn with the top centered and touching the troop numeral. They are only worn by persons currently holding the positions represented by the badge. See exception below for Den Chief Service Award.

Den Chief Cord.　　　Webelos Den Chief Cord.

Worn on left shoulder under epaulet and arm.

Joining Insignia

Boy Scout. This badge is worn the same as a badge of rank, but technically represents the joining requirements and *is not a rank.*

Boy Scout

Badges of Rank

These badges are worn centered on the left breast pocket of Scouts who have qualified for the rank. Only the highest rank earned is worn. See exception to placement in the case of Eagle.

Tenderfoot

Second Class

First Class

Star

Life

Eagle
(Embroidered)

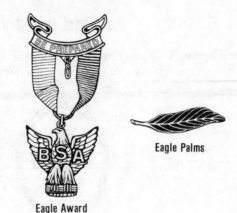

Eagle Knot

Eagle Palms

Eagle Award

Eagle Award. Worn pinned centered just above the left breast uniform pocket flap seam. This badge is worn only on formal occasions.

Eagle (embroidered). Worn centered on left breast uniform pocket.

Eagle Knot. Worn by adults above the left breast uniform pocket.

Eagle Palms. Worn pinned horizontally to the ribbon of the Eagle badge ⅛ inch apart.

Merit Badges

Sleeve. Up to six merit badges may be worn on the right sleeve (long-sleeve shirt) in a column of two starting 3 inches above the bottom edge of the sleeve cuff.

Merit badges can be worn on the right sleeve or the merit badge sash.

Sash. Merit badges may be worn in a column of two on the narrow sash and a column of three on the wide sash. The sash is worn over the right shoulder. It is worn only on formal occasions. No badges other than merit badges may be worn on the sash. Badges may be worn on front and back of sash.

Skill Awards

These are in the form of belt loops and are worn on the uniform belt by those Scouts who have qualified for them.

Camping

Citizenship

Communications

Community Living

Conservation

Cooking

Environment

Family Living

First Aid

Hiking

Physical Fitness

Swimming

Badges of Achievement

Recruiter. Worn as a temporary insignia on the right shirt pocket. May be placed immediately below any other temporary insignia attached to the pocket. Worn by a Scout who recruited a boy into Scouting.

RECRUITER

World Crest. The world crest is a cloth embroidered emblem with the international trefoil in white on a purple background and measures about 1-¾ inches. It is worn on the official uniform centered above the left shirt pocket 3 inches below the shoulder seam.

ITALIANO

Interpreter. If you are good at languages, a special interpreter badge is available to you. To earn this, you must be able to carry on a conversation in a foreign language or in sign language. You must write a letter in the foreign language (not required for signing). And you must translate orally and in writing from the language.

Youth Leadership in America Award for Senior Patrol Leaders. This award may be earned by any senior patrol leader who meets the six requirements and is approved by his Scoutmaster. This award makes the senior patrol leader eligible.

Webelos Arrow of Light Award. Worn just above the bottom seam of the left shirt pocket by Boy Scouts who earned the award while Cub Scouts. An adult may wear the square knot representing this recognition, if earned as a boy.

Den Chief Service Award. Worn in the same manner as den chief cord. May be worn with either of the above when serving in active capacity, or may be worn alone when Scout no longer serves as den chief. See *Den Chief Handbook,* No. 3211, for requirements.

Contest Medals. Worn centered over left breast pocket of the shirt by Scouts who earned the medal in troop or intertroop competition. Contest medals won as Cub Scouts are not worn on the Boy Scout uniform. Contest medals are worn only on formal occasions.

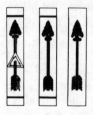

Order of the Arrow Sash. Available only from the Order of the Arrow lodge. Worn on formal Order of the Arrow occasions or service projects. Worn over the right shoulder under the epaulet. Only the 50th Anniversary Award and the 60th Anniversary activity awards emblems are officially worn on the Order of the Arrow sash. Any other items, including "sashbacks," are not authorized for wear.

Order of the Arrow Pocket Patch. Available only from the Order of the Arrow lodge. Worn on the right pocket flap by Scouts and Scouters who are lodge members in good standing.

 Order of the Arrow Ribbon Pin. Available only from the Order of the Arrow lodge. Worn suspended from the button of the right pocket from beneath the pocket flap by Order of the Arrow members in good standing.

Firem'n Chit. The owner of a Firem'n Chit has demonstrated knowledge of safety rules in building, maintaining, and putting out camp and cooking fires. For requirements see *Boy Scout Requirements,* No. 3216.

 Mile Swim, BSA. Worn on left side of swim trunks by Scouts who have earned the badge.

 BSA Lifeguard. Worn on the right side of swim trunks by Scouts who have earned the badge.

 Historic Trails Award. Worn on pack, blanket, or tent by Scouts who earned it as members of a troop meeting the requirements. A decalcomania is also available for paddle, canoe, or plaque.

 50-Miler Award. Worn on pack, blanket, or tent by Scouts who earned it as members of a troop meeting the requirements. A decalcomania is also available for paddle, canoe, or plaque.

When a Scout demonstrates that he knows how to handle woods tools he may be granted totin' rights. If he fails in his responsibility, his totin' rights may be taken away. See *Boy Scout Requirements*, No. 3216, for the requirements for carrying a Totin' Chip.

Paul Bunyan Woodsman. As a member of the Boy Scouts of America teach the Totin' Chip to a Scout using a hand ax. Then study chapter 6 in the *Fieldbook* and, using a ¾ ax, demonstrate to your Scout leader or other qualified person designated by him the following:

1. Cut a log 6-8 feet long and 4 inches or more in diameter into 2-foot lengths. Then split these 2-foot lengths into quarters.
2. With official approval and supervision do one of the following: (a) Clear trails or fire lanes for 2 hours. (b) Demonstrate how to fell a standing tree 4 inches or more at the butt. Lop branches, make brush pile; cut tree into 2-foot lengths and stack. (c) Trim down a tree, cut into 4-foot lengths and stack; make brush pile of smaller branches.

Badges of Participation

Attendance Pin. Worn just above the pocket flap seam of the left pocket. Requirements for qualification are set by the troop committee and Scoutmaster. Not to be worn by Scouters.

Attendance Bar. Attached between the year bar and the medal of the attendance pin by Scouts who have met troop qualifications for additional years.

Service Stars. Worn in a line centered ⅜ inch above the left pocket, ¾ inch from center to center of the stars. The line may be raised if necessary to allow room for decorations, medals, and other insignia prescribed for the left breast. Background of the star indicates where earned—blaze, Tiger Cubs; gold, Cub Scouting; green, Boy Scouting; brown, Varsity Scouting; red, Exploring; blue, Scouter. Service stars with numerals designating total service may be worn instead of multiple single stars. No more than 10 service stars may be worn.

Veteran Pin or Tie Tac. For nonuniform wear, except the tie tac may be worn with the uniform tie. Worn only by Scouters who have achieved veteran status.

National Jamboree Emblem. Worn centered immediately above the right pocket (above the nameplate if that has been moved because of an Order of the Arrow pocket patch). Worn only by Scouts and Scouters who have participated or are registered to participate in the jamboree represented by the emblem.

District, Council, Regional, and National Activity Badges. Except for jamboree badges mentioned earlier, these are all considered to be temporary insignia and are restricted to the wearing of one on the uniform at a time. The one selected shall be worn centered on the right shirt pocket. Additional temporary insignia earned may be used to replace the single insignia on the uniform or may be displayed on a campfire robe or as part of an emblem trophy display in the home.

District Insignia. Districts are operational arms of the local council. Individuals are not identified as residents of a district, but of the local council and the Boy Scouts of America. For this reason district insignia is not authorized for wear on the uniform. Where it seems desirable to identify district participation in council activities, district flags or banners may be authorized.

Jackets and Their Insignia

Red jackets in nylon, wool, and poplin are available for optional wear by Scouts and adult leaders. The proper universal emblem for the branch of Scouting the wearer is engaged in should be worn on the left pocket or, in case of a zippered jacket, above the pocket. The Philmont bull emblem is especially designed for the red wool jac-shirt to be sewn on the left shoulder above the pocket. Scouts may wear their leadership corps patch centered on the right pocket of the red wool jac-shirt. On all jackets the Philmont or high-

Official wool jac-shirt   Official lightweight jacket

adventure base emblems may be worn centered on the right pocket or in the same relative position if there is no pocket. The Order of the Arrow has adopted the jac-shirt as its official jacket, and members may wear the 6-inch national Order of the Arrow patch centered on the back. The large NESA, jamboree, and international participation emblems are approved to be worn on the back of the jacket. Only one such emblem may be worn at a time. In all cases, the lightweight jacket is an alternate for the jac-shirt, and this insignia may be worn on it in the same way.

Training Awards

The trained leader emblem, No. 280, may be worn by adult and junior leaders who have completed training for their current position.

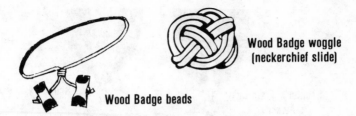

Wood Badge woggle
(neckerchief slide)

Wood Badge beads

Boy Scout Leader Wood Badge. Wood Badge is the advanced training program of Boy Scouting. It is designed especially for Scoutmasters and other leaders directly related to the program of a Boy Scout troop. Since it is advanced training, the leader must have completed Boy Scout Leader Basic Training and had an opportunity to put the learning to work.

Wood Badge training has two parts. The first is an outdoor experience where the Scouter lives as a member of a patrol, practices the skills of leadership and Scoutcraft, and learns how these can be used with boys. This practical training can be conducted either as a weeklong encampment or on a series of three weekends.

The second part of Wood Badge is the application of what has been learned. Each participant writes a "ticket"—a contract with himself as to how the new skills will be put to work. The ticket can be completed in as little as 6 months, but must be concluded within 2 years. When the ticket has been evaluated by the coach/counselor and the contract has been completed, the Wood Badge—beads, neckerchief, and woggle—is presented.

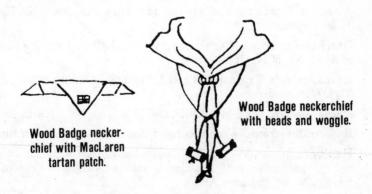

Wood Badge necker-
chief with MacLaren
tartan patch.

Wood Badge neckerchief
with beads and woggle.

Scouter's Training
Award

Scouter's Key

Scouter's Training Award and/or Scouter's Key. Worn over the left breast pocket, pinned just above the seam, by Scouters who have met the requirements. Since these awards also may be worn by Cub Scouters and Explorer leaders, a miniature Boy Scout device may be affixed to the ribbon and also to the square knot described below.

Embroidered Square Knots

Embroidered square knots are representative of metal pin-on awards and are designed for greater convenience of the wearer. There is no wearing sequence for the embroidered square knots on the uniform. They are worn above the left pocket in rows of three, with the order of wearing at the discretion of the wearer. The square knots are listed here in alphabetical order:

Arrow of Light, cloth, red and green knot, green to right, No. 5049, Scouter.

Award of Merit, cloth, silver overhand knot, ends down, No. 5021, district Scouter.

Den Leader Coach's Training Award, cloth, blue and gold, blue to right, No. 5047, Cub Scouter.

Den Leader's Training Award, cloth, gold knot on blue, No. 5046, Cub Scouter.

Eagle Award, cloth, red, white, and blue knot, No. 5018, Scouter.

Embroidered knots from other Scout associations, Scouter.

Explorer Silver Award, cloth, silver knot on red, white, and blue, red background to right, No. 5636, Scouter who holds this award or Ranger or Air Explorer Ace.

Heroism Award, cloth, red on white twill, No. 5057, member of the Boy Scouts of America who has received this award or its predecessor, the Certificate for Heroism.

Honor Medal, cloth, red knot on khaki, No. 5017, member of the Boy Scouts of America for lifesaving.

Medal of Merit, cloth, gold and blue, blue to right, No. 5180A, member of the Boy Scouts of America for meritorious service.

Order of the Arrow Distinguished Service Award, cloth, white knot on red, No. 6892, Scout or Scouter.

Professional Circle Award, cloth, black knot on white, No. MO144, Scouter. The **Fellowship Award** is indicated with the addition of the Boy Scout device, No. 5103D.

Quartermaster Award, cloth, blue knot on white, No. 5016A, Scouter.

Religious emblem, cloth, silver knot on purple, No. 5014, Scout or Explorer or Scouter; cloth, purple knot on silver, No. 5022, Scouter only.

Scouter's Key, cloth, green and white knot, green to right, No. 5013, Scouter.

Scouter's Training Award, cloth, green knot on khaki, No. 5015, Scouter.

Silver Antelope Award, cloth, gold and white knot , gold to right, No. 5012, regional Scouter.

Silver Beaver Award, cloth, blue and white knot on khaki, blue to right, No. 5010, council Scouter.

Silver Buffalo Award, cloth, red and white knot, red to right, No. 5011, national Scouter.

Silver Fawn Award, discontinued in 1974, wear Silver Beaver knot.

Silver World Award, cloth, red and white stripes, world, two stars to right, No. 5019, international Scouter.

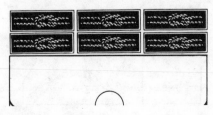

Embroidered square knots may be worn above the left shirt pocket in rows of three.

Chapter 18

Scouting Resources

WHEREVER you live in our country you are in a district, council, and region of the Boy Scouts of America. The aim of each level of Scouting is to help your troop succeed. Your district's commissioner staff and district committee are representative of and responsible to the chartered organizations within the boundaries of your district.

Your council, consisting of many districts, holds a charter from the Boy Scouts of America to administer and promote Scouting within the territory assigned to it.

NORTH CENTRAL REGION

WESTERN REGION

SOUTH CENTRAL REGION

Your region helps its councils secure qualified volunteer and professional leadership, develop effective financing, meet approved goals, and be effective administrators of Scouting in their territories.

The national organization provides the magazines, books and printed materials, uniforms, and equipment for Scouting. Each of these products reflects the continuing program development carried on by the Boy Scouts of America.

Six regions support the work of more than 400 councils located within the states and territories of our nation. Two councils operate beyond our borders. Through them, American families may enjoy Scouting while serving in the Armed forces or working in Europe or the Far East. For other American families in isolated locations around the world, Scouting is available through direct service from the national office located in Irving, Tex. The mailing address is Boy Scouts of America, 1325 Walnut Hill Lane, Irving, Texas 75038-3096.

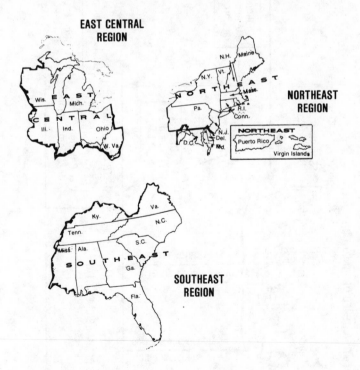

COUNCIL AND DISTRICT ORGANIZATION

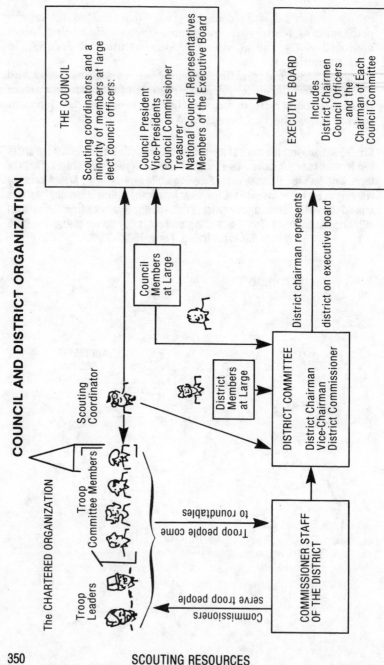

THE COUNCIL

Scouting coordinators and a minority of members at large elect council officers:

Council President
Vice-Presidents
Council Commissioner
Treasurer
National Council Representatives
Members of the Executive Board

EXECUTIVE BOARD

Includes
District Chairmen
Council Officers
and the
Chairman of Each
Council Committee

Council Members at Large

District chairman represents district on executive board

The CHARTERED ORGANIZATION

Troop Leaders

Troop Committee Members

Scouting Coordinator

District Members at Large

DISTRICT COMMITTEE

District Chairman
Vice-Chairman
District Commissioner

Troop people come to roundtables

Commissioners serve troop people

COMMISSIONER STAFF OF THE DISTRICT

COUNCIL AND DISTRICT RESOURCES

As a Scoutmaster, you have a lot of resources available to help you be successful in working with your Scouts. Your council is the focal point of all this help. It provides training for you, your assistants, and troop committee. It makes supplies, including literature, and badges and awards available. Roundtables serve to interpret recommended monthly troop programs.

Camping and outdoor facilities cost more to own and operate than most community organizations can afford. So your council owns and operates them for your benefit. Scouts grow from participation in council and district events conducted to enhance troop programs. Your professional staff coordinates all these services.

The council budget is developed annually by an executive board made up of adults from your local community. Most councils receive the bulk of their funds from the United Way.

Sustaining membership enrollment (SME) is conducted to secure enough funds to fulfill the objectives established by the executive board. Individuals throughout the community demonstrate their support of Scouting and its objectives by enrolling as sustaining members. The Boy Scouts of America believes each adult, family, or parent should determine for themselves the amount of their enrollment. An enrollment serves to demonstrate to the community at large the enthusiasm and desire parents and leaders have for a strong, active Scouting program in the community.

Resources available from the council and district fall into two categories—those things that will help you directly as a leader, and those that can be used to supplement the troop program.

Roundtables

Districts offer regular, usually monthly, roundtables. This is a name for a gathering of Scoutmasters of the district to receive program ideas for the coming month. It gives a chance to share ideas with other Scoutmasters. At the roundtable you will learn new games, ceremonies, songs, stunts, and crafts. Council and district activities for troops are outlined at the roundtable.

Your Commissioner

Successful Scoutmasters will tell you that they didn't do it all on their own. They had some help from others who had gone through the experience before them. Your commissioner is that kind of friend. Chances are that he has been a Scoutmaster. He has met most of the situations that may be puzzling to you. His job in Scouting is to help two or three troops like yours. If you succeed with his help, he is a successful commissioner.

As a matter of fact the commissioner staff and the professional staff of your council and district have wreaths on their badges of office. That wreath is a symbol of service to you and your chartered organizations.

Professional Scouter

Your commissioner is a volunteer. He isn't paid for what he does. The commissioner staff cannot do everything that needs to be done in your district or council, and for that reason a small, highly trained staff is employed to further the Scouting movement. Their work could be compared with the clergy. They are dedicated, hard-working Scouters who have chosen Scouting as their life work.

Because their work is to further the movement, your work is extremely important to them. Your council office and staff, therefore, are there when you need them. And what's more, they really want you to call when you need help.

Training Courses

Your district offers training courses for new Scoutmasters, assistants, and troop committee members. Your commissioner or the council office will have details. If there is not a course scheduled to take place soon, personal coaching is available from your commissioner or an experienced Scouter called a coach/counselor. He will help you to plan program and train your boy leaders to run the program. He will also help your committee provide program support for your troop.

Additionally, there are brief courses in these areas: Skill Awards, The Advancement Plan, Scoutmaster Conference, Leadership Corps, Merit Badge Counselor Orientation, The Troop Committee, Understanding Scouts With Handicaps, Couseling, Effective Teaching, Boy Scout Program Planning, Sports in Boy Scouting, Boy Scout Ceremonies, Troop Volunteer Resources, and Boy Scout Leaders' Roundtable.

Intertroop Activities

To provide for troops to come together from time to time, local councils and districts run intertroop activities, such as camporees, rallies, field days, and big shows.

There are only a few of these each year, and they are intended to supplement rather than supplant troop program. The preparation by troops, patrols, and individual Scouts stimulates good troop programs.

Participation in these activities is voluntary; each troop decides whether and how it will take part. But the troop that turns down such activities keeps its members from having some valuable Scouting experience.

Include the dates of these activities in your annual plan. As details of the events come out during the year, your patrol leaders' council should discuss the event and make a decision on whether to take part. It is hoped that the troop would participate in district or council events for these reasons: they look like they will be fun, will offer good troop programs in preparation, and will help to meet the objectives of the troop.

See'n'do. A 1-day Scouting activity designed to attract new Scouts and provide the entire community with an opportunity to participate. Held by the council or district.

Big Shows. These are great public demonstrations of Scouting. They are usually either booth type, circus type, or a combination.

In a booth show, each troop picks a Scouting skill, prepares to demonstrate this skill to the best of its ability, and then shows off in a booth on the subject. The public attends, and Scouts show them their stuff.

A circus type show has the audience seated, watching as Scouts put on skills in an arena out in front.

Tickets are usually sold by Scouts before such events, and the receipts from ticket sales are divided between the troops and some council project such as the purchase of camp program equipment.

Field Days. Here troops get together for 1 day of competition in the skills of Scouting. There are contests in such things as compass work, first aid, firebuilding, use of woods tools, nature lore, and fitness.

The Order
of the Arrow

The Order of the Arrow is a national brotherhood of Scout honor campers which originated in the early years of Scouting. It is a brotherhood of cheerful service. Scouts are nominated and elected by their fellow Scouts in their own troops. They must meet certain entry qualifications that are established by the Order of the Arrow. Each troop may hold an election once a year, supervised by a member of the Order. The number it may nominate and elect to Order membership depends upon the number of eligible candidates. All registered Scouts in the troop may vote. Since Order members are always in the minority in any troop, the majority who are outside the Order control the election.

There is provision for election of adults. They serve as advisers, as it is a boys' organization. Scouts are not admitted to Order ceremonies, which are based on Indian legend and lore, unless they are members. Scouters who wish to observe them are welcome.

The Order of the Arrow program in a council is conducted through a local lodge. These lodges conduct meetings, plan and carry out activities, organize service projects for Arrowmen, and develop summer camp promotion plans to help Scout troops prepare for camp. The Arrowman is expected to give richer service to his troop as a result of the honor bestowed.

Information on election procedures, local lodge practices, etc., can be obtained from your local Order of the Arrow lodge officers through your council office.*

Alpha Phi Omega

Alpha Phi Omega is a college service fraternity whose members are mostly former Scouts. If there is a college nearby with this fraternity, invite its help.

---

*The Scout executive of a council is the supreme chief of the fire in an Order of the Arrow lodge.

The Religious
Emblems Program

There is a close association between the Boy Scouts of America and virtually all religious bodies and denominations in the United States. Scouting is, of course, a nonsectarian movement. It is identified with no particular faith, encourages no particular affiliation, nor assumes functions of religious bodies. Hence it is important that you understand that the religious emblems program—really many programs—is a program of religious bodies and not of Scouting.

Qualifications for the religious emblems are established by the religious groups. The Scout works through his own spiritual leader in earning the emblem. The presentation is usually made at the local religious institution in which the emblem is earned.

It is appropriate for you to encourage Scouts who are interested to work for and earn the religious emblem for their particular faith. There is no connection between religious emblems and the advancement program of Scouting.

For sources of information regarding each see *The Official Boy Scout Handbook.*

National Eagle
Scout Association

Eagle Scouts may join the National Eagle Scout Association. Many local councils have active chapters on both a formal and informal basis. If your council has such a chapter, it can be helpful to you in your advancement program, particularly in planning and conducting Eagle courts of honor.

Chapter 19

A Short History of Boy Scouting

Baden-Powell

The Good Turn that
brought Scouting
to the U.S.A.

SCOUTING started in the mind of the founder, Robert S.S. Baden-Powell, whose first Boy Scout camp is described in the beginning of this book. After that camp, the next big step for Baden-Powell was the writing of a handbook for boys and a booklet for Scoutmasters. The handbook, called *Scouting for Boys*, was published in five parts early in 1908, and later that year in book form. It was an instant success.

Within a few months there were tens of thousands of Boy Scouts in Great Britain. They were guided by *Scouting for Boys* and a new weekly magazine, *The Scout*. Baden-Powell formed what was to become the British Boy Scouts Association.

Scouting had come to America even earlier than 1910. With the publication of *Scouting for Boys* in 1908, troops began forming at several locations in the United States, many in YMCA's, but there was no formal structure or organization for them.

The official birthdate for the Boy Scouts of America is February 8, 1910. It was incorporated on that date by William D. Boyce, a

Boyce   **Seton**   **Beard**

Chicago publisher, who had happened upon Scouting in 1909 while passing through London on a trip to Africa. Lost in a thick fog, he was approached by a boy who offered to help him. To Boyce's astonishment, the boy would not accept a tip because he said it was a Good Turn, and a Scout could not accept pay for such an act. Boyce went to British Scout Headquarters to find out what kind of program would have such an effect upon a city boy. When he sailed for home, he had a trunk full of Scouting literature, insignia, and uniforms.

Boyce willingly joined the common effort when he found others also trying to start a Scouting movement. Among them were two men whose influence on Scouting is felt to this day.

Ernest Thompson Seton, world famous as naturalist, author, illustrator, and lecturer on wildlife and the wilderness, was also the head of the Tribe of the Woodcraft Indians, a loose organization of boys who wrote to him after reading his nature books.

Seton was chairman of the committee on organization and the first Chief Scout of the BSA. He was also the primary author of the first *Handbook for Boys* published in 1911.

Daniel Carter Beard, another leader of an existing boys' organization, was a writer and illustrator of hundreds of magazine articles on outdoor life. His boys' organization was called the Society of the Sons of Daniel Boone. It stressed the lore and pioneering spirit of such great American scouts and outdoorsmen as Boone, Kit Carson, Davy Crockett, and Audubon.

With Seton, Beard merged his own boys' organization into the young Boy Scout movement. He became one of three national Scout commissioners, a member of the national Executive Board, and chairman of the National Court of Honor. Until his death at 91,

West

Beard was a familiar figure at any big Boy Scout event, unmistakable in the frontier garb he wore.

Late in 1910, as a small group of national leaders were struggling with the problems of a new organization, they brought into Scouting a man whose impact upon the movement was to be no less than that of Seton and Beard.

He was James E. West—a man as opposite to Beard and Seton as could be imagined. An attorney, he was then making a name for himself in youth work. From having spent his childhood in an orphanage, West knew first-hand some of the problems of the young. He was crippled throughout his life by a tubercular hip. Yet these handicaps had not prevented him from working his way through high school, college, and law school.

The founders talked West into taking the job of "executive secretary" of the BSA for 6 months, beginning January 1911. The 6 months lasted 32 years: West finally retired as Chief Scout Executive in 1943.

Seton and Beard had brought to Scouting the magic of the campfire and love of the outdoors. West brought limitless vision and administrative talent.

With the national organization beginning to take shape in 1911, national leaders turned their attention to local and regional organization, and to such vital matters as the Scout Oath and Law, rank requirements, and badges.

In the Scout Oath, the British version was closely followed, but the phrase "to keep myself physically strong, mentally awake, and morally straight" was added.

Baden-Powell's Scout Law contained nine points. They were adopted by the BSA with minor variations, and three were added: Brave, Clean, and Reverent.

As in England, Scouting swept the country as soon as boys heard about it. Even in 1911 there were 5,000 troops in the United States.

Scouting and Boys' Life have been helping Scouts and Scoutmasters since the early days of the movement.

There were a mere 14 merit badge subjects then, and 30 Scouts managed to earn a total of 83 among them that year.

To keep leaders and boys informed, two magazines began. *Scouting*, for adults, was first published in 1913, and *Boys' Life*, a young magazine for boys, was purchased by the Scouting movement in 1912.

When the United States entered World War I in 1917, the Boy Scouts of America was well known but not a household name. Scouting's work on the home front made it so. Fewer than 300,000 Scouts sold $3.5 million in Liberty Bonds after others had canvassed the field, raised over $43 million by selling war stamps, collected over 100 carloads of fruit pits for use in gas mask filters, operated 12,000 war farms and gardens, distributed 30 million pieces of government literature, and cooperated in numerous ways with many organizations. The value of Scout training came home to the American people, and Scouting became part of the American scene.

The services of Scouts in the years since 1910 make an incredible bank of statistics; more than 64 million Americans have been involved in the movement in these decades. The vigor and extent of the movement and its influence have long since grown far beyond the most extravagant dreams of its founders.

Yet Scouting is not just an American phenomenon. Every free country in the world uses the program. Although the United States leads the world in numbers of members, there are millions of Scouts around the world. It is said that one can raise his hand in the Scout sign anywhere in the free world and find a friend. World jamborees and other international visits and correspondence help to maintain and expand the brotherhood of Scouting.

Before he died in 1941 at the age of 83, Robert Baden-Powell issued a final message to Britain's Scouters and Girl Guide leaders summing up the achievements of the movement he had founded. Though decades old and addressed to British leaders, it seems appropriate as a closing to this book.

"Scouting's aim is to produce healthy, happy, helpful citizens, of both sexes, to eradicate the prevailing narrow self-interest, personal, political, sectarian, and national, and to substitute for it a broader spirit of self-sacrifice and service in the cause of humanity; and thus to develop mutual goodwill and cooperation not only within our own country but abroad, between all countries.

"Experience shows that this consummation is no idle or fantastic dream, but is a practical possibility—if we work for it; and it means, when attained, peace, prosperity, and happiness for all.

"Hundreds of thousands of boys and girls who are learning our ideals today will be the fathers and mothers of millions in the near future, in whom they will in turn inculcate the same ideals—*provided that these are really and unmistakably impressed upon them by their leaders of today.*

"Therefore you, who are Scouters and Guiders, are not only doing a great work for your neighbors' children but are also helping in practical fashion to pass God's Kingdom of peace and goodwill upon earth.

"So, from my heart, I wish you God-speed in your effort."

Baden Powell

Robert S.S. Baden-Powell

**The Scout trail sign for "I have gone home"
appears on B-P's grave in Nyeri, Kenya.**

INDEX

A

Ability groups, 203, 204
Acquiring camping equipment, 208
Activities assistant, 91
Activities
  along the hike, 188-89
  at your hike destination, 189
Activities among troops, packs, and posts, 111
Adult leaders, 61
Adult male association, 107
Advancement, 106, 224-45
Advancement badges, 333
Advancement, Four Steps
Adventure, 109
After the meeting, 90
Aims and methods, 98-111
Aims, the, 99-103
Alcohol, 130
Alpha Phi Omega, 355
Alterations of insignia prohibited, 333
Alternate Eagle Award merit badges, 139
Alternate solutions, 146
Announcements, 88
Annual planning conference, 157
Appointed Boy Scout leaders, 51
Arcturians, the, 8
Arrow of Light Award, 341
Assistant patrol leader badge of office, 336
Assistant Scoutmaster, 43
Assistant Scoutmaster badge of office, 336
Assistant Scoutmasters, 62, 91
Assistant senior patrol leader, 51, 91
Assistant senior patrol leader badge of office, 336
Attendance bar, pin, 342
Attention, sign for, 91, 134
Audiovisuals, 326

B

Baden-Powell, 6-8, 74-75, 286, 356, 360,
Baden-Powell patrol, 74-75, 248
Baden-Powell patrol requirements, 75
Badge, book, and candle, 314
Badges of achievement, 340-42

Badges of identification, 334-35
Badges of office, 336
Badges of other organizations, 334
Badges of participation, 342-43
Badges of rank, 226
Badge swapping, 334
Basic troop camping equipment, 210-12
Beard, Daniel Carter, 357-58
Beeline hike, 193
Beginner swim test, 203
Behavior problems, 122, 126-34
Be "in uniform," 312
Belt line punishment, 132
Belt tug, 301
Benediction, Scout, 37, 89
Be Prepared, 10
Big enough, 307
Big shows, 353
Blindfold compass course, 293
Board of review, 60, 228-29
Boating skill, 205
Bowline-sheet bend draw, 290
Boyce, William D., 356-57
Boy leaders trained to control, 124
Boy Scout, 231, 338
Boy Scout Leader Program Notebook, 155
Boy Scout program, 16-17
Boy Scout Program Helps, 153, 156, 157
Boys' Life, 154, 275, 359
Brainstorm time, 255-56
British bulldog, 299
Buddy system, 203, 205
Budget, preparing troop, 272
Bugler badge of office, 336
Building patrol spirit, 248

C

Cabins, troop owned, 201
Campfire ceremonies, 325
Camping and conservation awards, 219-22
Camping equipment, 164, 211-12
Camping facilities, 164
Camping in another council's camp, 200
Camping personnel, 164